GAMES
CHILDREN
PLAY II

Games to develop social skills,
teamwork, balance and coordination

First edition, *Games Children Play,* published 1996 and reprinted 1998, 2001, 2005.

Hawthorn Press

Published by Hawthorn Press, Hawthorn House
1 Lansdown Lane, Stroud, Gloucestershire, United Kingdom, GL5 1BJ, UK
Tel: (01453) 757040 Email: info@hawthornpress.com
www.hawthornpress.com

Cover design by Lucy Guenot
Typesetting and music setting by Winslade Graphics
Illustrations by Marije Rowling and Lucy Guenot
Printed by Short Run Press Ltd, Exeter

Every effort has been made to trace the ownership of all copyrighted material. If any omission has been made, please bring this to the publisher's attention so that proper acknowledgement may be given in future editions.

The views in this book are not necessarily those of the publisher.

Printed on environmentally friendly chlorine-free paper sourced from renewable forest stock.

British Library Cataloguing in Publication Data applied for
ISBN 978-1-912480-52-4

GAMES
CHILDREN
PLAY II

Games to develop social skills,
teamwork, balance and coordination

Kim John Payne M.ED
and
Cory Waletzko

Hawthorn Press

Contents

Part One
Exploring the House

Chapter One

Snow Games

Indoor/Rainy Day Games

Part Two
Beyond the Doorway

Chapter Three

Activities to Develop Spatial Awareness: 16+

Part Three
Considerations for Creating Inclusive Culture

Chapter Nine

Cultural appropriation vs. Cultural appreciation

In this games book, whenever there is mention of a cultural or ethnic tradition, we have done our best to hold up and honour the people and practices that inspired them. We have seen that when games are presented in this way, children can live inside the traditions they are playing out and develop familiarity and empathy for the culture that inspired the imagery. Above all it is our experience that when traditional games from around the world are described and presented respectfully to children eager to play, they can humanise and bring a deepened level of respect for cultures different from their own.

List of Game Contributors for Games Children Play II:

Rose, Barbara, Guido and Anna, Judit, Shirley, Simon and Nantia, Rebecca, Alison, Arlene and Natasha, Sally Cooper and Lesley Willis, Martin Baker, Rudolf Kischnick, Graham Whiting, Jaimen McMillan, Rob Sim, Craig Taylor, Jeremy Dunleavy, Paul Harnischfeger, Mashobane Moruthane, Julianna Lichatz, Jeff Tunkey, Will Crane, Torsti Rovainen, Susan Darcy, Kim Lebas, Bonnie Bolz, Katie Moran, Jaimen McMillan, Kevin Quigley, Josh Boyle, Pepper Williams.

Introduction

Our birth is but a sleep and a forgetting;
The Soul that rises with us, our life's star
Hath had elsewhere its setting,
And cometh from afar;
Not in entire forgetfulness
And not in utter nakedness,
But trailing clouds of glory do we come
From God who is our home;
Heaven lies about us in our infancy.

Wordsworth

Children move in play like young fish swim in water:
There are these two young fish swimming along and they happen to meet an older fish swimming the other way, who nods at them and says 'Morning, boys. How's the water?' And the two young fish swim on for a bit, and then eventually one of them looks over at the other and goes 'What is water?'

David Foster Wallace

Introducing this new edition

Confessions of a recovered (sort of) hide-and-seek player:

I would emerge sweaty and shaking from my hiding place long after the game had ended. 'It's just a game!', my childhood friends would say but I recall the feeling of my heart pounding in my chest and holding my breath while I was hiding. Complete stillness – complete darkness – this was a game of life or death. I would rather die than be tagged, and I was so good at hiding, I would never be found.

Even though it terrified me, I always played when I had the chance. These warring forces, the longing to play and the fear of playing, continue to tango in my soul to this day. Play is the perfect platform for this dramatic dance.

The Covid-19 global pandemic changed the rules of the game; no touching, no sharing, no singing, no hand-holding, no hugging, no breathing – unless you cover your face. Cooties are real. Not only are they real, but they could kill you. Keep six feet away. Stay home. Do not come out and play. Talk about a game of life or death!

As fate would have it, this new edition of 'Games Children Play' is being published just as many communities are re-negotiating the health and safety guidelines to allow for activities that have been off the table for a long time. For some of us,

we've not been able to play tag for over a year – we've been disconnected – literally, out of touch. This new edition features over 200 games that remind us how to reconnect – to ourselves and to one another – physically, emotionally, spatially, socially, even spiritually – to get us back in touch.

As a movement educator, my true teachers are the students. This last year in particular, they have taught me my most important lesson of all: We need to get tagged! We must be 'in touch'. It's okay to be afraid and it's fine to hide for awhile, but it's most fun to be found. My heart-pounding, sweaty, younger self, alone in her never-to-be-found hiding place, gets a do-over; I get to be 'found.' I'm in recovery through re-discovery.

The title of this book 'Games Children Play II' is also a play on words: 'Games Children Play, Too'. Meaning, we adults also get to play. We get to do things over. We get to learn and unlearn and learn again. It's not just a game – it's us evolving.

This edition was created by humans connecting with one another; sharing games, stories, cultures, customs, selves, and souls – and these connections keep connecting… through you! The game is on; we're all playing. The invitation is elemental and timeless ∞

TAG – You're it!

Cory Waletzko

Why play games with children?

An infant is born and as Wordsworth sees, is still enveloped in 'heavenly' forces. In the journey through childhood, each young person encounters and passes through what may be called 'thresholds'. This book is about those thresholds; about how children experience them and how we, their helpers, can identify and give them expression.

What makes this book different from other books on children's games?

The long journey to reveal or discover ourselves and our life's tasks is our life story; we can look upon games as the spaces or punctuation in this story, that give the text meaning.

The aim of this book is not only to outline ways of organising children's games, but also to give the reader a full and fascinating insight into why the game is appropriate for a particular age or stage of development. In this way it may be read both as a guide to child development and as a practical book about games.

Games often go wrong. Throughout the book examples are given of ways to help children who find it difficult to join in – whether they express this by withdrawing, or disrupting and even sabotaging; such children need to find a creative way of playing and also relating in a healthier way both to other children and adults.

Some children experience isolation and ridicule in games. Self-esteem is badly affected and often has lasting negative effects in other areas of life. The games in this book have been specifically developed to value all players regardless of their varying degrees of physical ability.

An enjoyable and satisfying role can be found for all those who play. In many of the games, examples will be given of how to work with introverted, unfocused, over-dominant or stubborn children.

The journey

We often say that children 'grow up' – as indeed they do. What would you think, though, if you were to hear that children also 'grow down' and 'grow in'?

Children grow through games. They first learn as infants about the world around them, and at times their gaze seems to look far beyond the new physical environment that they have come into. They exist partly in the periphery. Then as the years go by they spatially 'come closer' to themselves. They play finger games, clapping games, skipping, romping and running games. They grow more skilful as they learn about space and how to move in it; the games become more demanding, involving greater social complexity and negotiation. The journey from the young child playing finger games to the teenager playing basketball, is a process of coming 'in' and 'down', of growing heavier within the body. A dynamic exists between growing 'up' and 'down'; and also between 'growing in' to oneself and 'growing out' into the world.

Such a view is of special interest to the teacher or therapist; it increases our ability to perceive when a child has become 'stuck' in a particular stage, and to help her overcome the obstruction simply by getting involved in certain games and activities. This may be a controversial approach, but is also a fascinating concept worthy of exploration. Time and again I have witnessed difficult emotional and behavioural problems eased when the right activity is offered and taken up by the child. Suspicious or guarded reactions that may have existed in conversation, begin to fade when a particular game is introduced. The barriers to healing then also begin to fall away.

Kim John Payne

Hidden Treasures
Hints and tips for teaching games

Presenting games to children

Essentially there are three aspects to consider when presenting a game:

Abstraction: Some children have the ability to follow an explanation given in a verbal, diagrammatic, intellectual way. Young people in their middle to latter teens often have a developing capacity for this, and can therefore cope with such an emphasis.

Pictorial: Another group of children will relate more strongly to an explanation that has images, pictures or even a story to set out what needs to be done. The play area may be a jungle or a sea where tigers or sharks prowl. The tree or wall may be a castle, or have magic so that when you touch it you become invisible and cannot be tagged. A majority of children from about four to five until about 11 to 12 years old will be imaginatively enriched by these methods. It also makes the game more vivid and alive.

It may seem strange to suggest that children are not harmed by frightening images, such as sharks and giants which chase them. Many of the images children naturally bring into their play are mythologically-based monsters and creatures that are expressions of deep subconscious emotions. When these images are evoked in games, children are provided with an opportunity to bring up emotions that exist below the surface – to express and work through, in a child-like way, fears and aspirations they secretly harbour.

Another major advantage in presenting games in this way is that it takes emphasis away from the physical nature of the activity. It allows children of all abilities to find a role. It stimulates creativity, helps break down fear of the equipment. Many children, for example, have a fear of using balls; but when the ball becomes a sword that has to be avoided, or a precious treasure that has to be protected, it is amazing how cheerfully they will join in.

Children who focus too early on physical ability

unenriched by imagination, often experience frustration when they can't achieve the standards of those teenagers and grown-ups they are trying to emulate. They can become fanatical, over-interested in winning, and at times anti-social or even disruptive. Images help these 'spatially and behaviourally precocious' children to relax and play the game for its own sake and for enjoyment.

Imitative: Some children prefer to see the game or activity demonstrated. They need the leader either to show how it is done or place the players in their positions and have a 'walk through' before the real play begins. This is very strengthening for the child's will: she sees what needs doing and sets out to achieve it. This faculty is at its strongest in the first five to six years. Children will often learn complex finger or string games in minutes that have taken the adult hours to work out. It is at this age that the children will often imitate household activities such as washing up or digging in the garden. This is a very healthy kind of 'game' which is to be strongly encouraged (even if does take twice as long to finish the job!) It is the basis for healthy will-development that is vital for future inner strength.

In general

Although I have outlined these three aspects of learning and attributed them to various ages, this is only intended as a general guideline. For example, in introducing an activity to teenagers – such as shooting goals in basketball – the leader will draw on all three aspects. She may explain the technical approach – such as body and hand position; bring in an image – like imagining the basketball rim is a bookshelf that the player is trying to land the ball on; and then demonstrate how to do it. In doing so, she has touched the abstract, the pictorial, and the imitative learners.

Of course all of us have all three tendencies within ourselves. It is therefore more a question of which quality is dominant at certain ages and in varying situations. Potentially the most challenging aspect of this is that we as adults also have certain dominant tendencies; it is our task to become aware of them in order to include and stimulate all children in the group. We may for example have a tendency to explain in abstract form what is required; and when certain children in the group 'don't get it', we may look for other words to describe the task, yet still remain 'stuck' in the realm of abstract communication. If the child continues not to get it, she may begin to feel excluded, and even start to disrupt others. We may then end up disciplining or punishing the child, although it is ourselves and our lack of consciousness that lay at the root of the problem.

Using your own creativity

Use the children's own environments as much as possible. Don't only use images of the country, of rivers and mountains, but also of the city and of urban life when explaining new games and their rules. Only five per cent of the population of the U.S.A. lives in rural settings, and this trend is echoed in most western cultures.

Children often use games to connect with, or make sense of their environment, or their family or school situations. For example I once overheard a skipping rhyme in a playground that dealt with a child's experience and understanding of divorce. It went something like…

Mum and Dad went to war,
Went to the judge, found the law.
Mumma on Monday,
Daddy on Tuesday,
Mumma on Wednesday,
Daddy on Thursday,
Mumma on Friday,
Daddy on Saturday,
Sunday day of rest!

I am of course not suggesting that adults should make up similar rhymes, personal to the child involved; we can leave that to the children's own resources and self-expression. But we can think back to our own childhood and reteach some of the traditional rhymes, or we may even make up some new ones. It is so very satisfying to present a new rhyme to the children that you have especially made up for them, and for days and weeks afterwards hear them merrily chanting it.

Also use the seasons: games can be invented that use autumn leaves, the puddles in winter, and snow. For instance, I recently watched some children playing a simple game of tag. One child sat curled up, covered in autumn leaves, while the others approached him cautiously. Imagine the excitement when the leaves rustled, or when he finally burst out of the heap and chased them back to 'home'!

Language of the playground

With the onslaught of television, videos, computer games and computer based learning in school, many children are beginning to lose the old rhymes and traditional games that play such a vital role in our learning, creativity, and ability to interact socially in a healthy way. What I call 'playground culture' is today only a vague shadow of what, in the not-so-distant past, was rich, boisterous activity. The oral tradition, in which games and rhymes were passed down, is breaking down. Children are forgetting how to relate and talk to each other. The generation that was born in the 1950s, 60s and even the 70s is probably the last to remember something of these traditional games. Even in Asian and many African cultures, the stories and games are being lost. It is therefore up to us, as 'human reference libraries', to teach our children so that they in turn may teach each other. It involves us rolling up our sleeves and spending not only quality time, but fun time with our children. Once they are into the swing of things, we can quietly withdraw and leave them to it.

While initially you may have to help children sort out their disputes, it is good to gradually withdraw as they relearn the 'art of playing'. The disputes won't necessarily become fewer, but the quality of the resolution will become much fairer and clearer. Marbles, skipping, hopscotch, the many chasing games, wrestling and duelling games, ball games such as four square, all find a thirsty audience of children willing to try them out. The group quickly grows. At first the concentration span may be short, depending on how they have spent their leisure time; but slowly the 'healing' will take place. We can give children back a childhood – and one of the most potent ways is to reteach them a forgotten but once much-loved language, the language of games.

Bullying

Why play games to help counteract bullying? Games work at a deeper level on the dynamic of victimisation than our usual reaction of talking (or lecturing) to students, or giving somewhat meaningless or even harmful detentions or punishments. There are many games which you can play to help both bullies and their victims into more social ways of interacting with others. This is not to say that this is the only answer; but I have seen how games really can change the social constellation of a group of children, including unhealthy patterns like victimisation. Carefully designed and supervised games have the advantage of helping control the level of exposure and contact between the bully and victim without fuelling any particular crisis or conflict; at the same time, the whole group goes through the experience of the social dynamics of the game. The focus shifts from a personality conflict into a more situational or objective view. By means of a game, it is for example possible to transform a blanket statement such as 'I hate John', into something like 'I hate it when John does that'. A game can provide the opportunity for working on a problem area, without dismissing completely the person who is being bullied.

Games also give the bully (and the rest of the children) a chance to express the positive aspects of her strength as a leader. The child who bullies often has deep seated insecurities, which make her seek peer approval. She will try to seek this approval by taunting or tormenting others while being watched by her peers. The bully will very often pick on others who are weaker in some way than she is. Often the bully will be stronger than the victim – usually physically but also verbally. Games can use this

strength and energy in a healthy and positive way. In games such as Wolf and Sheep, Cat and Mouse House, or Coupe, the bully is called on to use her strength to protect someone weaker than herself.

Children who bully have often acquired or had this behaviour triggered in a myriad of differing ways: an environment of aggression at home or in the playground, family crisis, sudden change, learning difficulties and frustrations, role modelling from aggressive adults she sees at home, or from sports or music stars. Games can show these children how to channel their aggression in a more positive way. A child who continues to show aggression in an inappropriate way will often ruin the game and thus risk losing peer approval. It is interesting to note that the playground can be either the worst environment – breeding all sorts of unhealthy behaviour; or the best – where children learn to co-operate while still standing up for what they think is right. Playgrounds and play time at home can be transformed when teachers and parents take an active interest in reintroducing games. The 'Killing Fields' can become the 'Healing Fields.'

The poem *Back in the Playground Blues* graphically describes the bullying experience (page xvi).

As well as being weaker in some way, or smaller, the victim of bullying may often appear visibly different from others; e.g. wearing glasses, of a different skin colour etc. In games that are carefully planned, these differences can be 'defocused' – or the positive aspect of the difference can be emphasised. For instance, I have placed an overweight child as the anchor of a Tug-of-War – with much success! Or smaller children, who are often very nimble and quick, may be given tasks in a game that require these qualities (for example, in chasing games that demand fast, sudden changes of direction, such as many of the Cat and Mouse games). Slow thinkers often have an ability to picture: they catch on to games that are described in picture form much quicker than those who are more 'intellectual'. The shy, withdrawn child is often a good observer – and may well shine as a prison guard or watchtower person in a game. For instance, in *Storm the Castle*.

The victim will also benefit from the structure that

a game provides – all too often bullying occurs during unstructured times: break-times, after school, etc. I find that if I introduce a game that the children enjoy, they will continue to play during break-time; which means that there is less chance of bullying taking place.

If you play games that allow the potential victim to display her hidden talents, this will help her peers to see her strengths and she will win more peer approval. Lack of self-esteem and the loss of peer approval are the roots of much anti-social behaviour.

However, if bullying does occur:

- Quickly defuse the incident, and take attention away from it. Otherwise further polarisation will occur. Instead focus on the feelings and the implications involved.

- Do not punish or blame the bully. This will only increase the isolation and pressure on the victim so that bullying becomes more hidden.

- Don't berate the bully in front of her peers. This will only gain her status and reinforce her image as a 'bad girl'.

- Don't spend hours talking. Design fun outings or activities that the bully, victim and a couple of friends can take part in.

The main purpose of not 'blaming' the bully is that a culture of 'telling' needs to be cultivated throughout the school and the community. Anyone who sees bullying, or is being bullied, needs to feel they can speak up and 'tell', and know that they will not be persecuted for doing so. This can only be achieved if all concerned know they are safe and respected by teachers and parents, and that the issue will be dealt with thoroughly.

Work in small groups and listen to the children's ideas of how they think they can make things better.

How to pick teams

Letting two nominated team captains choose their own teams often leads to the strongest (or most popular) players being chosen first, and the weakest last. This situation can be difficult for individual children; so over the years I have used other methods to choose teams.

- A simple way is to make a circle and ask every second player (sometimes in pairs) to step forward, thus creating two circles. To make a circle ask all players to form a line behind you and simply set off walking or jogging with the children following, moving into a circle. Keep moving until the circle is evenly spaced.

- For 11 or 12 year olds and upwards, I ask first one team captain (of Team A) to choose a player, then the next team captain (of Team B) to choose someone of the same ability as the player just selected for Team A. If you can subtly ask the captains to vary their choices (e.g. not all the strong players first), it will be a more satisfying experience for the whole group. Alternatively if this does not work, the children can organise themselves into pairs of equal ability. If a team captain chooses one of the pair, the other partner joins the opposition team. The two captains take it in turns to have the first selection of each partner.

- Traditional counting-out rhymes can also be used. The players form a circle or a line and on each word of the rhyme the child doing the counting moves, touches or points to another player. The player touched when the last word of the rhyme is spoken, is on one team. The rhyme begins again, the process is repeated, but this time the last player joins the other side. This is repeated until all children have their team.

Going out

When a child fails to skip over the rope, catch the ball, etc. and 'goes out', I prefer not to make her sit out for the rest of the game. Most of the games therefore, suggest ways of not permanently excluding the player who goes 'out'. I usually have the children form a going-out/coming-in queue, as follows: Chris goes out, and becomes number 1 in the queue. He is joined by Patty, who is number 2. When Belinda is out, she joins the queue and becomes number 2. Patty is the new number 1, and Chris rejoins the game. So there are

Back in the Playground Blues

I dreamed I was back in the playground. I was about four feet high.
Yes I dreamed I was back in the playground, standing about four feet high.
Well the playground was three miles long and the playground was five miles wide.
It was broken black tarmac with a high wire fence all around,
Broken black dusty tarmac with a high fence running all around
And it had a special name to it, *The Killing Ground.*

Got a mother and a father, they're one thousand miles away
The rulers of *The Killing Ground* are coming out to play
Everybody thinking: 'Who they going to play with today?'

Well you get it for being Jewish
And you get it for being black
Get it for being chicken
And you get it for fighting back
You get it for being big and fat
Get it for being small
Oh those who get it, get it and get it
For any damn thing at all.

Sometimes they take a beetle, tear off its six legs one by one.
Beetle on its black back, rocking in the lunchtime sun.
But a beetle can't beg for mercy, a beetle's not half the fun.
I heard a deep voice talking, it had that iceberg sound:
'It prepares them for life' – but I never found
Any place in my life worse than *The Killing Ground.*

Adrian Mitchell (1984)

never more than two, or however many children you choose, in the going-out/coming-in queue. 'Forfeits' are also a very traditional way of dealing with a mistake that is made within a game. These often take the form of an agreed penalty. If you get hit in a skipping game, for example, you may be asked to make three jumps on only one leg. If you can do this then you are allowed to go back to two-footed skipping.

When explaining the game

Expand the context by using imaginative pictures. It can help to have younger children sitting on the ground around you while you tell them the story of the game. I call this the 'huddle', where we form a tight little group, all sitting; this allows me to talk quietly to the children about what it is we are about to do. I often tell them a short story that contains in it the picture of the game we are about to play.

Alternatively, for children who are a little older, explaining a game while they are standing (or sitting) in a circle is also effective. I often ask the children to form a 'toe circle', meaning that we should stand in a circle looking at our feet and make sure that a perfect circle is achieved, so that all our feet are side by side. This gives the players something to focus on, and it is surprisingly quick to achieve a form that otherwise may take some time.

In ball games, always keep the ball in your hands when clarifying or explaining. We sometimes use what we call the 'talking ball'.

This means that only the person holding the ball may speak; all others must remain quiet and listen. When she has finished talking or asking a question, the ball is passed back to the game leader who then may pass it to another child who wishes to speak. I have found this very helpful; accepting it helps the children learn to respect each other's right to speak, and, what's more, to be heard.

Endings

It is very important for the players, especially for young children (3–9 years old) that a game has a definite ending. Just as a story has an ending, a journey has a destination, and a letter a closing greeting, so should a game have a defined outcome. The leader should tell the children before the game begins how the ending will come about. While this may seem obvious, some games that begin enthusiastically end in a sloppy or, worse, an argumentative manner, because the ending has not been clearly defined.

It is very important for players from about 10 years old and upwards, to review the game just played. This allows them to develop reflective thought, quietens them and allows a conscious finish to the game-time. I would even go so far as to suggest that a moment of complete silence, perhaps 10–15 seconds at the very end, helps the young person 'absorb' on a deeper level all the bodily activity that she has been engaged in while playing the game. With the younger ones, a simple story echoing the game's character will serve the same purpose. Children playing freely in their own time tend to do this 'review' quite naturally. When walking home they can often be heard discussing the failures and triumphs of all that occurred.

Breaking The Rules:
Sabotaging the game… conflict

Why? How do we deal with it?

Children seek the security of behavioural boundaries. It is partly the way they learn about the world and what is acceptable. They will often create very elaborate rules for a game and then have to develop consequences when one of the players infringes these. The rules are often quite sophisticated and the penalties harsh. However, when the game is played the next day it may well develop a new dynamic; someone has a good idea, and therefore the rules will adapt. In this way a great deal of our social abilities are learnt and refined.

Some children are habitual rule-breakers. It is almost as if they can't help themselves. Others may do it less often. Some will do it very openly, even in a challenging way. Others will be more secretive. This tendency may exist for a number of different reasons and have just as many implications for the rule-breaker as for other children.

There is a reasonably common correlation between the children who regularly break rules – and more importantly, resist attempts to be held responsible and accept the consequences – and the particular kind of life they lead outside the game environment. This usually falls into one of two categories.

The first, and the most common, is the child who has an abnormally loose home-life, where she seldom experiences restrictions, or, if there are any, the consequences for breaking them are either ill-defined or not followed through. Such a child may have a great deal of unsupervised leisure time. She has difficulty in relating to the rules. She will seldom take the opportunity to participate in their formation and will either show little interest in others who bend or break them; or overreact, displaying little understanding of the situation. If the matter is pressed by the other players she will threaten to withdraw, at times very vocally, or the others will have to find a way to adapt the rules to suit her. They may even turn a blind eye to further infringements.

In a supervised situation where an adult is present, this child will be helped if encouraged to be a central part of the game. You may choose her to be one of the team captains, or have an important role. You may try to encourage the child to take part in the rule forming. She will also be helped by sharing in the 'ownership' of the game. This can be achieved, for example, by giving her responsibility for being the only one to hold the ball in certain situations, or to give out the various pieces of equipment that may be needed. When a rule is broken, encourage the rule-breaker to find a new rule if she disagrees with the present ones. This is a helpful tone to adopt with a child who is lacking in form.

The second is the child who experiences the other extreme; who is subject to very authoritative, abnormally restrictive parenting, for whom the consequence of any disobedience is swift and unbending and does not easily take mitigating circumstances into account. Such a child will usually seek to be central in the rule-forming process and try to impose rules and consequences which are unimaginative and rigid. If accused of an infringement this child will argue strongly, and if pressed may even seek to redefine the rules so as to accommodate her action. If this fails, she can often become extremely upset and demonstrate threatening behaviour, in much the same way as she has perhaps been treated by parents.

Initially she can be asked to help mediate in the disputes of others, which is a task she will relate well to; however she must then also nominate another, or a small group, to take the role of judge. She may argue a case and be heard but should also be encouraged to agree to accept their decision. Eventually this child may be given the task of adapting the rules whenever the need arises. It may be necessary to inform the parents of her difficulties and of how you intend to help her.

Behaviour disturbance and the Temperaments

But there are also other types of rule-breakers. Some children naturally relate to rules better than others. This is a more deep-seated attribute than has just been outlined – which may be called acquired behaviour. This more deep-rooted quality is generally known as disposition or temperament. It does have

an important bearing on children's relationship to rules and consequences.

Considering children according to only four main categories of temperament may seem to be a pigeon-holing, rigid approach. In fact the opposite is true. There are few greater gifts one can give another person than a sincere attempt to understand them. This is particularly true if some of their actions seem to be negative and even bring you into conflict with them. Trying to empathise on a deep, insightful level can defuse what may have become a cycle of destructive behaviour, and open up new possibilities of relating. The idea of temperaments is a very useful aid to developing this understanding and empathy.

The first and most important step is to try to define your own temperament as objectively as possible. Be as honest as possible in identifying your own dominant tendencies. One of the best ways to identify your own or another's temperament is to ask: 'What temperament/s am I not?' This should leave you with the answer. Of course we have all four temperaments within us, but usually one or two will be dominant. After observing yourself for some time you may notice that one temperament will tend to come to the fore in certain situations.

The second task such empathy asks of you is to put aside preconceived feelings you hold for the other person. Listen and consciously observe their behaviour, without being judgemental. The fact that you can do this often brings a new clarity into the relationship.

Thirdly, what can you do to help the situation? What follows may both stimulate recognitions and indicate possible ways forward:

The Napolean…
the Choleric, the Fire Breather

There are those who see rules as constricting boundaries, infringements of their rights. Such people are normally extrovert and dominant; they may well be stocky and thick-set and dig their heels in when walking. Their speech is emphatic and deliberate. They see games as a personal challenge providing them with the possibility for conquest.

They may often have a poor memory and a restless nature, impatient to act before the explanation of a game is finished.

Sometimes they break rules simply because they have either forgotten them or did not listen in the first place. They will seek to blame others for their own mistakes. This tendency can cause problems, as many other players will see that it was the choleric's own fault and that it is therefore not fair to blame anyone else. This in turn will lead to a 'digging in of the heels' on the part of the Napoleon.

Such children need careful handling in a conflict situation as they have a strong sense of pride. Speak to them quietly or, in more extreme circumstances, defer the conversation until they have calmed down. If you insist on 'having it out there and then', you may well harden their attitude, and their behaviour will become more reckless and outrageous. Be careful with criticism, especially in front of others. Affirm their positive deeds, particularly those that involved courage or daring. Draw on their leadership ability; for example if they have withdrawn or are refusing to let the game continue, you may tell them that the game needs their input, that they are very strong players. Whilst the cause and particularly the solution may seem clear to you, the only way this type of child can become 'unstuck' is if she can still continue to feel in control, and not lose face. Any solution that you may whisper may well be taken up by such children and loudly proclaimed to the other players as their own idea, which everyone should take note of.

Be discreet yet strong. Make sure that once a decision is made it is final. Don't waffle, be to the point. You may even challenge such a child by saying that she has stopped playing because she's not up to it; or that you will ask someone else. Whilst the choleric will push you to change your mind, you will win her respect for standing firm.

In Australia when a bush fire is burning out of control, the fire fighters sometimes light a 'back burn'. This involves deliberately lighting another fire that is carefully calculated to collide with the initial, uncontrolled blaze. The destructive bush fire can then be extinguished, for there is no more fuel to burn. This principle can also be used to help a choleric child who has got to the point of shouting in anger; you can reply with the same, or even with increased intensity. It is vital that this is not done in anger but with a conscious wish to help her. If at all possible this should not be done in front of others and should be used only occasionally.

The Butterfly... the Sanguine, the Air Rider

These children do not really break rules, they disregard them. They see rules as applying mainly to others who have the misfortune to need them. They like to move freely from one situation to another, never stopping for too long at any one place. They are often slender and well built, lively, graceful and eloquent. Their friendships are frequently fickle and changeable. Like the choleric they have a poor memory; but they do have an ability to notice much of what is going on around them. They relate very much to the present moment.

Sanguines do not feel overly challenged when accused of violating rules, and will seldom get into an argument. They seem to accept all that has been said; other players may often feel they have sorted the problem out, only to find that the butterfly child has taken very little notice and has repeated the breach. This will sometimes provoke others' fury, because 'she keeps messing thing up'. The only way to deal with it seems to be either to tolerate this charmingly infuriating behaviour or to exclude the child from the game. But the sanguine can also at times have wild temper tantrums, which can be quite disturbing to the other children; if you the adult, though, don't get caught up in the whirlwind, but instead remain calmly detached, assuring the others that this is just something that she does from time to time, you will often find that the tantrum ends quickly.

The butterfly child has what may be called a 'hit and run' method of expressing anger or discontent. She may say or do hurtful or outrageous things and then very quickly change the subject or leave the room, leaving others (particularly the melancholics) to cope with the destruction and mop up the mess. She may later deny that she meant anything, saying that it was just a joke or that it is everybody else's problem for taking things so seriously. Sanguine children do this (often with real skill) in an attempt to avoid what causes them great discomfort – consequences.

Attempting to point out to sanguines what they have been responsible for, and asking them to take the consequences, is like trying to catch a butterfly or a grasshopper on a warm summer's day. The only way to stand any chance of success is to use a net. When working with groups the best 'net' that can be used is to involve as many people as is manageable to reflect back to the sanguine the effects of her behaviour. Invite others to tell the sanguine how she is both positively and negatively influencing what is being said or done. Do this with lightness yet directness. Use the same words often. Identify a word or a phrase that can be called out, one that playfully exposes when the 'hit and run' tactics are being employed.

However, there are other ways. In a supervised situation where conflict occurs, act immediately. If you delay, the sanguine may well have moved on to the next adventure and will show little interest in a problem that is past. The sanguine's ability to sympathise can be called on. Ask her to try and appreciate how frustrating it must be for the others. Alternatively you may ask her to remedy the situation as a personal favour to you. The 'butterflies' respond with great warmth to the cultivation of personal contact. Whilst their interest in many aspects of life may seem superficial, their real devotion can be awakened through personal connection.

The Comfort Zone…
the Phlegmatic, the Water Dweller

The phlegmatics have a love of the rules. 'For everything a place, and a place for everything' could be their motto. They seldom break the rules, but if they do and agree that they did, they will accept the consequence with good grace. If however they don't agree, they will refuse all penalties and stubbornly insist they were not in the wrong. They may become quite immovable no matter how much pressure is brought to bear. Normally slow to complain or express anger, they can

react with intensity when someone breaks a rule and won't own up.

The phlegmatics are often round and fleshy and walk with an ambling, constant gait, and have slow but well-defined gestures. They are logical, amiable but somewhat withdrawn. In a game situation, they will – if interested – be good team players and will adopt a supportive role; if they know the game well they may also occasionally emerge as leader. They are strategists, able to make elaborate plans if given the time. They need lots of warning about anything new. If told to do something that they don't want to, they will prefer to be quietly non co-operative, rather than openly disagree.

The anger of the phlegmatic is like a tidal wave, which forms far out to sea – slowly, silently swelling and growing – but then strikes land with a devastating force. It is all-consuming and reckless, anything that gets in its path is engulfed. The previously gentle, lapping waves and predictable tides now wreak havoc. If one carefully observes phlegmatics, early warning signs of an approaching outburst can be detected. Just as the regular patterns of the tides begin to change erratically before a tempest, so too do the phlegmatic's normal responses. The normal easy-going attitude may become a little touchy; she may become less tolerant or withdraw deep into herself. Her all-important routines may become disrupted. Or you may simply feel that something is not quite right. Of course you may ask if there is anything bothering her and show a patient and unthreatening attitude; but if that doesn't work, then batten down the hatches and head for high ground, putting in any damage limitations that you can think of – like warning other members in the family or class not to take it too personally or get too involved in her anger.

Screaming matches will achieve little. She will particularly need you and others around her to be in good shape to comfort her in the aftermath, and to help her begin the reconstruction process. You will not be so effective in this if you get too involved in the accusations and anger.

A tidal wave also often alters the old shore line, where water meets the land. The sea will recede far beyond its normal mark, exposing much previously submerged terrain. This earth is bare, uncultivated and unmapped. This has obvious parallels with the phlegmatic's rare outbursts. Not only does the anger affect and challenge many old forms and routines, it also offers the potential for new growth and change. This is a delicate time. It may take quite a few days of you consoling and reassuring her, before you can gently suggest areas of positive change. You will need to give her time to think this over as her processing of thoughts and ideas resembles the tortoise more than the hare, but let her know that's fine. She will be feeling raw, perhaps guilty and almost certainly exposed. Phlegmatics' possibility for change is inextricably bound up with their anger.

When the phlegmatic becomes 'stuck' either in her dreamy apathy or her stubbornness, don't be afraid to speak immediately, sharply and consciously. One does not need to raise one's voice, though; a calm intensity is the right tone. This usually serves to jolt her a little out of her problem. You can also draw on her strong mothering instinct, perhaps pointing out to her that there are many in the game that need her care.

A phlegmatic will often be heard to say wearily 'This is boring'. In these instances you may choose to take her boredom to its limits. Ask her to sit out of the activity and do nothing, absolutely nothing! She may well enjoy it for a while, but stay with it; and every time she comes back ask her to sit out again so she may fully 'enjoy' her boredom. Let her know that you are not angry with her, but make little attempt to engage. It may take several sessions; but eventually she will probably idle up to you and ask if she can join in, at which point she is warmly welcomed. Superficially this may seem like a small thing, but on a deeper level it is an important developmental shift – one that may well have positive implications for her life in general.

The Wilting Lily…
the Melancholic, the Earth Carrier

What particularly leads the melancholics into conflict is their self-absorption. They are amazed, hurt and sullen if accused of wrong-doing. They are so engrossed in themselves that they cannot easily see another player's point of view. The melancholic hears every complaint as a wounding attack aimed only at herself. She may lash out with personal, subjective comments about the players who are challenging her, but will not easily focus on the source of the problem at hand – such as the rule-infringement. She is very sensitive to sarcasm directed at herself, yet will freely use it towards others. It is these tendencies that combine to make the melancholic an open target for teasing and bullying.

The melancholic's anger sometimes resembles a sniper sitting hidden in a safe or camouflaged area, shooting hurtful or destructive comments at anyone who is a perceived threat and comes within range. The more one aggressively searches for the sniper, the more she retreats behind her cover and redoubles the shooting in an attempt to protect herself. This is dangerous for all concerned. Even if you do manage, often wounded, to expose her hide-out, you will have to try to take hold of a prisoner whose only options are to try to escape or give in to your will.

Far better to assure the melancholic that you understand her pain and that you are no threat. Wave a white flag and walk the ground between your position and the place she has retreated to, slowly letting her know that you don't blame her for what she has done, but that it is causing both herself and others some pain; and that you would like to help sort it out. Only then may the sniper allow you to approach. While she may not give up her weapon, the next time a conflict occurs she will recognise you, which may make your negotiation easier.

The melancholic finds it difficult to join in even though she would like to. She stands on the edge of situations, restrained by imagining injury, insult, intimidation and generally all the bad things that may happen if she gets involved. She is often thin and willowy, her demeanour resigned, her complexion sallow. She may speak haltingly, pausing to consider what people think of her. She has a low pain threshold, feeling every bump and knock. Her friends will be few; she prefers to make special bonds with one or two others. She likes solitary activities such as reading and painting; and long walks in nature where she takes note of all the small details she sees. She has a long memory when it comes to things she has been involved in, and a strong relationship to the past.

But for each of these difficult traits the melancholic displays, there exists a positive one. A bridge needs to be constructed from her introverted self, over the perceived dangerous waters, to the world on the other side, the world that exists outside herself.

It does no good to try and console the melancholic with statements like 'Never mind, it wasn't that bad really'. This merely confirms for her that no-one understands; and increases her feeling of isolation. Far better to empathise, or try to imagine the melancholic's sense of all the bad things that have happened or may happen. If you observe her watching a game from the sidelines, it's helpful to talk to her about how hard it is to join in. Sympathise with her, for example, about that situation two years ago when someone called her an awful name: 'If the same child does it again', you can say, 'just feel sorry for him that he has to do such a thing to make himself seem important'. The melancholic will have to try and overcome the hurt; you as the adult can reassure her that you will notice if such a thing happens again.

Melancholics also have a well-developed capacity to notice suffering in others. This can be a wonderful quality if they are helped to see what they can do to assist other people. If they feel that they are making a sacrifice, they may well go to great lengths to be of service.

While it is important to show understanding to the melancholic, be wary of going too far and becoming morose. Sympathise with past events and future fears in a kindly but matter of fact way, showing that while you understand her feelings, there is also a steady hand safely directing the situation.

The adult reaction

Children who break the rules can be annoying, even infuriating to the adult. You can have the feeling that no matter what the situation, the same child will inevitably try to disrupt or become difficult in some

way. It gets to the stage where you are anticipating it, even warning the child that you will not stand for it again.

This can result in an escalating conflict situation where your reactions become somewhat unconscious. Looking back in the evening, you will perhaps be disturbed less by the actions of the child than by your own lack of control.

The type of response we give in a conflict situation is seldom straightforward. However, there are a few basic 'checks' that you can do. First and foremost, examine your own temperament. For example, do you have choleric tendencies? When the child shouted at you in front of others, did you react too forcefully because you could not stand to lose face? Or were you so keen to 'get on with things' that your explanation of the game was too quick? This may have resulted in some children not knowing what to do and therefore misbehaving.

Did the situation spiral out of control because of your sanguine nature, which prevented you noticing the warning signs? Was your explanation of the game so disjointed that the conflict arose because some players disagreed about what to do?

Was that caustic, sarcastic comment you made a result of your melancholic nature? Did you feel personally wounded by some of the children telling you that the game was 'dumb' and that they would not play anymore?

Were you over-connected to the form of the game you had so carefully and slowly planned, that when the child sabotaged it you reacted strongly?

These are just a few examples of the many reactions we may have that are influenced by our own disposition. It is essential that we not only look at the part the child played but more importantly at our own response. It is the adult's responsibility to reach the child, not the child's to reach the adult. There may be some difficult situations that you feel you handled well. Look at these, learn from your successes. Why is it that the child was able to calm down and accept what you suggested?

It is often helpful to look at your own biography, particularly at that part of it which relates to the same age as the child or group that you had the difficult situation with. For example you may ask yourself: 'Is there a connection between my overreaction towards that child who was picking on a smaller boy, connected to my own small stature and the fact that I was bullied at that age?' or: 'Is the reason I don't really grasp the difficult situation due to an unconscious fear of conflict? Are my reactions connected with defensive or avoidance tactics?' These questions and others may arise if we have the willingness to look into ourselves. Addressing a difficult situation may not only help the children to grow up stronger, but also help the adult to deal with some of her own unresolved feelings. The child unconsciously respects the adult who is able to deal with her own weaknesses in a searching way.

Equipment

Use of equipment

It is important that the children are active in setting up and putting away equipment – if this is practicable. When the children are active in these processes, they not only get more exercise but are also helped to feel 'ownership' of the game. They tend, therefore, to place a greater value on what goes on when playing it. They also learn how to set up games for themselves, and thus no longer have to be wholly reliant on an adult to get a game started and finished. This idea can be taken even further in the actual designing, making or collecting, of equipment for the game. Old pieces of wood can become goals or bats; blankets or sacks become bases, screens, caves etc. Many hours of real enjoyment can be had transforming 'junk' into equipment that will be used over and over again. The child experiences process. I firmly believe that what may be called 'process-less-ness' is at the root of many of the social ills that afflict our young people today. Making up a game and fashioning a bat or other equipment, is no small thing in helping the child to develop strong, individual values, empathy for others, and the ability to see something through to the end.

The portable gymnasium

Very few schools or clubs around the world are lucky enough to have a gymnasium or even a well-kept and defined playing area at their disposal. Over the years I have used a simple way to define a play area. I buy a long rope, which is normally very cheap, of at least 100 metres in length, and lay the rope down on the ground as a perimeter. If children leave this area, they are 'out'; I usually ask them to come back in through the 'door', which I 'open' after letting them stay outside for a while. The 'door' is where the rope has an end and where it meets itself. For example you may lay out a circle or a rectangle, using all or part of the rope according to the game and the number of players. If you want a really top-of-the-range 'portable gym' you may buy several hundred metres of rope and a winder (usually found in garden shops) that is normally used for winding up garden hoses. In this way, setting up, packing up, and storage, are easy and efficient.

You may wish to supplement this set-up with a few witches' hats or cones (never, of course 'borrowed' from road-side works) to give a good profile to your court area.

This cheap and simple piece of equipment is very helpful – particularly in chasing games, in which the more determined chaser and escaper may disappear over the distant horizon, much to the alarm of the leader and the amusement of the children!

Playing-balls

For chasing games where children 'brand' (i.e. strike) each other with the ball, a **Foam Practice Volleyball** (non-sting) is recommended. These can easily be bought from any good sports shop or catalogue. Instead of this you can also use a slightly deflated volleyball, or more sturdy beach ball. What is important is that when you are branded with the ball, you are not hurt in any way. The fear of being hurt by the ball is very common for many children and prevents them from entering into, and gaining valuable experiences in games. These 'softy' balls are perfect; they allow the strong players to hurl the ball as hard as they like whilst the more sensitive players know that they can enjoy the game without being intimidated.

Of course you may vary the size and weight of the ball according to the game and the age of the child. It is a wonderful thing to make a ball with the help of children. I have tried many different designs. One of the most successful is made by wrapping a large amount of old woollen thread round and round a tennis ball, until the desired weight and size is achieved. Then sew strips of cotton, woollen or polyester material together to form a rough sphere-shape. Finally place the thread-wound ball inside the material – and you have a wonderful play ball. You may substitute real wool, not yet spun, instead of yarn. This makes the ball lighter. Other variations are to first cut a small hole in the tennis ball and pour in some sand, which makes the end product heavier. If you have a lot of old stockings you can put the wool-wound ball inside it and sew it up. Build up the layers of nylon stocking by repeating this last step over and over until you have a good strong covering.

These balls are ideal for inside- or rainy-day use as they are a little more forgiving on the lightshades and other objects; but they can also be used out of doors on dry days.

Tennis balls

Tennis balls can be used for ball games if necessary. For games that involve branding, I make the tennis ball softer by piercing a hole in it with a sharp object. Alternatively, wrapping some woollen thread around them will soften them. Low impact tennis balls are also on the market at the moment. They are generally used for 'short tennis'. The advantage of these balls is that they are not quite as bouncy as ordinary tennis balls and are much easier to control. I remember playing against-the-wall-type branding games as a child, in which the tennis ball was dipped in water to

make it really sting when it hit you! This was a game for the 'hard core', tough, branding players.

Whilst not advocating this game as a builder of world peace, it is interesting that some children will naturally, of their own accord, toughen up some games in order to test themselves and take things to the limit. As adults we may be alarmed at such activity, but some children need and want it.

Mini basket balls

These are useful for introducing rounders as they offer a bigger surface area to hit. However, they don't tend to fly so far when struck – which can lead to over-crowding around the hitter. They are also fine for playground games such as *Four Square*, but are not as good as slightly softer and bouncier playground balls. They should be slightly deflated to the size of a large grapefruit. If they are too hard, little fingers can be hurt. These balls are terrible in branding games.

Hula hoops

These are useful to mark a small area e.g. *Shipwrecks* (game 112), *Trains and Stations* (game 141). They can also be held up as targets and of course used in their own right.

Coloured bands

Bands or bibs to identify teams or individuals are always useful, e.g. *Crows and Cranes* (game 51). I have often been astonished at the prices of these in sports shops. They can be made very cheaply and easily. Cut up a single-coloured, sturdy piece of material into strips about 4–5 foot long and 2–3 inches wide (120–150 by 5–6cm). Sew both ends together, making a band that is worn 'sash-like' across the chest and around the back. For a professional job, use a sewing machine and fold a little of the band-edge back on itself; sew along it, making a hem or seam. Make as many as you need in one colour and repeat the process with another.

Whistles

These are not appropriate in games for children up to 10 years of age. The voice is so much better. Even after the age of ten, a clear, loud direction is better than a whistle. Only in formalised sport is regular use of whistles necessary; even then it is better to use your voice where possible.

Ropes for skipping games

Many people comment on the beautiful ropes that I use with the children. They are reasonably heavy, woven, soft and silky. I get them from boating suppliers who are very helpful (and rather amused when I tell them what I want them for). They usually have a huge range of ropes to choose from in any length you want. They are often very much cheaper than the ropes bought from a shop. Lovely wooden handles can be carved with the help of the children.

Wooden staffs

There are many games that can be played using wooden staffs or rods (e.g. *Bird in a Cage*, game 200). These should be approximately 3'6" long (about waist high on an adult) and about 3/4" in diameter (100 x 2cm). Broom handles can be used, although dowelling from timber yards is often better quality. I usually round the edges off by sanding them down and give them a lovely finish by oiling them with linseed oil every six months or so.

Beanbags

These can be made from any pulse or bean e.g. kidney beans, lentils etc. Just make sure the bags don't get damp or wet! If you ever plan on taking them out of the country make plastic-bead ones as bean-filled bags will be confiscated by the customs. The making of these bags can be a popular 'rainy day' activity. The standard size is about 3 x 2 inches wide, and about 1 inch deep (7.5 x 5 x 2.5cm). Alternatively you can buy one from a sports or toy store and copy the design. For the younger children I sometimes put a little 'tail' on the bag. You can do this by sewing on a 6–8 inch (15–20cm) piece of ribbon to one edge. This makes a lovely tail behind the bag when it is thrown, making the flight path of the bag more obvious. It also makes it much easier to catch.

If you are making juggling bags these can be quickly and easily done by filling a balloon with a small amount of grain, about 2–3 tablespoons. Then cut off the neck of a second balloon and put the first balloon, which contains the grains, inside it. Repeat this step over and over until you've built up about five layers of rubber.

If using 'edibles' such as beans or lentils, you'll need to store them in such a way that critters will not get into them as a winter snack. Game leaders who have outdoor storage spaces, make sure you store these in tight plastic tubs.

Each person will need to make at least three juggling balls/bags. Alternatively you can make a pyramid shaped juggling bag out of cloth, which is excellent for beginners. Each side of the pyramid has a base of 2 inches (5cm).

Marbles

There are many different types and sizes of marbles, each with their own character and value. In a marbles craze, certain colours and designs become much valued 'hard currency'.

Quoit or rubber ring

These are commonly available and cheap to buy. You might be lucky and find the lovely old hemp rope type, however most are now made from rubber. They usually measure around 6–8 inches across (15–20cm).

Floor mats

Most sports stores or catalogues have these thin gymnastic or judo tumbling-mats. They are not cheap but are worth the outlay; once acquired the children use them very frequently. They are available in many sizes. The most standard size is around 5ft x 3ft long (150 x 90cm) and about 1–2 inches thick (2.5–5.0 cm). Some have the added advantage of velcroing together if you have more than one.

Drums and other percussion instruments

Many of the games in this book involve either music, singing or percussion sounds. Many games can also be adapted so that the element of listening or tension is created through the use of musical instruments.

Skittles

The best sort are the old-fashioned wooden ones, but these are difficult to obtain. Most toy stores have plastic ones. The heavier the better. They usually stand around 10–12 inches high (25–30cm) and are shaped like an old fashioned Coca-Cola bottle with a smaller base. I have never really been successful in making these out of scrap wood but a friend has made me some beautiful ones on a wood-turning lathe. Alternatively you can use tin cans of various sizes that have had the sharp edges made safe.

Acknowledgements

Heartfelt thanks to Cory Waletzko, who so playfully worked in the compiling of the new games in this book. Also to Martin Baker, Rob Sim, Knut Ross, Jaimen McMillan, Graham Whiting and Kate Hammond for their inspirational colleagueship. Thank you to the students both past and present of Wynstones, Mt Barker Waldorf, Michael Hall Steiner School, Emerson College and Bothmer Movement International. And to my father who embodied, in all he did, the spirit of fair play.

Special admiration and gratitude to Thom Schaefer and Jaimen McMillan for holding the Olympiad torch high and spreading its light across the world.

Kim John Payne

Special thanks to Tate Benson for LGBTQ+ consulting, and to my masterful movement teachers from whom I've learned (and looted) and with whom I've laughed (and loved): Mashobane Moruthane, Julianna Lichatz, Jeff Tunkey, Will Crane, Torsti Rovainen, Susan Darcy, Kim Lebas, Bonnie Bolz, Katie Moran, Jaimen McMillan, and Kevin Quigley.

Thank you to Kim John Payne for starting this game of author-tag so many years ago, and for the team at Hawthorn Press for their stamina and vision. Huzzah!

Great, gooey gratitude to my powerful peer collaborators, willing to read and give feedback, even in the eleventh hour: Josiah Proietti, Joey Brenneman, Lauren VanHam, Merideth Jackson, Fonda Black, and Kevin Quigley (the oceanfrog, indeed)

A Spacial ∞ shout-out to Jaimen McMillan and the Spacial Dynamics© Institute (modern-day Hogwarts): and to my family for gearing me up with such excellent training along the way, that I now get to play for a living!

Cory Waletzko

Note:
Pronouns alternate between 'she', 'he' and 'they' throughout the text.
Modifications are included throughout to incorporate players with differing physical abilities and mobility adaptation needs.

PART ONE

Exploring the House

Games For 7–12 Year Olds

Chapter One
Snow Games – Mixed Ages

1. Fox and Geese

The snow geese love to return every year to their favourite frozen lake, their pit-stop on the long journey south for winter. They are having a peaceful rest when a fox comes bounding along to try to catch as many geese as he can for his supper.

After a freshly fallen snow, the group stomps a large circle with eight or so paths to a small middle spot. The fox starts in the centre of the 'wheel' and the geese are on the outside. When the game begins, the fox chases the geese to tag them. All must stay on the freshly-made path. If a goose is tagged, they go into the 'pot of goose-stew', an area marked out of bounds where they can build a snow fort, make snow sculptures, or 'snow-vegetables' to go into the 'stew'. Any player who steps off the path must go to the 'pot of stew'.

Variations:

- Any activity can be chosen for the geese who have been tagged (snow-play, building snow sculptures, making snow angels, etc.).
- When a goose is tagged, they become the new fox.
- When a goose is tagged, they become a fox helper. Eventually, all players are fox helpers and only one goose remains. The final remaining goose is the new fox in the next round.
- Can play with two (or more) foxes at the start of the game. The game leader can give the duo a minute to strategise before the game begins.

Hints to the leader:

- The game leader can stand near the 'pot of stew' to guide interactions of the geese who have been tagged.
- The game leader may call a new fox or have the fox choose a buddy to help them if they are getting tuckered out.

AGE RANGE: Multi-age

PLAY AREA: Outdoors in winter – after a fresh snowfall; large circle at least 20 paces across, made with fresh footprints in the snow, 8 'spokes' that come out from the centre like a wheel.

NUMBER OF PLAYERS: 6–30 (or more)

EQUIPMENT: None

For children who may struggle to play this game:

- For more sensitive players, it can be too much pressure to be the only one left at the end, the sole target of the fox(es.) In this case, the game leader may call an end to the round when there are two geese left, not just one.
- The game leader may wish to call a struggling child to the out-of-bounds space (the pot of stew to build snow sculptures) before they are tagged by the fox, to redirect them before a potential meltdown may arise.

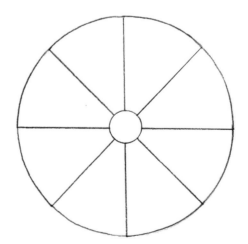

2. Jack Frost / King Winter

The cold weather is on its way, and two tricksters have come to freeze everything (and everyone) in sight! Jack Frost is an excellent icicle maker, while King Winter makes fantastic snowballs. How long will this cold snap last?

AGE RANGE: 7–9

PLAY AREA: Outdoors in winter, 25 x 25 paces (larger for more challenge, smaller for less challenge)

NUMBER OF PLAYERS: 7–30 (or more)

EQUIPMENT: Cones or other outer-boundary markers

Players form a circle holding hands. One player is chosen to be Jack Frost, another is chosen to be King Winter. The two stand in the centre of the circle before the game starts. When the game begins, the circle breaks up and the players run away to avoid being tagged. When they are tagged by Jack Frost, they become an icicle (arms out, feet wide), when they are tagged by King Winter, they become a snowball (sitting on their heels in a curled 'ball', heads down near the knees.) Frozen icicles can be 'melted' (freed) when another player crawls under their legs.

Snowballs can be 'melted' when another player rolls over their back. Jack Frost and King Winter count how many icicles and snowballs they can 'freeze'. Players count how many icicles and snowballs they can 'melt'.

Variations:

- This can be played with just one of the characters (i.e. Jack Frost as the only 'it.') Let the players get used to these movements. Then play a round with King Winter as the only 'it.' After players have been introduced to both characters, then add them together in the same round.
- There can be a 'Secret Sun' – the only player who has the power to 'melt' an icicle or snowball. The game leader chooses them by asking all the children to close their eyes and put their hands behind their backs, palms up. The game leader walks around and taps that player's palm, and then asks the players to open their eyes. The Secret Sun then tries to keep their identity hidden from the taggers. If the taggers guess the true identity of the Secret Sun, that round ends and a new game begins. A new Secret Sun is chosen.

Hints to the leader:

- Have the players practise 'melting' one another, icicles and snowballs, before playing in the heat of the game. Players may try to free an icicle from different directions and must make sure they don't bump heads.
- Remind those that are 'it' that they may not tag a player who is freeing another. They must wait until that person is back on their feet before they try to tag them – putting in place a 'count-to-three-pause' rule can be helpful.

For children who may struggle to play this game:

- Some children have a hard time accepting being tagged. The game leader can join in the game and model becoming an icicle/snowball along with the other players. (It's actually quite fun to have someone melt you!)
- The rolling-over-the-back movement to 'melt' the snowballs provides a sense of deep pressure that some children are actually seeking when they engage in off-task behaviour. This motion can be done in slow motion by the game leader, providing a satisfying sense of 'heaviness' that can serve to relax them.

3. Helmet, Goggles, Skis & Poles

This is a twist of the classic, 'Head, Shoulders, Knees and Toes' game/song for those that live in ski-friendly areas. It is played in the same way as the classic, and each time the song is sung, a section of the song is omitted (players are silent) while the moves continue.

AGE RANGE: Multi-age
PLAY AREA: Any
NUMBER OF PLAYERS: Any
EQUIPMENT: None

Helmet, goggles, skis and poles, skis and poles
Helmet, goggles, skis and poles, skis and poles
And hat, and gloves, snow pants, and coat
Helmet, goggles, skis and poles, skis and poles

The moves:

Helmet (Hands on head)
Goggles (Hands make circles over eyes – like binoculars)
Skis (Touch toes)
and *Poles* (Arms out to sides – hands in fists as if holding ski poles)

Hat (Hands on head)
Gloves (Both hands up, fingers spread)
Snow Pants (Each leg steps into pants)
and *Coat* (Zip up coat from navel to throat)

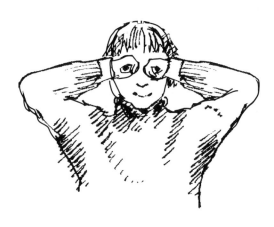

The game leader can call players 'out' if they mess up the words/moves. Players who are 'out' step to the side and continue to sing the song. Players try to stay in the game as long as possible. Last player to be called out wins the round.

Variations:

- Can be done in other languages.
- Players can make up their own moves/words.

Hints to the leader:

- Players will want to do the moves to 'Head/Shoulders…' The group should practise multiple times before playing a round with 'outs'.

4. Snow Cone Relay

A relay race perfect for snowball-packing weather!

Divide the players into even teams. Have the teams make as many snowballs as they can in a period of time. Line up three (or however many teams there are) cones or cans on a low bench or stumps. The players form lines for this relay. Each player gets one snowball throw to try to knock over a cone and then goes to the back of their team's line. Depending on the ages of the players, they can work together for 'good luck points' or each line can compete for the high score of knocked-over-cones. If a cone is knocked over, the game leader calls, 'Freeze.' Players must not throw in a 'freeze' lest they lose a point. The game leader rights the cone, gets out of the way, and calls 'Unfreeze', and the game begins again.

Variations:
- To make it easier, place the starting line closer to the cones; for more challenge, further away.
- For more challenge, have the players throw with their non-dominant hand.

Hints to the leader:
- Encourage teams to build their snowball piles where they won't get trampled in the excitement of the game.

> **AGE RANGE:** 9+
> **PLAY AREA:** Outdoors in winter; snow that is 'packable'; best with a bench or stumps on which to place the cones
> **NUMBER OF PLAYERS:** 6–30 (or more)
> **EQUIPMENT:** Three cones or cans, a bench or tree stumps

- This activity promotes snowball throwing, so be clear with the players that this game's aim is at the cones, not the people! The game leader may choose another activity before going back indoors so that children are not tempted to throw snowballs at each other after the game is over.

For children who may struggle to play this game:
- Snowball throwing can be overstimulating to some children. As an alternative, a child may be chosen to be the 'Eagle Eyes' for the game, standing next to the game leader and calling the freezes, resetting the cones, or tallying up the team scores.

5. Roman Wrestling: Snow Style
Created by Julianna Lichatz

Two teams face one another in two lines – facing off. One pair at a time tries to wrestle the other to the ground and pin them on their back for three seconds. Rules: no head/neck grabs, no kicking or tripping, no faces in the snow. The first person to pin the other on their back for three seconds wins the round.

Hints to the leader:
- The process of creating teams can make or break a given game. Older players can be given the chance to choose a partner that is a good match for them. Ideally, both players agree, and if not, a different match is sought.

> **AGE RANGE:** 12+
> **PLAY AREA:** Outdoors in winter, flat area of fresh, soft snow
> **NUMBER OF PLAYERS:** 6+
> **EQUIPMENT:** None

6. Sled Dogs

In the snowy tundra, the villagers must call on their sled dogs to pull them through the snowstorm to deliver a very important message to the villagers in the next town 'Take cover, get indoors, there's a giant blizzard on the way!' There is no way the villagers could make it on foot, so they depend on their trusty huskies to get them there.

Children gather in groups of three. One sits on a rubber base (or small sled/cardboard pizza box) and holds the middle of a jump-rope with elbows close to their sides (rider), two others hold the ends of a jump rope and pull the child on the base (sled dogs.) The riders are pulled to the far end of the field and back to the starting line before they switch places. Players take turns so each gets to be a rider and a sled dog. This can be done for fun or for speed with teams like a relay. Great for core strength, stamina, and cooperation.

Variations:

- Have players experiment with different techniques for the turnaround.
- Rider may prefer to put the rope behind their back rather than hold the rope.
- To make the numbers even, there can be one sled dog pulling one rider.

AGE RANGE: Multi-age

PLAY AREA: Outdoors in winter, packed snow on flat field

NUMBER OF PLAYERS: 3+

EQUIPMENT: rubber bases, small sleds, or cardboard pizza boxes, jump-ropes, cones to mark start/stop points

Hints to the leader:

- Riders need to lean back so they don't get pulled off their sled.
- Sled dogs must work together to go the same speed, no lone-wolf running ahead!

For children who may struggle to play this game:

- For some children who have not yet developed core strength and are still negotiating their balance, they may get pulled off their sled as their eager sled dogs race ahead, and end up being dragged rather than riding. In this case, the jump rope should be wrapped behind them at the waist rather than held in their hands.
- For more anxious players, the game leader can remove 'racing' aspect. The activity is fun in and of itself and does not require the element of competition.

7. Polar Bears and Seals
Created by Julianna Lichatz

Polar bears and seals don't need ski poles, so neither do we! – A playful introduction to cross-country skiing.

The game leader is the polar bear, standing in the middle of the snowy field and the players are the seals, all lined up at one end. To start the game, the game leader calls to the players, 'Come little seals and glide across my ice field', at which the players then kick-and-glide across to the other side. Meanwhile the polar bear tries to tag the players. If tagged, they join the polar bear in the middle of the field and try to catch the seals the next time they run across.

Variations:

• This game can be played without skis. The game leader and players may create new animals and ways those animals chase and are chased (i.e. penguins, reindeer, snow leopards).

Hints to the leader:

• Cross-country skiing is a sport that can be enjoyed for a life-time. As a movement activity for young children, it is not only a fun way to stay active in the winter, also helps with the following:

– The cross-lateral patterning helps with midline integration.

– Rhythmical movement helps with breathing and circulation, bringing a sense of calm/order to internal systems.

– Helps develop balance.

– Students learn to initiate their own will to get from point A to point B, as opposed to downhill skiing where they sit passively as they ride up the lift and allow gravity to propel them back down.

– Students must learn to stop their movement to stay in control.

AGE RANGE: 7–10

PLAY AREA: Outdoors in winter, rectangular field full of snow, large enough for group to be challenged getting across

NUMBER OF PLAYERS: 8+

EQUIPMENT: Cross-country skis and boots for all, no poles!

8. Cold & Spicy Buffalo-Style Yoga Ball
Created by Jeff Tunkey

Who says it's too cold to play outside? Cold and Spicy Buffalo-Style Yoga Ball will keep you warm!

This is a snow-soccer game, but with only one kick – the kick-off! Best played when the snow is soft and snowsuits provide plenty of padding for the players.

Two teams, each side has an 'end zone' marked by the corner cones. After a kickoff, players can shove, roll, carry or throw the ball across the goal line. Usually a few players will self-assign as goalies. The rules are: no kicking after the kick-off, no neck or head grabs, and don't hurt anyone… very much! *(Say that with a knowing smile on your face, and send anyone who's playing too rough to the 'penalty box'.)*

Variations:

- If the field is icy, this game can be played with all players on their hands and knees – no standing.

Age range: 8–11

Play area: Outdoors in winter. 40 x 40 paces (soccer-sized field)

Number of players: 6–30 (or more)

Equipment: Four cones or other boundary markers, 24" yoga ball

Hints to the leader:

- Best to start with a no-physical-contact rule. Once players get the hang of it, and when the snow is fresh and players are bundled up (and padded) in snow gear, 'rough and tumble' element may be added.

9. Hands-and-Knees Hockey

Too slippery to run on the ice? No problem!

This game was created as a solution to the playing field at our school icing over. No one could walk on it without slipping, and we certainly couldn't run. Because everyone was all bundled up with snow gear, we decided to crawl around on the ice. One child found an old frisbee that had been left out and buried in a snowbank, and it slid across the ice so smoothly, it soon became a hockey puck. The rules of this game are basically the same as in hockey, but instead of using sticks, players move the frisbee across the ice with their hands in a gliding motion.

Variations:

- This game can be played with or without goalies. If the group is small, it's more fun for the players to be in the action, defending the goal only when needed.
- The goalie position can be used for players with limited mobility.

Age range: Multi-age

Play area: Outdoors in winter, icy surface (frozen pond/lake – or a field with poor drainage that ices over in winter!)

Number of players: 6–30

Equipment: An old frisbee/disc, 4 cones to mark goals, snow pants and gloves for all players

Hints to the leader:

- The more puffy the snow pants, the more fun this game can be; knees in particular need protection while crawling around on the ice.

10. Ramparts in the Snow
Created by Julianna Lichatz

Finally, permission to have a snowball fight!

Divide the group into two teams. The teams go out to an area away from the normal playspace (wooded area or field out of vision from youngers) and build snow forts and an 'arsenal' of snow balls. At the signal from the game leader, they are allowed to 'attack', some hiding behind the forts and others serving as spies and infantry out in the field.

Hints to the leader:

• Make sure that there are no rocks or chunks of ice that may get packed into the snowballs.

• If playing in a school environment where there are younger children on campus, it's best that this game be reserved for the older students and played in a space that is not observed by the younger children, especially if you have a 'no snowball throwing' rule at the school. Remind the older students that this is a special occasion, and when the game is over, that means the game is over… cease fire!

AGE RANGE: 12+

PLAY AREA: Outdoors in winter, woods or field with fresh packing snow

NUMBER OF PLAYERS: 6+

EQUIPMENT: None

Indoor/Rainy Day Games – Mixed Ages

11. Sleepy Jay

Sleepy Jay was so sleepy, she didn't have the energy to do anything, let alone get out of bed and go to school! She was too sleepy to make her breakfast, too sleepy to tie her shoes, and too sleepy to get up off the couch and go to school. She decided to disguise herself as a 'little old lady' so that others would offer her their seat on the school bus. But no such luck, the children saw through her disguise, and they were not about to be fooled into giving her their seat!

AGE RANGE: 7+

PLAY AREA: Indoor, medium-sized room.

NUMBER OF PLAYERS: 7+

EQUIPMENT: As many chairs as there are players, a shawl/hat/other prop for 'Sleepy Jay'

The game begins with each child sitting in a chair with one chair empty. Chairs are all facing different directions with about two paces between chairs. One player is chosen to be 'Sleepy Jay' and they are standing up when the game begins. Sleepy Jay may only move toward the empty chair by shuffling their feet with a slow pace to get there. The other players are trying to keep Sleepy Jay from sitting down, but as soon as they stand or move to switch chairs, they may not sit back down in that same chair but must keep the motion going toward a new chair. Players may not run, they must walk to a new chair. If Sleepy Jay finally gets a seat, Hooray! – a new Sleepy Jay is chosen.

Variations:

- For older players, add a soft ball for passing. New rule is that a player can only switch chairs when they have the ball. The rest of the players then work together to thwart Sleepy Jay.
- Once the above variation has been practised, a second ball may be added.

Hints to the leader:

- When learning the game, players will be tempted to try to sit back down in the same chair that they were leaving. Gently remind the players that once they make a move to change chairs, they must commit.
- To begin, the game leader can take the role of Sleepy Jay, modelling the shuffling motion of the feet to establish the slow pace of the game.

- The game leader may preview and practise a 'freeze' setting for the game. Players practise moving from the motion of the game into a 'freeze' position – like statues. This allows the game leader to control the pace and tenor of the game so that it doesn't move too fast or become too noisy.

For children who may struggle to play this game:

- This game can arouse squeals of excitement! For more sensitive players, challenge the group to do a round in silence – no squealing allowed!

12. Rabbits and Carrots

The farmer planted his carrots all neatly in a row, but there were some very hungry rabbits who lived on the other side of the field that just loved to pull a carrot to the burrow and eat it all up. However, a fox also lived in the field and the fox liked to sneak up on the rabbits and catch them.

Half of the players are the carrots who lie in a row, face up, arms extended outwards towards the rabbits. Half the players are rabbits who are safe in their burrow behind a marked line.

There are one or two players who are the foxes and wear pinnies or coloured bands.

If a rabbit successfully pulls a carrot back into the burrow, even if just the fingertips are over the burrow line, then that carrot becomes a rabbit.

When rabbits are tagged by the fox in the field, they become carrots and lie down where they are. Rabbits are not safe anywhere beyond their burrow and can be tagged even when holding onto a carrot.

Hints to the leader:

- Do not allow any rabbit or fox to jump over a carrot! Carrot safety is a must.

AGE RANGE: 9–11

PLAY AREA: Indoor, 20 x 20 paces, size is adjusted to the number of players.

NUMBER OF PLAYERS: 10+

EQUIPMENT: Pinnies or coloured bands to identify the foxes, cones or ropes to mark the boundaries

- Talk to the rabbits about gently letting go of carrots if they ever have to run away in a hurry.

- The game leader should begin as the fox to manage the flow of the game. They can ease off if the rabbits need a little help, and increase the challenge when there are plenty of rabbits.

- Many children love to be chased and will run out to get caught even when a rabbit is pulling the last carrot into the burrow. If this doesn't produce a cheer and a natural end to the game, then call the end of the game.

- If the children who are carrots start moving on their own, tell them that the farmer plants the stationary carrot variety, not the motorised ones; self-propelled carrots are not allowed!

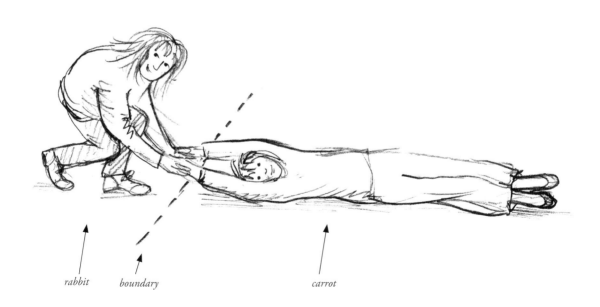

rabbit   boundary   carrot

13. Catch the Signal

Sometimes, when you're really quiet, you can hear the secret message of the wind. Shhh… there it is now… can you hear it?

This is a quieting game that cultivates focus, also known as 'pass the pulse'. The group of players takes hands in a circle. The game leader squeezes the hand of a person next to them in a certain rhythm. The 'signal' then gets passed around the circle from one player to the next.

When the game leader receives the signal after having gone all the way around the circle, they reveal the signal they sent versus the signal they got by clapping the (possibly) two different rhythms; like the game 'telephone', but using movement rather than words.

Variations:

- For more challenge, the game leader may challenge the group to close their eyes.

Hints to the leader:

- The game leader should start with a simple pattern that is easy to remember, and get more complicated as the group finds success.

- Much of the time, the signal changes, which can tempt players into blaming others – 'who messed up?' To minimise this, the game leader can frame it as a wonderful mystery, 'The winds do change sometimes, don't they? How fascinating!'

AGE RANGE: 7–11
PLAY AREA: Any
NUMBER OF PLAYERS: 6+
EQUIPMENT: None

14. Coin or Stone?

Once there was a magpie who loved to collect shiny objects. She sometimes saw a bright flash of copper light out of the corner of her eye when she flew over the village, spotting the bright shiny pennies she sometimes saw in the villagers' hands when they paid for a loaf of bread. The magpie let out a shrill 'CAW!' begging the villagers to give her their penny.

The villagers agreed to give the magpie their coin, as long as the next time she flew into town, she would repay it. Will the magpie repay the coin or will she try to trick the villagers by keeping her precious shiny penny and giving them a stone instead?

AGE RANGE: 7–9
PLAY AREA: Indoor, any room
NUMBER OF PLAYERS: 8+
EQUIPMENT: One coin, one stone

The group stands in a circle. The game leader can begin as the 'magpie' or choose another player. The magpie starts by holding both a coin and a stone in their hand. They skip around the circle of players. The rest of the group holds their hands behind their backs with their palms turned upward so that either object can be placed in their hands by the magpie. If a player receives the stone, they then chase the magpie back to their spot, attempting to tag them before they get there. If a player receives the coin, they are to make no motion whatsoever, standing completely still like a statue.

For players who receive a stone, if they are able to tag the magpie before they get back to their place, the tagger then gets to be the new magpie. If they are not able to tag the magpie before the magpie makes it back to their spot, they turn into stones (sit down in their spot).

The players that have been turned into stones can be saved if a player receives the coin from the magpie and is able to stand perfectly still. In this case, the stones all stand back up and rejoin the game. If a player receives the coin and makes any movement, that player is turned into a stone. The game is over if/when the magpie has managed to turn all players into stones.

Variations:

- 'Right Shoulder/Left Shoulder' – Same rules as above, but with no objects needed. If a player is tapped on the right shoulder, they stand still. If they are tapped on the left shoulder, they chase the 'it' back to their spot, trying to tag them. If they flinch when tapped on the right shoulder, they sit down. If they chase the 'it' and fail to tag them, they sit down. When tapped on the right shoulder, if a player is able to be perfectly still, they are able to save those that are sitting; all seated players then stand up and the game keeps going.

- For players with limited mobility, the role of 'Eagle Eyes' can be added – the player who watches for any motion coming from the players in the circle, serving as a helper to the referee.

Hints to the leader:

- Before the game begins, give the players a chance to feel the coin and the stone in their hands. Pass the objects around in a circle. This helps players to literally get a feel for the game.

- It is very challenging for players to not flinch at all when handed the coin. The game leader can determine how strict to be. Perhaps in the first round, a player is allowed to move their head only, or their eyes only. As the players get more familiar with the game, the game leader may choose to enforce the no-movement rule more strongly.

15. Cheerio!

Two neighbours meet on the opposite side of town. They are very polite and courteous, always making sure to shake each other's hands, and ask each other how they are doing. But, there is one word, one very special word, one purely magical word that, when it is spoken, no matter what may be happening, a lightning bolt strikes from out of the sky and all players that are connected by the hand are suddenly given the superpower of lightning speed. Who will be the first neighbour to hightail it back home?

This is a more complex version of 'Duck, Duck, Goose.' The group stands or sits in a circle. The game leader chooses one player to be 'it.' The group then decides on a magic word. Once the magic word is determined, the player who is 'it' skips around the circle, eventually tapping one of the players on the shoulder. The person who was tapped then stands up and skips the opposite way around the circle as the 'it,' and the 'it' player skips around the other way, and both people meet on the opposite side of the circle. They shake hands and proceed to have a very civilised conversation (a chance to practise conversational skills!) The script goes something like this: 'Good morning, neighbour!' 'Good morning, neighbour!' 'How are you on this fine day?' 'Oh, quite well, neighbour, and you?' This back and forth banter of pleasantries continues until the 'it' player says the predetermined 'magic word.'

When the magic word is spoken, both players run (in opposite directions) to try to get back to the empty spot on the circle. Whoever gets there first gets to stay, and the game continues with the person who did not get back to the empty space skipping around the circle and tapping a new player on the shoulder.

AGE RANGE: 7–9
PLAY AREA: Indoor, any room
NUMBER OF PLAYERS: 8+
EQUIPMENT: None

Variations:

• Can be played seated or standing.

Hints to the leader:

• It can be fun to extend the pleasantries and to build the anticipation as the players await the magic word. Encourage the players to keep hold of hands (via the extended handshake) until the magic word is spoken. Then they can let go of hands to run.

• If playing the seated version, make sure the person running back to the seated position does so without running into the neighbours. The game leader may add a rule such as 'no sliding' to ensure the safety of the seated players.

• It takes awhile to get the shape of this game. The 'it' player can always begin by skipping around the circle clockwise, and after they tap a shoulder, they continue around the circle clockwise until they meet the player on the other side. Then, when they shake hands, both players will end up running the same direction that each of them is facing. The 'it' player always travels clockwise; the tapped player always travels counterclockwise.

16. Psychic Tag

Everyone thinks of a number between one and four (in secret), then silently walks about the room shaking hands with other players with the number of shakes that matches the number they thought of. If their shake matches that person, they are a 'family' and hook arms and continue shaking until everyone in the room is paired up.

AGE RANGE: 9+
PLAY AREA: Indoor, any room
NUMBER OF PLAYERS: 8+
EQUIPMENT: None

Variations:

- The game leader can time the group to see how long it takes for everyone to be paired-up / linked-up. Then the goal is for the group to beat their fastest time.
- Depending on the number of players, the range of number options can increase or decrease. For larger groups (20+) players may choose a number between one and five, etc.

17. Who or What or How Many?

This is a guessing game where each player has some bit of information stuck to their backs, and they are trying to guess what it is. Depending on the variation, players can be historical figures, animals, vegetables, numbers, etc.) The catch is that, since they cannot see their own 'Who, What, or How Many,' but other players can see it, they have to ask the other players questions about their post-it, but they may only ask questions that can be answered with a Yes or a No.

When playing with numbers, questions can be 'Is it higher than _____?' or 'Is it lower than _____?'

AGE RANGE: 12+
PLAY AREA: Indoor, any room
NUMBER OF PLAYERS: 6+
EQUIPMENT: Post-its, pencils

Variations:

- If played in a school setting, the game leader may wish to choose a theme based on what the players are currently studying. (Geography, History, Chemistry, etc.)

Hints to the leader:

- The game leader should collect all the post-its before the game to make sure they are legible, on-theme, and that there are no repeats. The game leader may also wish to distribute the post-its, ensuring that players receive post-its that suit their level/learning style.

18. All For One, One For All (aka *Stayin' Alive*)
Created by Kim Lebas

Fun is contagious, and the fun is spreading! How long will it take to 'spread the fun' to the rest of the players? Are we having fun yet?!

Two players begin as 'It' wearing pinnies or coloured sashes. They are trying to tag all the other players with the ball while the ball is in their hand (control tag). Pinnied players may not run with the ball, but they can pivot and lunge to tag players, and they can pass the ball to each other. If you are tagged, you don a pinnie. The goal is to 'stay alive' by being the last remaining player without a pinnie.

Hints to the leader:

- This is a non-contact game, no physical contact allowed except for the 'control tag' of the ball. Players may not throw the ball at players to get them out – no 'pegging'.
- Encourage the 'Its' to pass to each other quickly and often, 'give and go,' so as not to give the other players too much time to evade.
- Some of the more timid players may stick to the corners of the room, inadvertently cornering themselves into being tagged. Encourage players to keep moving.

Variations:

- **The Musketeers – 1**
  (Teams challenge each other to a duel – En garde!)
  Similar to the above game, but with teams: two teams, two balls. Two different coloured pinnies or sashes for each team. Each team is trying to tag players from the opposite team in the same fashion as above. Goal is to see which team is first to get the other team out. To begin, each team starts with a ball. As above, players may not run with the ball, but can pass to each other. In this version, players may intercept the balls as well, regardless of whether their team began with that ball or not.

> **AGE RANGE:** 12+
>
> **PLAY AREA:** Indoor, 20 x 20 paces (not too big)
>
> **NUMBER OF PLAYERS:** 8+ (fun with larger numbers in a not-so-large space)
>
> **EQUIPMENT:** : Pinnies or coloured sashes (as many as there are players), one soft ball

- **The Musketeers – 2**
  - To increase the sense of drama, when players are tagged, rather than immediately being 'out', the game leader can add a 'three-strike rule': When tagged the first time, go out of bounds and count to 50 then re-enter the game. Second time, count to 100 then re-enter the game. Third time, you're out!
  - Players who are 'out on a count' can take on various fitness challenges, a more active variation than just standing and counting: i.e. when tagged first time, 10 push-ups then re-enter the game. Second time, 10 push-ups, 10 sit-ups then re-enter the game. Third time, you're out!)

- **Chameleon**
  Similar to the above game with two teams, but in this variation, each team is trying to 'convert' the players to join their team. When a player is tagged, instead of going out, they step out of bounds briefly and switch their pinnie or sash to the other team's colour. First team to flip all players to their team wins that round. This variation encourages players to play for the fun of it, to not get overly attached to one particular team/colour (and the added challenge of remembering what colour they are!)

  Variation of *Chameleon*:
  The game leader may add the 'three-strike rule' (as above) – counting, or fitness challenges to stagger the re-entry of the players.

Hints to the leader:

- This game (and all the variations) is best played within a small playing area, preferably indoors. If it is played outdoors, the game leader can assign one or two helpers whose job is to grab the ball if it goes out of bounds and pass it back to the 'Its'.

- A common strategy for the 'Its' is to target specific players and work together to get them out. This can intimidate some players, so the game leader may wish to start the game with 'no targeting' rule.

For children who may struggle to play this game:

- Some children may be afraid of the ball. When possible, outside the pressure of a game, practise passing the ball back and forth so that the ball comes toward the chest area, not the head ('chest pass').

- For players that may be hesitant or new to the game, the game leader may add the role of 'Shadow Whisperer.' The game leader chooses a child that knows the game well to be the Shadow Whisperer. During the game, the Shadow Whisperer whispers helpful tips to the child that is new, telling them where to go next and helping them to see the game better from that new standpoint. The Shadow Whisper can get an extra life for helping. If the team mate that they are helping gets out before they do, the Shadow Whisperer does not get the extra life. This bonds the children together, as they are both helping the other.

tagger

taggee

ball

control tag

19. Rickety Bridge

Suspended over a deep gorge hangs an old rickety bridge. No one knows how long the bridge has been there, but it's been long enough that the elements have taken their toll. Travellers who wish to cross from one side of the gorge to the other do so at their own peril – one false step and the rickety bridge may collapse, sending the traveller into the muddy depths below!

AGE RANGE: 7+

PLAY AREA: Any room

NUMBER OF PLAYERS: 2–20

EQUIPMENT: At least 7 hula hoops or coloured 'spots', piece of paper, pencil

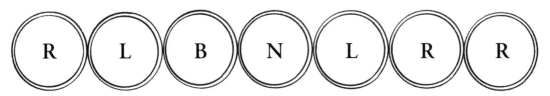

Set out seven hula hoops in a row. This is the bridge. One player is the 'map maker' and creates a specific path pattern, writing it down on a piece of paper, and keeping it hidden from the other players. Path options for the map maker: in any given hoop, a player may use their Right foot, their Left foot, Both feet, or No feet. (Map maker uses R, L, B, N on their written map to indicate the path.)

Each player takes their individual turn to cross the bridge to guess the 'correct' path. If a player uses the foot in a given hoop that matches the map, the map maker makes no sound – they are 'safe'. If a player uses a foot in a given hoop that does not match the map, the map maker makes the sound of a big splash, and that player leaves the hoop and goes to the back of the line. The players build on each others'

successes in order to figure out the correct path across the bridge. The first player to make it all the way across the bridge without a 'splash' wins the round and gets to be the new map maker.

Variations:

- Similar to the multiple and creative ways players create rules for *Four Square* (game 151), players may create new ways to cross (i.e. feet crossed, heels together, toes together, squats, hands, etc.). Wait until the group has played the original version multiple times before adding new path options.

- To take the focus off of the individual achievement of the player and to focus on the collective wisdom of the group, the game leader can present the game as a group challenge – how many turns does it take the group as a whole to discover the pattern? This variation is recommended for younger players. Then the challenge is to see if the group can beat their score the next round, to guess the pattern in fewer tries.

Hints to the leader:

- This game is good for teaching right/left sides. If a player is still developing the ability to distinguish which is right and which is left, the game leader can ask that player (or all the players) to give their right leg a few taps so they have a kinesthetic sensation that will help them. ('My right leg is the one that feels tingly.')

- Some children may need coaching on how to be a map maker (i.e. not making the pattern too difficult, or not being too harsh with their 'splashes'). The game leader should be the map maker until the group has played enough to become familiar with the lay of the land.

20. Boom!

An old colonial pub game adapted to be family-friendly: From the ages, for all ages!

The first person rolls one dice. The number on the dice is their number for the round. They then roll all three dice. If they get their number on one dice they yell 'Boom' and take one trinket. If they get their number on two dice they yell 'Boom Boom' and take five trinkets. If they get their number on all three dice they yell 'Boom Boom Boom' and it's an automatic and immediate win for that player. The player's turn is over when they have a roll in which their number is not present. Then the next player starts their turn.

Keep going with the next person rolling one dice to get their number for their turn. The first player to get 15 trinkets wins. If a player gets over 15 trinkets, however, they have to put them all back in the pile and start over.

AGE RANGE: 8+

PLAY AREA: Any room, requires a surface on which to roll dice

NUMBER OF PLAYERS: 2+

EQUIPMENT: 3 dice, 15 'trinkets' per player (i.e. natural objects work well – stones, acorns, leaves, etc.)

21. Zoo Run

The animals have escaped from the zoo! The zookeepers are on a mission to capture the animals and take them back to the zoo. The animals are enjoying their freedom and will not make it easy for the zookeepers. Who will win the day?

The game leader divides the group into two teams: animals and zookeepers. The zookeepers are seated, facing a partner at least 10 paces away. They have one soft ball between them. The animal team is standing in a line and, one at a time, they have a chance to make their 'zoo run'. At the start signal, the first player in the animal team line tries to run to the opposite side of the room and back without getting pegged by a rolling ball. If they make it there and back, they get two points for their team. If they run to the opposite wall and hesitate for more than three seconds, they can then stay at the opposite wall and try to run back home when the next animal makes their zoo run. If an animal is pegged by the ball while running, they are out and they go to the back of the animal line. The round continues until each animal has had a chance to run. The zookeepers may only roll the ball to their partner and back (no zigzag rolls) but they can roll as many times back and forth as they wish. When all animals have run, the teams switch places.

> **AGE RANGE:** 8–12
> **PLAY AREA:** Indoor, regular-sized room
> **NUMBER OF PLAYERS:** 12+
> **EQUIPMENT:** At least 3 soft balls that roll

Variations:

- The game leader may determine that the group plays a certain number of rounds or up to a certain score, depending on time.

Hints to the leader:

- This is a good game to play before introducing any dodgeball games that involve 'pegging'. Since the balls may only be rolled, the running players get to experience a sense of challenge/danger that does not cross over into complete chaos, as is experienced in some dodgeball games. The player knows where the balls are going to be, they just don't know exactly when they will be there.

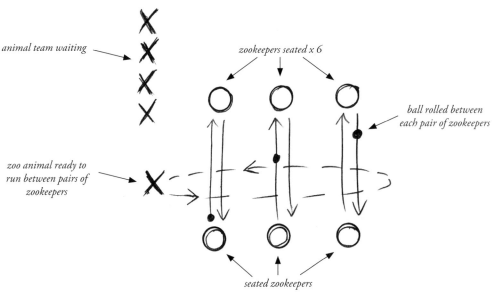

animal team waiting

zookeepers seated x 6

ball rolled between each pair of zookeepers

zoo animal ready to run between pairs of zookeepers

seated zookeepers

22. Tournament Rock-Paper-Scissors

You win some, you lose some.
If you can't beat 'em, join 'em!

At the start of the game, all players mill about the space until they come upon another player. The two players do 'Rock, Paper, Scissors, Shoot!' to determine the winner of that match. The person who loses that match then stands behind the person who beat them (optional: with their hands on that person's shoulders), cheering that person on by, literally, having their back. This continues in an add-on fashion, and the lines of players get longer and longer. Eventually, there is one final match between the two players who have all of the rest of the players behind each of them, and the victor is determined.

Variations:

- Game leader or players can use alternative moves (i.e. Salmon, Bear, Mosquito or Wizards, Elves, Giants, etc.) Team-building exercise could be for the group to create their own moves.

- 'Conga-Line' – simplest version as described above – creates a long line that can then bend around in a snake-like fashion behind the victor.

- 'V for Victory' – the first two players who lose to the victor place only one hand on their shoulder (one person off their right shoulder, one person off their left shoulder), creating 2 separate lines that form a 'V-shape' with the winning player at the centre.

- 'Branching Out' – for very large numbers – same as above, but each losing player behind the victor (and every other losing player after that) ends up having a losing player off of each of their shoulders – expanding exponentially.

Age range: 7+
Play area: Any room
Number of players: 8+
Equipment: None

- For players who do not want to put hands on shoulders, the game leader can give jump ropes to each player. Players begin with the jump rope tied around their waist so that their hands are free. Losing player then stands behind the winner player and loops their jump rope through the winning player's jump rope, and once again ties their jump rope around their waist. Lots of tying and untying. Slip-knots work best.

Hints to the leader:

- This is a non-running game; no tagging involved.

- For younger players, practise the hand gestures beforehand. Encourage players to make their 'Shoot!' choice clearly and confidently, no half-way gestures and no hesitating.

- The game leader may use this as a get-to-know-you game, making a rule that you can only have a match with someone whose name you do not yet know. Before their match, players introduce themselves to one another with a handshake.

- This game cultivates an 'easy come, easy go' attitude that is so essential in life. This game is recommended for any child who has a hard time accepting being tagged in more high-pressure, fast-paced games. Playing this game regularly can alleviate the need to win at all costs.

23. Counting Game – Don't Crash!
Adapted by Kevin Quigley

The group sits in a circle. Start with the group counting, one-by-one, around the circle, from one to the total number of players. This determines the target number that the group must collectively count to. For a group of 20 players, for example, the target number is 20. The goal of the game is for the group to then count to the number 20. Everyone must speak once and only once, but there may not be any overlaps (crashes). If two (or more) players speak at the same time, that is considered a crash and the group must then start over.

Additional Rules (optional)

- *No same-starters* – no single player may start a round of the game more than once.
- *No signals given* – no hand signals, no talking, no patterns, and so on.
- *Sing-Crash* – some groups find it helpful to sing the word 'CRASH' when a crash happens to help them all come to attention to start another round more quickly.
- *No Neighbours* – until the group has gotten half way through their total, no one may speak immediately after a neighbour on either their right or left.
- *Starting Rest* – require the group to come to a true group silence where all players are attentive and still before anyone may start the round by saying the number ONE. This silence should last at least the length of a single heartbeat, but may last longer.
- *Louder* – for more advanced players, add the rule that each number must be spoken more loudly than the previous one. Players build up the volume so that the final number spoken is also spoken the most loudly (very challenging!)
- *Softer* – the first number spoken is the loudest and each number spoken after that is spoken more softly. The last number, then, is spoken in the faintest whisper (nearly impossible!)

> AGE RANGE: 12+
> PLAY AREA: Any room
> NUMBER OF PLAYERS: 10+
> EQUIPMENT: Enough chairs for each player

Variations:

With each successful round, another challenge may be added:

- *Laughter:* Say your number in a voice that is intended to get at least one other person in the room to laugh. If there is any laughter that is also considered a crash.
  - Tip: Gravity and Levity. Have them send energy down into the group. Laughter is rising energy, so an imaginary beam of light or extra growths from those tree roots, can often allow the laughter to rise into the eyes, but not become vocal.
- *Control:* **All** extraneous vocal sound is considered a crash: sneezes, burps, giggles, talking – all of it. Very difficult to do, but the control of the impulse is an important one for adolescents to master.
  - Tip: Most of these sounds are rising elements. One can delay even a sneeze or a cough for a few minutes before it becomes vocal. They will be amazed at how much control over even involuntary noises they will be able to achieve.
- *Prime numbers:* Incredibly difficult! First, practise having them clap together as a group. Someone will say the word 'clap' after which, the whole group will clap and make one single sound. It will take them several tries before the group understands just how long they need to wait after the word in order to all clap together. Then, once they are able to do that, they will play the game as normal, but the entire group must clap together in unison after each prime number is said. After non-prime numbers, they do nothing. Crashes are caused when someone claps after a

non-prime number, when someone **fails** to clap after a prime number (they need to be honest about this), and when there has been a sloppy, non-unison clap.

- *Non-prime numbers:* After a while they will learn the pattern of primes and it will get easier and easier. So, even if they haven't succeeded, have them clap on the non-primes and stay silent on the primes.
- *Primary colours:* Continue with the clap technique, but now they have to pay attention to each other – so there is no predictable pattern. If a student is wearing a top or shirt that is a primary colour (red, blue, yellow), clap. Otherwise, no clap.

Hints to the leader

Tips to test:

Do the following make a difference in the group's efficacy?

When working with middle schoolers, give them an opportunity to find out, 'What Works?'

- *Posture* – not too forward and not leaning back, both of these things can put you to sleep, mentally. Sit up in a ready position to play and instrument or sing, and the group, which often has been crashing around four, can make it to seven in their very next try.
- *Gravity* – both feet flat on the floor.

No crossed legs, or turned ankles, no feet on furniture. This creates a sense of ensemble and really helps with the listening needed to do well.

- *Rhythm* – the initial count around the circle must be on a single pulse that neither speeds up nor has a break in it (because someone wasn't paying attention). This begins to synchronise the heartbeats of the participants which helps them avoid crashes.
- *Levity* – Have them put a light in their eyes and to actively look around the circle and meet each other. This helps participants to stay awake and invested in doing well.
- *Connection* – Before the first number is spoken, have them imagine roots growing out of the soles of their feet into the earth beneath them, these roots grow towards all the other players and tangle together beneath the surface and, like the roots of trees in a forest, helps them communicate silently with each other. This can lead to a group's first success at counting the whole way through.

24. Not a Knot

Try to make this knot, not-a-knot!
Classic ice-breaker game.

The group stands in a circle. Each player reaches their arms out in front of them, crosses their arms, and then moves toward the centre of the circle to eventually join hands with other players: right hand to right hand (same with the left.) Make sure that no one ends up taking hands with the person standing directly beside them. Wait until all the 'stragglers' have found a connection. This forms a giant 'knot' that the group then tries to undo without letting go of hands. Moving slowly, without breaking the connection, the players try to untangle the knot. Players are allowed to shift their hand grips, just as long as they maintain the connection. If any players lose connection, the group lets go of hands, shifts up their places in the circle, then tries again.

Variations:

- The element of time and/or competition may be added whereby, a group tries to untangle their knot either faster than their previous time, or faster than the group next to them.
- Silent round – no talking (and no telling other people what to do!)
- For more experienced players, can add blindfolds to all but one person who is assigned the role of the leader.

> **AGE RANGE:** 9+
> **PLAY AREA:** Indoor or outdoor, any area
> **NUMBER OF PLAYERS:** 10+
> **EQUIPMENT:** None

Hints to the leader:

- It's important for the players to move slowly as they negotiate their knot, and to take into consideration the diverse range of physical ability within the group.
- Sometimes it seems impossible for the knot to get untangled – but in most cases, there is a solution. The game leader should ensure that the group has sufficient time to work it out.

For children who may struggle to play this game:

- This game requires close contact. To allow more space, rather than actually holding hands, the game leader can provide handkerchiefs – players then take hold of the handkerchief corners rather than holding hands.

25. The Source

Mysteriously, the group is moving all together, but there is one player who is the secret source of all the motion… Who is it?

The players stand in a circle. The game leader chooses one player to leave the room while they choose one player to be the 'Source'. The Source, while staying in their same place in the circle, slowly begins to move their arms, and the other players follow their moves. All players on the circle are trying to move in such a way that does not give away the identity of the Source. Once the motions have begun, the game leader calls the player back into the room. The guesser stands in the middle of the circle and tries to guess, 'Who is the Source?'

Variations:

- This can be done in a seated circle.
- The game leader can ask the guesser to close their eyes rather than leave the room.

Hints to the leader:

- The game leader should model being the Source

AGE RANGE: 9+
PLAY AREA: Indoor
NUMBER OF PLAYERS: 8+
EQUIPMENT: None

so that players practise slow and controlled movements. Then, the game leader may decide to choose the Source by seeing who is able to make their movement the most fluid.

For children who may struggle to play this game:

- Some children will be tempted to be tricky to the players on the circle when they are the Source by moving in ways that are difficult to follow, and/or get carried away by the feeling of power of controlling the movement of the group. If this happens, the game leader should switch out players and not allow the player to take advantage of their position.

26. Scrambled Eggs

Can you put all your ducks in a row, even when their eggs get scrambled?

The game leader chooses five players to stand up in a line facing the group. The rest of the group is given a short period of time (10–20 seconds) to memorise the order, then they must turn around or close their eyes while the game leader scrambles the order. The game leader then calls for the group to turn around or open their eyes. The group tries to guess the original order.

Variations:

- Depending on the skill level of the group, the game leader may choose more players (eggs) to scramble.

AGE RANGE: 7–9
PLAY AREA: Indoor, any room
NUMBER OF PLAYERS: 10+
EQUIPMENT: None

Hints to the leader:

- The game leader may ask the players to raise their hands and be called on to guess the order. When a person is guessing, encourage the group to keep their comments to themselves, since they will get their turn to guess.
- This game works well in a classroom where the guessers are seated at their desks and the 'eggs' stand up in front of the room.

27. Heads up, 7-up

The game leader chooses a certain number of players to stand at the front of the room. They are the 'taggers'. The rest of the group stays seated at their desks until the game leader says, 'Heads down, thumbs up'. The seated group follows those commands and then the 'taggers' roam about the room and must tap a seated player's thumb and then come back to the front of the room.

If a seated player has their thumb tapped, they then put their thumb down. Once all the taggers have made their thumb-tags and are standing back at the front of the room, the game leader says, 'Heads up, 7-up, whoever got tagged, stand up'. The game leader then gives each standing player a chance to guess who it was that tagged them. If they get it right, the players switch places. If they get it wrong, they must wait until everyone else has had a chance to guess before the identity of the taggers is revealed. The game leader then chooses new players to be taggers and the next round begins.

AGE RANGE: 7+

PLAY AREA: A regular classroom with desks and chairs

NUMBER OF PLAYERS: 7+

EQUIPMENT: None

Hints to the leader:

- To avoid players only choosing their friends in this game, the game leader may add a rule that taggers must choose a person they have not chosen before in the game, or other variations to keep cliques from forming.

28. Bob the Rock

The group forms a circle. One person comes inside the circle to try to spot 'Bob'. Bob can be any object that can be handed behind the backs of the players in the circle without the person in the middle being able to spot it. As the circle is passing Bob from one person to the next behind their backs, the circle says over and over, 'Bob the Rock, keep it movin', keep it movin'…'

Anyone on the circle may hold up Bob at any time when the person in the middle has their back turned, but if anyone on the circle sees Bob when he is held up in the air, they must say, 'I see Bob!' The person in the middle can point to the person on the circle that they think at that moment holds Bob. If they guess correctly, the person who was holding Bob then takes the place of the person in the middle.

AGE RANGE: 10+

PLAY AREA: Any

NUMBER OF PLAYERS: 9+ (larger numbers work well too)

EQUIPMENT: A rock or any hand-sized object that can be passed from person to person

29. Assassin

There is a top secret assassin among you; their mission – to eliminate all but one player. Who will solve this murder mystery, before it's too late?

The players stand in a silent circle. The game leader asks the group to close their eyes and then walks around the outside of the circle, tapping one player between the shoulders. That person is the assassin. The assassin's job is to 'poison' as many of the other players as possible. They do this with a scratch on the wrist when shaking hands with another player.

To begin the game, the leader counts down from three to one and, when possible, turning the lights out at one. (There is no speaking during the game. If the game leader witnesses conversation or hears any talking, they must eliminate that player by calling their name and saying, 'Die!')

Players mill about the room shaking hands with each other, and seeing if they can witness the assassin poison another player. If they believe they have spotted this and determined who the assassin is, they may stop and stand with their feet together and their hand raised high in the air.

The game leader calls on them by name, and the accuser will say, 'I accuse' (they name the player.) If the named player **is** the assassin, they confess and the round is over. The accuser has won. If that player is **not** the assassin, the accuser is eliminated.

For obvious reasons, dead players may not accuse.

The assassin is not required to scratch with every handshake. Players who have been scratched do not react immediately in any way. They begin a silent count to ten in their heads. Once they have reached ten, they 'die'. The particulars of this death may be as simple as stepping to the edge of the play area and leaning against the wall or taking a seat.

A player's death is the only moment that it is allowed for a player to make a vocal sound. Some players prefer to make a very dramatic death and fall to the ground and remain lying on the floor. Some spaces will allow this to safely occur and others may not work with this model. If players are allowed to dramatise their

> **AGE RANGE:** 12+
>
> **PLAY AREA:** Room with a light switch
>
> **NUMBER OF PLAYERS:** 10+ (larger numbers work well too)
>
> **EQUIPMENT:** None

death, they must do so safely and can not knock into other players or furniture and may do no harm to the people or objects in the room (including themselves). If vocalisations are allowed, they may not raise their voices loudly enough to disturb anyone beyond the confines of the room. Blood-curdling screams can be quite a shock to hear in the hallway.

Variations:

- An alternative method of determining the assassin role before the start of the game is to use the same number of playing cards as players – all red except for the Ace of Spades – which marks the assassin. The cards **must** be collected each time before the game begins.

Hints to the leader:

- When the game leader is assigning the assassin, no one may touch their neighbor in any way. No physical contact allowed until the hand-shake portion of the game begins.

- It is rare that an assassin will be able to murder all the other students (but one). An assassin that can make it that far in the game without being accused is certainly to be commended!

- Sometimes, a particular student is selected more than once in a particular year, and some students will complain that they 'never' get picked. When the game leader uses the element of chance in determining who the assassin will be, players must accept the random nature of it.

- No one may refuse a handshake; if the game leader witnesses someone avoiding a handshake, that player receives one warning. If they are seen doing this again, they will be eliminated by the game leader.

30. Stella Ella

Form a circle – palms face up; right hand on the top, left hand on the bottom, so that players' hands overlap with palms resting on or holding up their neighbor's. The game leader moves their right hand across their body to 'slap' the player's hand standing to their immediate left, the the motion continues clockwise around, with each player slapping their left neighbour's hand. Each 'slap' is a beat of the song and the slaps go around. At the end of the song, on the count of 'five', the person on the receiving end of the slap tries to move their hand away before their neighbour slaps it. If they do not move their hand away in time, that player steps to the middle of the circle and is 'out' for the next round, watching the action from the centre of the circle. If the player is able to move their hand away in time, then the player who was slapping on the count of 'five' is left to slap their own hand, and thus they get themselves out and must take the place of the person in the centre of the circle.

Stella Ella Oh La
Quack Quack Quack
Singing Es Teega Teega
Teega Teega Shack Shack
Es Teega Teega Va Lo, Va Lo,
Va Lo, Va Lo, Va Lo Va
One, two, three, four, five!

AGE RANGE: 8+
PLAY AREA: Indoor, any
NUMBER OF PLAYERS: 8+
EQUIPMENT: None

Variations:

- The person who is out goes to the middle of the circle to watch the action. When the next person gets out, they go back in. Only one person in the middle at a time.

- For more challenge, the game leader may add a rule that the person who is out can try to distract the players in order to make it harder for the group to concentrate. Specific rules can be added to the 'distractor' (i.e. no sounds, only motions or no physical contact)

- For more challenge, the game leader may add the rule that the group must close their eyes. Anyone who breaks the rhythm or misses a player's hand

is out. In this variation, the game leader (who keeps their eyes open) is the only one that can call players out.

- Pick up the tempo each time to make it more and more challenging.

Hints to the leader:

- This is a good transition activity that can be played while some of the group is ready, but others are finishing up some other task (i.e. putting on their outside shoes, putting away equipment from another game, etc.)

- Start by just practicing making contact around the circle without the pressure of the rhythm so that players get a feel for it.

- Encourage players to find the 'sweet spot' of slapping – not too hard, but not too light. The result should be a satisfying sound that keeps the beat of the song.

- The game leader can choose a different player to begin each time and/or have the circle mix up and find a new space each time so that no one knows where the final slap will land.

For children who may struggle to play this game:

- Keeping a rhythm can be very challenging for some players. The game leader should start the game with a slow tempo. Only build up speed once all players have the hang of it.

- The game leader should seat a struggling player next to them, preferably on the game leader's left, so that they know they'll be getting the pulse from the same place/person each time.

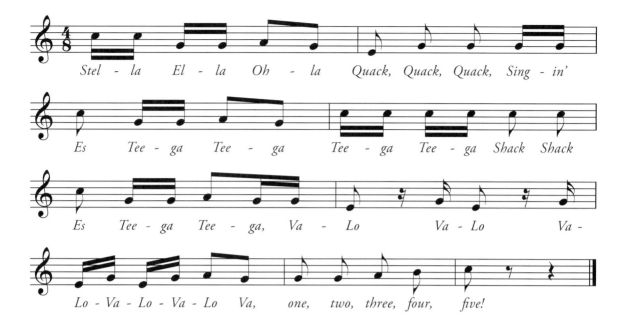

Stel - la El - la Oh - la Quack, Quack, Quack, Sing - in'

Es Tee - ga Tee - ga Tee - ga Tee - ga Shack Shack

Es Tee - ga Tee - ga, Va - Lo Va - Lo Va -

Lo - Va - Lo - Va - Lo Va, one, two, three, four, five!

31. Ninja

The object of the game is to slap your opponent's hands to get them out. The players begin by standing in a circle. Everyone stands with their own palms together (hands in prayer position.) The players then, all together, jump out from the centre of the circle and simultaneously yell, 'Ninja!' while striking a ninja pose. The first player to make their move (chosen beforehand) begins the action.

The first player decides (in secret) if they want to attack the player to the left or to the right of them. On the attack, the player makes one fluid motion with the goal goal of slapping that player's hand. They may only take one step with one leg or jump towards another player with both feet. If they fall, they're out.

The opponent may dodge the attack. When the first player makes their move, the defending player attempts to avoid being slapped. The motions then go around the circle, each player attempting to either attack or dodge an attack, only allowed to use one fluid motion. Every player begins the game with two hands, and if one of their hands is hit, they put that hand behind their back and continue the game one-

AGE RANGE: 10+
PLAY AREA: Indoor or outdoor, any
NUMBER OF PLAYERS: Any
EQUIPMENT: None

handed. A player is out when both of their hands have been hit.

The turns keep going in order around the circle until there are two players left, at which point the game restarts with only those two players. They strike their ninja poses and take turns attacking each other and dodging until there's only one ninja left standing.

Variations:

- Can add 'Revenge Rules' – A player who has gotten out may go back in when the person who got them out gets out.

Hints to the leader:

- A good strategy for success is to fluidly move from your dodge into your attack, so that the person you attack won't be prepared for it.

Skipping Games

Running through the rope

The 'classic' threshold ages of seven, nine, twelve, fourteen and so on, are becoming less clear. In the past, outer signs of change – such as the change of teeth – would almost exclusively occur around the age of seven. Now it can occur at any time between four and ten – or even twelve in some instances. Likewise, puberty can begin at any time between the ages of nine and sixteen. In the past, emotional and physical maturation was more closely linked; nowadays, early physical and late emotional development is becoming increasingly common. The stress, insecurity and behavioural changes that are often associated with these thresholds is thereby prolonged.

When introducing skipping (jump rope), it is good to start with group activities, and then move towards individual tasks. Running through the rope in pairs, for instance, will be easier for a child who is just beginning to skip, than doing it alone. The chanting of rhymes helps the skippers to participate in the rhythm of the moving rope: so it is important to speak the verses (or sing the songs) as rhythmically as possible. Also, the verses and words invite the child to cross a threshold, to have the courage to approach the moving rope.

Skipping is beneficial for the six to eight year olds, for it is now that they really begin to experience the world as separate from themselves. The rope symbolises an external object that needs coming to terms with, a force that exists outside themselves, that has its own rhythm which must be understood and accepted.

32. Come In, Come In

With the children on your right, swing the rope clockwise. Ask children to run through in pairs while saying this verse:

> Come <u>in</u>, come <u>in</u>
> Come <u>knock</u> at my <u>door</u>.
> Run <u>through</u>, run <u>round</u>
> And <u>back</u> for <u>more</u>

On each underlined word, the rope touches the ground. Then ask one child in the pair to close his eyes. The other child leads him through.

> I <u>take</u> my <u>love</u>
> And <u>knock</u> at the <u>door</u>
> Run <u>through</u>, run <u>round</u>
> And <u>back</u> for <u>more</u>.

Now they must run in and jump once over the rope, and then run out, while this verse is said:

> Come <u>in</u>, come <u>in</u>
> Come <u>knock</u> at the <u>door</u>
> One <u>skip</u> and <u>out</u>
> And <u>back</u> for <u>more</u>.

Once the children have mastered this, keep them on your right but turn the rope anticlockwise. Now they must jump over the rope and immediately run out.

When the children are a little older and more proficient, you can begin to turn the rope in an anticlockwise direction (relative to where the children are queuing up for a turn to skip), because

> **EQUIPMENT:** A rope for skipping

this is more challenging: it does not invite them in, as a rope turned clockwise does.

Skipping helps the children become aware of the world around them. The moving rope is a barrier outside themselves that they have to conquer. They have no control over it – and this can be quite threatening to some. Some children will reject skipping because they fear that their failure to succeed will be exposed. It is helpful when introducing skipping to explain to the children that skipping takes courage. Find an image or a picture that they can identify with – for example, the picture of a knight who is brave enough to go near the dragon's jaws.

33. The Teeth of the Dragon

> The <u>teeth</u> of the <u>dragon</u>
> They <u>open</u> and <u>shut</u>
> <u>Run</u> for your <u>life</u>
> And <u>don't</u> get <u>cut</u>!

Leading a person through with shut eyes is a good exercise to counteract bullying – I tend to pair the bullies with their victims, so that each child has a turn to lead the other, in a caring and responsible way.

> **EQUIPMENT:** A rope for skipping

34. The Rocking Boat

This game can be done in pairs holding hands. The pairs, once they have made it through, split up and circle back to the line on opposite sides, where they meet again. This particularly helps children who are less confident.

> We <u>went</u> to <u>sea</u> in a <u>pea</u> green <u>boat</u>
> In a <u>pea</u> green <u>boat</u>, with a <u>big</u> warm <u>coat</u>

The rope rocks gently back and forth, while one at a time, the skippers jump over the rope.

> The <u>first</u> wave <u>rocked</u> and <u>rocked</u> <u>around</u>

The rocking of the rope gets bigger.

> The <u>snakes</u> they <u>slithered</u> with<u>out</u> a <u>sound</u>

The rope is laid on the floor and moved left and right by the turners.

EQUIPMENT: A heavy skipping rope

> Then <u>two</u> waves <u>rolled</u> and <u>rolled</u> <u>around</u>

The rope is pulled tight across the floor by the turners. One turner flicks the rope and sends a wave-like motion down the length of the rope to the other turner. The turner who recieved the wave now returns it using the same technique. The wave that is created is about 18 inches / 45cm high.

> And <u>turned</u> the <u>boat</u> <u>upside</u> <u>down</u>

Now the rope is turned over in traditional skipping style so that they may run through without having to jump.

> <u>Upside</u> <u>down</u>, <u>down</u>-side <u>up</u>

Repeat as above.

> And we <u>all</u> dried <u>off</u> in a <u>fisherman's</u> <u>hut</u>.

Repeat as above until all the children have had a chance to try to run through; and then begin again at the beginning.

35. High and Lows

Turn the rope clockwise, with the children on your right. The children run in and jump over the rope to the following verse:

> <u>High</u>, <u>lows</u>, <u>stars</u> and <u>peppers</u>
> <u>Scissors</u>, <u>turn</u> around, <u>touch</u> the ground.
> Faster…

The rope touches the ground when the underlined words are spoken.

The rope is turned at an increasing pace while the verse is said quicker and quicker.

Variations

> **EQUIPMENT:** A heavy skipping rope

When the child fails to jump clear or is caught by the rope, he remembers at which part of the verse he stopped. This gives him his own 'task': he has to see how many star jumps, high jumps or whatever, he can do.

If you have a large group of children, a second rope can be used for the 'tasks'.

Highs

Lows

Stars

Peppers
(jumping over the rope as quickly as possible)

Scissors

Turn around
(the child turns around while skipping)

Touch the ground

36. Fishes, Fishes

Fishes, <u>fishes</u>
<u>I</u> need <u>fishes</u> to <u>put</u> in my <u>pot</u>
And <u>eat</u> for <u>dinner</u>.
<u>Some</u> are <u>thin</u> and <u>some</u> are <u>fat</u>

But <u>catch</u> some <u>soon</u>
And <u>that</u> is <u>that</u>.
<u>Some</u>times <u>high</u> and <u>some</u>times <u>low</u>
And <u>which</u> fish it <u>catches</u>
We'll soon <u>know</u>

Sit in the centre of the circle of children. You are going to 'fish' with the skipping rope and the children are the fish in the pond. Swing the rope round the circle, and the children jump over the rope and ring ('the fishing hook') as it comes past. When you say the words 'sometimes high', pause in the verse and swing the rope around above the children's heads. Tell them to crouch down while you do this. Then bring in the rope and make it swing near the floor again ('sometimes low').

Hints to the leader:

• Pass the rope behind your back as it moves in a circular motion, in this way the rope whizzes around without you becoming very dizzy.

> **EQUIPMENT:** A heavy skipping rope; rubber ring (also known as a quoit)

• Before the rope goes up above the heads of the children, pull it back closer to yourself, increase the height, then let it out again. Make sure it is a soft rubber ring and that it is kept well above the heads of the skippers.

• What to do if a child fails to jump clear of the rope? You can tell children who fail to jump clear of the rope to 'go to the edge of the pond'. When the third child goes to the edge of the pond, tell the first child to rejoin the circle of fishes. With older children you can instead tell the children who don't jump clear to skip over the rope in a different way from the others. The first time, the child might do a step jump; on the second fault, a star jump; on the third fault a turnaround, and on the fourth fault become a 'frog', to crouch and jump over the rope from that position three times successfully.

• Recently, however, when I was playing this game with a group of children, one who was 'sent out' of the pond became upset. The rest of the children were quite disturbed by his feelings. So I wondered if I could find a different 'consequence' for those children who failed to jump clear of the rope. When discussing this with a group of student teachers, one made a suggestion that I hadn't thought of during all the years I have played this game: the child is still sent to the 'edge of the pond', but if the rest of the 'fishes' jump clear of the rope for the next three times, the 'fish out of water' is allowed to return to the pond. I thought this was a very useful suggestion: the group helps the 'excluded' child to return to the circle and he is then unlikely to feel outcast or rejected.

Creating Your Own Skipping Rhymes

Creating your own verses, rhymes and skipping games is not as difficult as you would imagine.

For instance, a class of student-teachers were given the example of a skipping game *(The Fisherman's Hut)*, and then asked to produce some games of their own.

Here are three that were written:

37. Waves on the Sea Shore

<u>Waves</u> on the <u>sea</u>-shore
<u>Roll</u>ing, <u>roll</u>ing
<u>Waves</u> on the <u>sea</u>-shore
<u>Roll</u>ing, <u>roll</u>ing
<u>Fish</u> in the <u>wat</u>er
<u>Swish</u>ing, <u>swish</u>ing
<u>Fish</u> in the <u>wat</u>er
<u>Swish</u>ing, <u>swish</u>ing
<u>Light</u>ning and <u>thun</u>der
<u>Flash</u>ing and <u>crash</u>ing
<u>Light</u>ning and <u>thun</u>der
<u>Flash</u>ing and <u>crash</u>ing
<u>Don't</u> get <u>wet</u>!
<u>Don't</u> get <u>wet</u>!

Rose, Barbara, Guido and Anna

38. Oh Look! The Winding Brook

<u>Oh</u>… <u>look</u>! The <u>wind</u>ing <u>brook</u>!
<u>Have</u> you <u>seen</u>… the <u>rip</u>pling <u>stream</u>?
<u>Let's</u> be a <u>swim</u>mer, <u>in</u> the <u>riv</u>er!
<u>Now</u> jump <u>free</u> through the <u>tum</u>bling <u>sea</u>!

Judit, Shirley, Simon and Nantia

39. Down by the Pond

<u>Down</u> by the <u>pond</u> where the <u>fish</u> do <u>play</u>
<u>In</u> jumped a <u>frog</u> and <u>scared</u> them all a<u>way</u>
<u>Down</u> by the <u>pond</u> where the <u>frogs</u> do <u>play</u>
<u>In</u> jumped a <u>duck</u> and <u>scared</u> them all a<u>way</u>
<u>Down</u> by the <u>pond</u> where the <u>ducks</u> do <u>play</u>
<u>In</u> jumped a <u>fox</u> and <u>scared</u> them all a<u>way</u>
<u>Down</u> by the <u>pond</u> where the <u>foxes</u> <u>play</u>
<u>In</u> jumped a <u>croc</u>(odile) and <u>scared</u> them all a<u>way</u>
<u>Down</u> by the <u>pond</u> where the <u>croc</u>(odile)s <u>play</u>
<u>Along</u> came <u>Rebecca</u> (use child's own name)
And <u>scared</u> them all a<u>way</u>

Rebecca, Jayden, Aaliyah, Michael

Here are some more skipping rhymes overheard in playgrounds around the world:

40. There Was an Old Woman Tossed up in a Basket

There was an old woman tossed up in a basket,
> (the rope is swung up and the skipper runs in)

Ninety-nine times as high as the moon,
> (the skipper calls out the number of skips he has to
> do before continuing the rhyme)

And where she was going I could not but ask it.
> (skipper shakes his head)

For in her hand she carried a broom.
> (skipper pretends to hold a broom)

'Old woman, old woman, old woman' quoth I,
> (skipper pretends to hunch over like an old lady)

'Whither are you going to up so high?'
> (on the word 'up' the skipper must jump so that his
> knees touch his chest)

'To sweep the cobwebs out of the sky'
> (skipper pretends to jump high and sweep the sky
> with his broom)

'May we go with you?' 'Aye bye and bye'
> (the skipper jumps out of the rope and a new
> skipper comes in. Alternatively the original skipper
> stays in and is joined by another. They then skip
> together. At the end of each successful rhyme a
> new skipper joins. In this version you can see how
> many skippers join in before a mistake is made)

It's interesting to note that playground skipping chants often reflect social issues, such as addiction:

41. I Like Coffee, I Like Tea

I like coffee, I like tea,
I want Jonathan in with me.
I don't like coffee, I don't like tea,
I don't want Elizabeth (skipper calls a child's name)
in with me.

All in, a bottle of gin,
> (one by one all the skippers attempt to join in)

All out, a bottle of stout.
> (one by one all the skippers attempt to run out of
> the rope; the first skipper in is the first one to leave,
> and so on).

42. Teddy Bear, Teddy Bear

The skippers take it in turns to complete the verse and its tasks.

Teddy bear, teddy bear, touch the ground.
> (the skipper touches the ground)

Teddy bear, teddy bear, turn around.
> (skipper turns around while skipping)

Teddy bear, teddy bear, walk up the stairs
> (skipper mimes action; one knee lifted at a time)

Teddy bear, teddy bear, say your prayers
> (holds hands as if praying)

Teddy bear, teddy bear, turn off the light,
> (mimes action.)

Teddy bear, teddy bear, spell 'good night'.
G.O.O.D.N.I.G.H.T!

43. Johnny over the Ocean

Johnny over the ocean, Johnny over the sea,
Johnny broke a tea cup, and blamed it on me.
I told Pa,
Pa told Ma.
Johnny got in trouble, Ha, ha, ha !
Salt, honey, mustard, PEPPER !

When the word 'Pepper' is called, the rope-turners turn the rope very fast.

44. Keep the Kettle Boiling

Keep the kettle boiling,
Don't be late,
Keep the kettle boiling.
Call the rate.

All the skippers line up. One at a time they run through the rope and back round to the starting side. For each turn of the rope, one skipper should run through. If the skipper does not make it back in time or gets caught with the rope, he becomes the next rope-turner. If there are lots of skippers playing, an object may be touched after the run-through, before the skipper can return to try again. This may be a nearby tree or wall. When 'Call the rate' is said, one of the skippers may say a number like 'one' or 'three'; this means that you must skip the number that was called before trying to get out.

45. Down by the Ocean

Down by the ocean,
Down by the sea,
Simon went fishing,
With Daddy and me.

How many fishes did Simon catch.
One, two, three, four, five, six, seven…

In this case the name of the skipper is Simon. It is changed as each new skipper comes in. The rope is kept turning as the number of skips is counted. As the number increases the rope gets faster.

46. Everybody, Everybody

Everybody, everybody,
Come on in,
The first one that misses,
Takes the end.

The first skipper to get caught by the rope has to take the place of one of the children who were turning it.

47. Changing Bedrooms

Changing bedrooms number 1
Changing bedrooms number 2
Changing bedrooms number 3
Changing bedrooms number 4

The skippers run in from each side, changing places with one another as each number is called. They do this by timing their move and jumping in a 180 degree turn. Of course it is much harder to run into the moving rope when you are standing on the side: you have to jump straight in.

48. All In Together Now

All in together now,
How do you like the weather?
January, February, March, April, May…

Each skipper runs in when she hears the month she was born in called out. When all the skippers are in, the rhyme is repeated and each skipper jumps out when her month is called.

Children's Feet

Children's feet need to develop naturally, and should not be formed from the outside by shoes that impose a pre-designed shape. Sports shoes may do this, particularly those with a pronounced cushioning heel. I have seen children who usually wear such shoes actually bruising their heels when they come to run or walk with bare feet. They do not actually 'meet the earth': they are semi-permanently cut off from fully meeting the resistance and solidity of the ground beneath them.

The sayings we have in everyday speech, such as 'standing on firm ground', 'digging your heels in', 'having the world at your feet', or 'a well-grounded person', are made nonsense of by the footwear that popular fashion now dictates. Contrary to popular opinion, built-up arches in shoes do not always counteract such problems as fallen arches. In fact, wearing shoes that mould the feet can lead to less malleability and strength in the arches as well as in the lower leg muscles. Problems with foot formation may develop which in turn adversely affect the ankles, knees, hips and spine. At this stage it may be helpful to seek expert advice, and in some cases specific corrective inserts are placed in the shoe.

Current footwear fashions are almost like an inversion of the much derided tradition of foot binding carried out in China and Japan in the past. The result is similar, since the foot loses the ability to form itself in a healthy way. Sports shoes should be worn for sport only. At other times, the wearing of plain thin-soled shoes and sandals – or, when the weather or situation permits, running about bare-footed – and the playing of games that increase foot flexibility, will contribute to the child's overall health.

49. The Water Bird

Ask the children to take off their shoes and socks. Scatter the marbles on a tumbling-mat or carpet. Tell them that they are water birds, and must see how many marbles they can pick up, only using their toes, while the rhyme written below is said. (Children should not bend down to transfer the marble from the foot into the hand. They should try and lift the foot as high as possible, without dropping the marble!)

> Standing in the lake
> Is a long, tall crane
> Little fishes in the water
> In and out again.
>
> With his feet he gathers
> All his food for the day
> As many little fishes
> As a tall crane may.

When I do this with the children, it becomes very clear to me which of them wear shoes that mould the feet, and which don't. The children who wear only training or

EQUIPMENT: A bag of marbles of mixed sizes; a tumbling mat or carpet

sports shoes often do not have the flexibility and control in their feet that is needed to pick up small objects, such as marbles; this has far-reaching consequences.

50. Crows and Cranes

Divide the class into two groups. Give the groups names that begin with the same letter: e.g. Cranes and Crows. Each group has its own demarcated territory – at each end of the playing area, not more than 50 paces apart. This may be a line drawn with chalk, it may be a tree. (If you are playing this game outdoors it is particularly important to demarcate the two territories.)

The drum is beaten and the first sounds of the names, (e.g. 'Crrrr…') is called out. The groups advance towards one another, taking one step for each drum beat.

The drummer calls out the name of a group, e.g. '**Cranes!**'. The Cranes turn round as quickly as possible and run back to their village with the Crows in hot pursuit. (You don't necessarily have to call out the names of the tribes alternately – life isn't always fair!)

The fleeing group is safe when they get back to their tree. The prisoners that have been caught are proudly led back by their brave captors to the victorious group. They are then ordained as members of that group. The process is repeated over and over until all of one group has been caught.

Variations:

- This game can be played with four groups. Then it is important to have enough arm bands of four different colours, so the children know who is who.

- I have also played this game as a water game, in swimming-pools.

- If a player who is pursuing another, crosses the line and into the fleeing players' territory, the fleeing player may turn around and capture his pursuer.

> **EQUIPMENT:** Drum (not essential, but good to have); arm bands – one for each child (optional)

Crows and Cranes is a popular game with eight to nine year olds, and also provides the opportunity to learn some very valuable things about oneself. It places children in situations where they are faced with the consequences of the kind of person they are. For instance, the children who have bold and loud natures, (referred to as the Napoleons in the section on 'Breaking The Rules') will march so confidently, so eagerly into battle, that they will often forget to take their army with them. Then they are very likely to be captured and have to join the other group.

But the children who are more timid and quiet by nature usually don't get caught by the other group until the end, because they take small, cautious steps and so remain closer to their territory. Towards the end of the game, they are likely to be left alone facing a huge advancing group. This situation provides them with an opportunity to transform their timid natures by showing courage. This enables the game leader to work with the children, rather than against them. If you were to force a timid child to take big steps, this might well lead to tears and fear. When the game itself presents the child with the consequences of his behaviour, he can learn to change more easily and 'organically'.

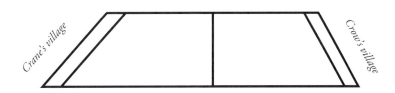

51. Hop

Divide the players into two teams. Each team lays out a 'ladder' of staffs, about 45cm / 18 inches apart, on the ground in front of it. There must be a staff for each player in the team. When the teams have lined up behind their 'ladder', the leader gives the sign for the race to begin. The first player of each team hops on one foot over each staff, picks up the last staff in the row, and hops back over the rest of the staves.

EQUIPMENT: One wooden staff per player

They tag the next player, who repeats their actions.

Players must not put the other foot on the ground or touch a staff by mistake. The first team to pick up all its staves wins.

52. Hot Potato

Tell the children that the beanbag is a very hot potato. They must pass it round the circle, throwing and catching it as quickly as possible, so that it doesn't get a chance to burn their hands.

Begin by passing one beanbag around the circle. Later introduce a number of other beanbags. You can also decide to change direction when a beanbag is dropped. This means that the children have to listen carefully for the word 'Change!', while throwing and catching. Try to encourage the children to pass and give the beanbag in one action, so that they

EQUIPMENT: 1–4 beanbags

don't actually hold the beanbag still at any one time. The beanbag will then pass around the circle in one continuous movement.

It is good to encourage children to explore other ways of throwing and catching. Now describe the 'hot potato' as a 'heavy pumpkin'. Show the children how to let the 'weight' of the pumpkin determine the arc of the passage.

53. Wind, Moon and Rainbows

When introducing a game such as *Wind, Moon and Rainbows* to young children, it is pedagogically sound, as well as helpful, to present an imaginative picture of the game and its rules. This can most easily be done by telling a story. The children can huddle round while you do so. The next game is presented in a story form, as an example:

'Once upon a time, the north wind decided to make chaos in the universe. So it blew with all its might, and scattered the moon, stars and planets to the far reaches of the world. An old man, a wizard, saw what the north wind had done, so he wandered all over the universe, and wherever he walked, rainbows formed. But when the north wind found out what the wizard was doing, it flew off, blowing beneath the still and beautiful rainbows and making them scatter hither and thither.

'The wizard decided that he needed help. So he journeyed to the moon, and asked her if she could help him. Then he went to the morning star, and asked her if she could also help. Then the moon and the morning star began to look for the rainbows, and when they had found them, left them shining quietly again, gently touching the earth. But the moon left the north wind until last; at last, with the help of the morning star, she brought their mischief to an end.'

One child is the north wind. One child is the moon, another the morning star. The other children are quietly shining rainbows, who are scattered across the universe. (The rainbows make an arc with their bodies by touching the ground in front of them with their hands.)

The north wind frees them by nipping beneath this arc. But the moon doesn't like the chaos the wind has made, so with the help of the morning star he finds each rainbow and touches it gently; then the rainbow finds a place to rest on the earth. (The rainbows sit down once tagged.) Finally, when all the rainbows are quietly on the earth, the moon catches the north wind.

This game presents a picture of order and chaos to the children. Although life can appear unordered and without structure, it is possible to find peace and stillness, without losing a sense of life (the rainbows continue to shine once they are on the earth). Paradoxically, there is also a sense that the rainbows do not have much control over their fate – they are blown around by the north wind, and settled by the moon upon the earth. But each individual suffers the same fate: not only are the rainbows touched by the moon, but so is the north wind eventually, who caused all the trouble in the beginning. Perhaps one can say that this picture is one of final justice – that everyone will finally meet his or her own destiny.

54. Go Forth! [1]

If you are playing outdoors near trees, you can tie a rope to a tree, so that children can use this to swing across between logs.

Divide the children into two 'groups'. The aim of the game is for the whole group to complete their journey home – to jump from log to log round the whole circle without falling off.

The groups start their journeys – they start at the same point in the circle, but one group goes clockwise and the other anticlockwise round the circle. But on

> **EQUIPMENT:** Sections of logs arranged in a circle

the way they meet their friends. Unfortunately they meet them on a narrow path on the side of a cliff / in the middle of a deep marsh. They have to grit their teeth and try to pass one another without falling into the marsh, or down the cliff. However, if a member of the group falls, both groups have to retreat and start the journey again.

55. Go Forth! [2]

Again the children can be a group who are journeying. However, this time there is only one group who must pass over the treacherous marsh without falling in and drowning, and reach their village (the other side) safely.

If one member of the group falls off a log, then everyone must return and start again. But eventually they reach a log that they cannot jump to (a bit out of their reach), and then some problem-solving is needed.

I usually place the planks, without comment, in a pile on one side of the play area, and wait to see who thinks of using them. Once they realise the planks can be used, the group can make them into bridges for crossing the marsh. But if a bridge falls into the marsh, it is lost. They have to take the bridges with them when the last member of the group has crossed – otherwise their village will be in danger of attack from enemies.

When children are about eight years old, they begin to experience the world as separate from them. They may also start feeling separated from the other children; though this is a painful experience, it is also a sign of their growing individuality.

Both versions of *Go Forth!* allow children to explore their newly-emerging individuality through the outer effects of their actions. For instance, in *Go Forth! (1)*, the Napoleons of the class will probably take charge, organise their groups, and boldly set off. But when they meet the 'leader' of the other group, they are

> **EQUIPMENT:** Sections of log, planks of various widths and lengths (3 or 4 are enough)
>
> **PREPARATION:** Set out the logs, carefully matching the distance between the logs and the planks – so that the longest plank can only be used in one place

faced with a dilemma. What they wish to do is throw the other one off the cliff – but that would mean everyone would have to begin the journey again. I have seen two choleric children meet face to face like this – but then find a socially healthy solution: they used their strengths and abilities to support those children who had to pass them.

I have also often seen a group help a very sanguine child who would set off gaily skipping from log to log – but in such a dreamy way that he inevitably fell. Then the others, with a loud groan, would all have to return to the start. The sanguine child might repeat this many times before realising what he was doing, and how it was affecting all the other players. Finally, another surer-footed and slower child would take his hand so that they could reach the other side successfully.

In *Go Forth! (2)* it is often the melancholic child who will notice the planks lying on the side of the play area. The other children will then look at him in a new way – he has provided a solution to their problem!

56. Wolf and Sheep

One child is the wolf. He is in his 'den'. Another child is the shepherd. He has a hut, but is looking after the sheep. The rest of the children are the sheep. They are playing in a meadow: they stand in a circle and hold hands. They skip around the circle while singing this song:

> We are playing in the woods
> while the wolf is not about.
> If he were a-bout,
> we would all look out!

Then they call out, 'Wolf! Wolf! Where are you?' The wolf answers, 'I am getting out of bed' (while miming the action). The sheep sing the song again, call out to the wolf, and he answers again. For example, 'I am putting on my boots.'

The sheep sing the song and ask the question, and the wolf answers, describing how he is getting ready to go out – each time mentioning and miming another activity (e.g. combing my hair, taking a shower.)

But then the wolf is finally ready to chase the sheep, and in answer to the sheep's question, he now calls out, 'I'm ready for my BREAKFAST!' The wolf chases the sheep and tries to tag as many as possible. When they are tagged they go to his den. But the shepherd can save the sheep from the wolf's den, by accompanying them, holding them by both hands, to his hut. The wolf, though, can try to tag them on the way. If he gets them, then the shepherd has to return the sheep to the den. If they reach the hut, the sheep is free.

> **PLAY AREA:** Choose a place for the wolf's 'den' at one end of the play area (it could be a tree, or a bench), and another for the shepherd's 'hut' at the other end. If you have no trees, stones etc. you can draw two small circles on the ground for the den and the hut.

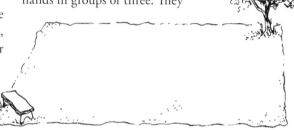

The sheep can also protect themselves from the wolf by skipping around as they hold hands in groups of three. They can stay in this safe circle while they sing the song – but not for longer.

Variations:

- If five sheep circle the wolf, they can hold him captive while they sing the song once through, and he stands asleep in the centre of the circle.

- Five sheep can circle the wolf, but he can try to escape by climbing beneath the sheep's arms. (Never let the children climb over each other's arms – they can easily fall onto their heads, which makes it rather dangerous!)

The game ends when the wolf has caught all but three of the sheep. I would let these three sheep, as reward for their survival, choose the next wolf and shepherd. If, however, the wolf is not managing to catch the sheep, and the game is dragging on for too long, the leader may call through the woods for another wolf to help his friend. (Choose one or two of the captured sheep to become wolves.)

We are playing in the woods, while the wolf is

not a-bout If he were a - bout, we would all look out!

57. Bunnies and Burrows

One child is the fox. The others are bunnies. The mats are burrows. If the bunnies are in their burrows, they are safe.

The fox tries to tag the bunnies when they are running between burrows. When they are tagged, they sit out in the fox's den. As fewer and fewer bunnies remain, some of the burrows 'collapse' (remove one or two of the mats or hoops). When the fox has caught all (or nearly all) of the bunnies, a new fox is chosen and the game begins again.

Variations:

- As soon as the first bunny is caught, they become the new fox and takes the vests from the old fox, who becomes a bunny.

- For older children, the fox has a ball. They have to brand the bunnies with the ball while they are running between the safety of the burrows. The fox is allowed to run with the ball.

- The fox is not allowed to run with the ball. However, you can increase the number of foxes in

> **EQUIPMENT:** Four or five floor-mats, or hoops; one practise volleyball; three bibs or vests

the field, perhaps three or four, and then they can throw the ball between themselves.

- Allow only a limited number of bunnies per burrow – e.g. three. When there are more than this number, the fox is free to enter the burrow and tag them.

- A fox's lair is demarcated (with a hoop usually). When the fox catches a bunny, he must go into the fox's lair, and wait to be freed by one of his fellow bunnies. A bunny can free a friend by taking his outstretched hand and running with him to a burrow – they both have to return to a burrow before freeing another imprisoned bunny. Now it is essential to have two foxes – one to guard the bunnies who are imprisoned in the fox's lair, and the other to freely tag the running bunnies.

58. Water Bunnies and Burrows

This game can easily be adapted for playing in a swimming-pool. For the burrows, demarcate a number of areas on the sides of the pool (one pace long). Place some in the shallow area of the pool, and others in deeper areas.

There can be a time limit placed on the various 'burrows' – a count of ten for safety areas in deeper water, a count of five for those in shallow water, for instance.

Variations:

- This is such a simple and universal chasing game, that it is very easy to create variations. For instance, I adapted it into *Tree Tag* (game 154) for a playground in Australia, so that the children would remain out of the sun, and mainly run in the shade of the trees. The safe areas ('burrows') were trees marked with ribbons – and instead of bunnies and foxes, the characters were possums and dingoes (a native dog). I introduced new rules for older children, such as a specific times allowed at each tree – a tree with a larger trunk would be able to support a possum for longer than one with a thinner trunk.

59. The Four Elements

The players stand in a circle. The leader stands in the centre of the circle with the ball. As she throws the ball to a player, she calls out the name of one of three elements (fire, air or water.) In this example, 'Air!' The player catches the ball, and has to think of a creature connected to air: so he says for example, 'Eagle'. He then throws it back to the leader.

This is repeated over and over again, but the person in the middle will vary the element that is called. A player may only hold the ball for three

> **EQUIPMENT:** One soft play ball

seconds. (A player is not allowed to name a thing that has been mentioned before.)

However, if the leader calls 'Fire!', the player must not touch the ball at all, but let it fall... If a player fails to think of a response, or catches the ball on 'fire', they are out and join a going-out/coming-in queue to one side of the circle.

60. Circle Cat and Mouse

The players form the mouse's house by standing in a circle, holding hands. One player in this circle is chosen to be the mouse. He stays holding hands within the mouse's house. Outside the house is a cat who tries to catch the mouse. The mouse runs away from the cat, by moving with his 'house'. (The circle can rotate away from the cat.)

Hints to the leader:

- You may find that the children do not keep in a circle. Two suggestions:
  - Stand in the centre of the circle so the children have a point of reference.
  - Make a circle on the ground with a rope – tell the children that the circle they form must stay within this rope.

Unlike later versions of *Cat and Mouse*, the mouse is within the house, and part of it – he is not separated from the group's protection. Also, this game does not have a movement from outside the circle to the centre, or from the centre to the outside; it is therefore less spatially demanding.

61. Grandma's House
Devised by Sally Cooper and Lesley Willis

One child is the wolf. Three players form a small circle by holding hands: they are Grandma's house. The wolf chases the children, and tries to tag them. If he tags them, they go into the centre of Grandma's house, where there is a big pot.

If they wish to escape, they can 'knock on the door' of Grandma's house, by holding onto the wrists of the three children forming it. They then become part of the house as well, so that it gets larger and larger as more players seek refuge.

The game can have various endings:

1. The wolf either catches all the children or everyone has joined in Grandmas' house, hence there is no one left to chase.

2. When only one child is left who is neither a part of the house nor in the wolf's pot, he may try to free all the children in the pot by linking hands with Grandmas' house.

3. The same as number two but this time the last player left uncaught has to get inside Grandma's house, take one child from the pot and try to get him out of the house without being caught by the wolf. Remember that the wolf cannot enter the house or the pot, but in this instance he tries to catch the last player and the person he is rescuing as they emerge from the house. If the wolf does not succeed in doing this, then the last child wins on behalf of the whole group. Once inside, the last player only has a count of ten in which to try and make his rescue, otherwise the wolf wins.

62. Monkey in the Middle

The circus has come to town, and the animals have learned all sorts of special tricks! The monkey would love to join the circus, so he's trying to tag the animals as they run by him, to take their place.

The group stands in a circle, each player standing behind a low cone or marker. One person in the middle who is 'it' (the monkey.) When the game starts, the players make movements/signals to each other. When one player picks up the movement/ signal from another, the two of them make eye contact and then run to switch places, both of them trying to avoid being tagged by the 'monkey.' If a player is tagged, they become the new monkey, and the old monkey takes the place of where that player was heading – thereby 'joining the circus'.

Variations:

• For non-running players, a new role can be created: 'The Change Caller' – this person exclaims when there's a change (for example, 'Now,_____ is the new monkey.') This also helps the group keep track of the fast-paced changes.

> **AGE RANGE:** 8+
>
> **PLAY AREA:** Indoor or outdoor; regular sized room or field, 20 x 20 paces
>
> **NUMBER OF PLAYERS:** 10+
>
> **EQUIPMENT:** Cones or markers for each player to stand behind

Hints to the leader:

• Some players may have a hard time coming up with moves and be more likely to simply follow another's lead. The game leader can do a brief warm-up, introducing four or five moves, or adding a new move to the warm-up each time the game is played. This can increase the movement 'vocabulary' for all.

• This game is fun and silly, and can get the players very excited. Consider following this game with a more focused/quieting exercise before sending the group back into the classroom. *Catch the Signal* (game 13) is a good one for this.

63. Shoo-Fly

*We're going to journey to the other side of the world.
All join hands and don't let go!*

Group takes hands in a circle, facing the inside. The game leader chooses two players to be the 'magic arch' under which the group will all travel to eventually turn the circle inside-out.

Shoo-fly, don't bother me,
  (Forward four steps towards the centre)
Shoo-fly, don't bother me,
  (Back to place)
Shoo-fly, don't bother me,
  (Repeat)

For I belong to somebody.

I feel, I feel, I feel like a morning star,
  (Leader brings the players through the 'magic arch')
I feel, I feel, I feel like a morning star,
  (Keep singing these lines until the turning is complete and the circle is turned inside-out.)

Variations:

- Once the circle is turned inside-out, players let go of hands, turn around and face the centre of the circle, and the game leader chooses a new 'magic arch.' The group takes hands and start again.

AGE RANGE: 7+
PLAY AREA: Indoor or outdoor, any
NUMBER OF PLAYERS: 8+
EQUIPMENT: None

- After the circle is turned inside-out, without letting go of hands, repeat all of the moves, but facing the other way. This then eventually brings the players back to their original places.

Hints to the leader:

- As the circle turns inside-out, encourage players to move slowly – no pulling on arms. The players that were the 'magic arch' are the last to unravel and have the trickiest transition. If there is a 'break' in the chain, this is the most common moment for it to happen.

For children who may struggle to play this game

- When playing the role of 'magic arch,' some children may be tempted to bring their hands down onto the other players as they are crossing under. The game leader can position them next to her/him to be a 'leader' rather than the 'magic arch'.

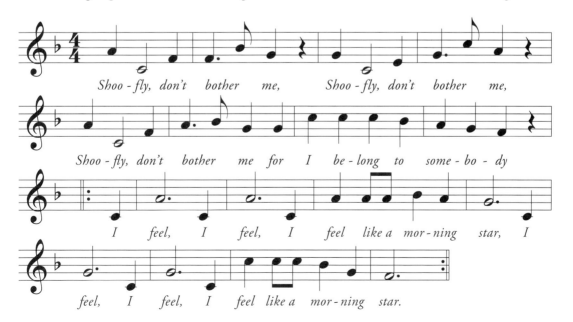

64. Gnomey Ball
Created by Josh Boyle

Players form a large circle, legs spread out with each player's feet touching their neighbours'. Players bend and the waist and are able to touch the floor. The ball is passed by way of rolling (never bounced). The object is to send the ball through the legs of another player to score a goal. When a goal is scored, players commiserate with a 'gnome dance'. Each player stands in the circle. The game leader calls out each action individually: 'Elbows in, knees together, thumbs up, eyes closed, and tongue out'. After the players are prepared for the dance the teacher sings: 'A tootie ta, a tootie ta, a tootie ta ta – A tootie ta, a tootie ta, a tootie ta ta', All players circle around themselves one way, and then unwind the other way – the 'gnome dance' is complete.

> **AGE RANGE:** 7 year olds
>
> **PLAY AREA:** Indoor or outdoor; players form a large circle
>
> **NUMBER OF PLAYERS:** 10+
>
> **EQUIPMENT:** One playground ball

Variations:

- The game leader may call any number of 'actions' for the 'gnome dance' – or make up new ones.

Hints to the leader:

- This can be a lead-up game to *Gaga Ball* (game 172), a playground game in which players try to get each other 'out'. In *Gnomey Ball*, all players stay in; this works well for younger players.

65. Ro-Sham-Bo Tag

Absolute chaos has broken out, and everyone is trying to tag everyone! No arguing allowed! There is only one way to solve disputes: Ro-Sham-Bo, Ready, Steady, Show! Conflict resolution 101.

Everybody's 'It'! Everybody is chasing everybody. Players may only tag above the waist. If there is any question or disagreement, it is settled with, 'Ro-Sham-Bo, Ready, Steady, Show!' (aka – Rock, Paper, Scissors.) If you are tagged or lose a Ro-Sham-Bo, you go down on a knee. You are back in when the person who got you down goes down.

Variations:

- For young children , the game leader can give an image of grasshoppers in a field of tall grass who love to play together. They love crouching down and hiding in the tall grass and then hopping back up to surprise their friends and chase them.

- For players unable to run, perhaps in a wheelchair or seated/stationary position, they can be the 'place' that players go in the event of a tie – the first one to get to the non-running player gets to have the non-running player Ro-Sham-Bo on their behalf.

> **AGE RANGE:** 7+
>
> **PLAY AREA:** Indoor or outdoor; 25 x 25 paces (larger for more challenge, smaller for less challenge)
>
> **NUMBER OF PLAYERS:** 6+ (the more the merrier)
>
> **EQUIPMENT:** Cones or other boundary markers

Hints to the leader:

- This game can establish a culture of conflict resolution through a simple/doable act that is developmentally appropriate, quick, and effective. It allows children who have trouble accepting being tagged a way to 'roll with it' since it is the basic building block of the game.

- When forming a group, this game helps build a sense of unity, cooperation, and how to work out differences because it 'invites conflict' from the beginning.

- This game works with multi-age, good for ice-breakers or get-to-know-you events.
(Adults love it too!)

66. Dragon in the Mountain
Created by Kevin Quigley

*The forest sprites have no interest in gold. It's just boring metal. But they **do** like to see amazing and awe-inspiring things – like dragons flying about!*

The players begin as forest sprites all in a line. The game leader has placed the balls 'within the Dragon's lair' (behind a hula hoop, which represents the mouth of the cave.) One by one, the forest sprites enter the mouth of the cave (the hoop held aloft by the game leader) and take a single piece of treasure (any one ball) back out through the mouth and they place it somewhere in the play area. It may not be hidden under or behind anything and must remain in plain sight and easily reachable. They do not want to anger this dragon, just to coax it out to play!

Once all of the balls have been placed around the space, the forest sprites sing the mysterious *Dragon in the Mountain* song. As the song is being sung, each player moves around to the back of the mountain and in to the cave. The first to arrive (a player whose name is called by the game leader) stands in the mouth of the cave, the other players line up behind the first in line and put their hands on the waist of the student who is immediately in front of them. The first player is the head of the dragon and when they get to the word 'Fly!_____' in the song, the whole dragon, in one streaming, snaking line, jogs out of the cave to seek its treasure. The teacher may call for a particular ball (by colour or some other characteristic. i.e. 'Collect the giant, purple gem of the Elvish Queens!') and the line of the dragon snakes about the play area to locate the required treasure piece, picks it up, and flies back to the cave to deposit the treasure.

Additional rounds may be played with each 'head of the dragon' remaining in the cave to

> **AGE RANGE:** 7 year olds
>
> **PLAY AREA:** Indoor or outdoor, 20 x 40 paces, a field or a large room
>
> **NUMBER OF PLAYERS:** 8+
>
> **EQUIPMENT:** 1 large hoop (held vertically by the teacher) and 1 ball per player, the balls may be of different colours

watch over that treasure, while the other children become their forest sprite selves again, to pick up a piece of treasure and to find a new place in which to put it. When they are placed, the mysterious *Dragon in the Mountain* song begins again.

Dragon in the mountain,
Sleeping o'er his treasure,
He is dreaming of the days
He'd roar and breathe a fiery blaze!
And all would fear his shadow.
Dragon in the mountain,
Sleeping o'er his treasure,
Hoarding all the jewels and gold,
He keeps it in his mountain hold.
And to search for more,
He'll spread his wings and fly!
Fly! Fly!
Then back to his cave he'll go.

67. Bowser the Hound
Created by Bonnie Bolz

Peter Rabbit loved to eat all the juicy vegetables from the farmer's garden. One day, the farmer decided to catch that pesky rabbit by putting his hound, Bowser, on Peter's trail. Bowser the Hound had a keen sense of smell, so he set off to chase Peter, following the scent of the trail.

Players sit or stand in a circle with a good double-arm distance between them; they are the trees/bushes that make up the forest through which the chase occurs. One child is chosen to be 'Peter Rabbit'. One child is chosen to be 'Bowser the Hound'. Peter Rabbit runs around the trees creating a pathway that Bowser the Hound must follow exactly. The chase is over if:

- Bowser catches Peter.
- Bowser 'loses Peter's trail'.
- The race has gone on for a while, then the game leader counts down to finish the round.

Variations:

- Easier: Remove the element of tagging and have Bowser simply follow Peter Rabbit as precisely as possible.
- More Challenging: Players who are trees can create a variety of forms for Peter to master: (legs spread apart to crawl under, curled up like a stone to hurdle or vault over, make an arch with a partner to form a tunnel, etc.)
- When there is a tag, players switch roles.
- Game leader can choose different movements for the chase (i.e. hopping on one foot, crawling on all fours, etc.)
- Game leader can call out 'Trees' or 'Bushes' to the players in the circle, and players must stand/sit according to the call.

AGE RANGE: 7–9
PLAY AREA: 20 x 20 paces, size is adjusted to the number of players
NUMBER OF PLAYERS: 10+
EQUIPMENT: None

Hints to the leader:

- Make sure there's enough space between the children who are sitting/standing as trees to make safe pathways. Branches/arms need to be tucked in to prevent stepping on fingers.
- The trees are encouraged to follow the 'Trail' that Peter Rabbit creates and see if Bowser the Hound can follow it exactly.

For children who may struggle to play this game:

- Adjustments for a child who cannot sit still could include having a 'Trail Watcher' who sits outside of the circle of trees and watches the trail.

68. Rabbits in the Bushes
Created by Susan Darcy

Once upon a time, there was a colony of rabbits that lived in a warren in a beautiful meadow. But the foxes were beginning to hunt the rabbits with such success that the rabbits decided to find a new home. They sent out a scout to search for a suitable new home, and the scout came back to describe a lovely spot far in the southlands that would be the perfect place to build a new warren.

So, they made a plan to move all the rabbits to a new home without the foxes finding them, and their plan involved a very clever trick. They put a rabbit at one-mile intervals all along a road in the opposite direction of the southlands. This road full of tricks for the fox led far to the north.

Hidden in a clump of bushes every mile there was a rabbit waiting. The last rabbit to leave the warren was the littlest rabbit that volunteered to be the first one to trick the fox that had so long terrorised them. The littlest rabbit hopped along at a rapid clip, making sure the fox was on her trail. She knew exactly where the hiding place would be that held the next rabbit and quick as a wink, she disappeared into a clump of bushes beside the road, and the first hiding rabbit ran out from that same bush to keep up the chase. The fox, not realising the trick, thought this was still the same little rabbit that had left the warren earlier that morning.

The rabbits continued, mile by mile, to play the same trick on the fox, leading him farther and farther north, farther and farther away from their new home in the southlands. The fox got so tired, his tongue began to hang out of his mouth and his tail began to drag in the dust. The rabbits kept this up, one after the other, ducking into a clump of bushes while another rabbit leapt out to trick the fox. Eventually, the fox could go no farther. He ceased the chase and dragged himself off to find a place to rest where he collapsed into a long and very tired sleep. The little rabbits were able to travel safely in the opposite direction to their new home in the southlands.

.

> **AGE RANGE:** 7–9
>
> **PLAY AREA:** 20 x 20 paces, size is adjusted to the number of players
>
> **NUMBER OF PLAYERS:** 10+
>
> **EQUIPMENT:** None

The game leader assigns roles to the players. Some are bushes standing at random places on the field, some are rabbits crouching down in front of the bushes – one rabbit per bush. One player is chosen to be the fox, and another is chosen to be the littlest rabbit who starts the chase. When the chase begins, the rabbit takes refuge in any of the bushes by standing behind a bush and tapping the bush, who in turn taps the rabbit crouched down in front, who then races out and is now being chased by the fox. The bush then crouches down and becomes a new hiding rabbit, the original rabbit stands behind and becomes a new bush and the fox is left chasing each subsequent rabbit. If the fox catches the rabbit before it is safely behind a bush, the roles reverse – the fox becomes the rabbit and the rabbit becomes the fox. This is a fast-paced game.

Hints to the leader:

- Once the players have practised the moves, the game leader can add a time-element countdown. The rabbit who is being chased has to tag-out before the countdown, or they automatically become the fox (or are replaced by a new fox of the leader's choosing).

- This game can be confusing! It underscores the difference between 'impulse' and 'reaction time'. We want to cultivate impulse control and enhance reaction time! Make sure to have the players make their tags clear when switching from rabbit to bush, and from bush to rabbit. Encourage the players to wait until they get an actual tag before they dash into action. Every time we play, the children 'jump the gun' in their anticipation of being the next rabbit to zoom out of a bush. Sometimes two rabbits will be running around because someone mistakenly came out of a bush. Be prepared to freeze the game momentarily to get players back to their right places and then continue. It is fun once they get the hang of it.

- Sometimes the ability level of the fox and the rabbit is unequal, and the fox has no chance of catching the rabbit. This can be fine, unless the child who is the rabbit is so fast and wants to run so much that they dominate the whole game and never take refuge in a bush. In these situations, the dynamics can erode rapidly and certain children may get frustrated with themselves or with others. Be prepared to shift things around, create variations, and make new rules as needed. Keep it fun.

For children who may struggle to play this game

- This game is less about an individual rabbit running and avoiding capture, and more about quick changes, finding a safe bush almost immediately, and the quick succession of new rabbits into the chase. The quicker the turnover, the more satisfied the players feel because everyone gets a chance, and no one is allowed to monopolise the opportunity to be the running rabbit. Look for this dynamic. It is a selfless act to find a bush quickly. Those children who are not mature enough to do this will be the ones who delay the game by running and running. Emphasise that this game is not only about the individual, it is about the group.

69. Wolf in Sheep's Clothing

It's a warm, breezy day, and a shepherd watches over her flock of sheep. Some of the flock are new baby lambs, still finding their footing and not wishing to stray away from the safety of the flock. The shepherd closes her eyes, 'I won't fall asleep, I'll just rest my eyes for a moment' The little lambs are content, skipping happily among the flock. What harm could come if I shut my eyes for just a little while…'

Without anyone noticing, a very clever wolf has slipped into the flock, disguised as one of the sheep – wearing the fleeces of one of his victims. While the shepherd's eyes are closed, the wolf tries to tag as many sheep as he can, but he has to be sly, lest the shepherd discover his true identity.

> Little lambs of springtime,
> skipping all around,
> one among you in disguise,
> the lambs you will bring down.

Players stand in a circle. They are the sheep. The game leader chooses one player to be the shepherd to stand (or sit) in the middle of the circle, and a secret wolf (by winking at them or tapping them on the back while the group has their eyes closed.) Once the wolf has been chosen, the whole group skips in a circle around the shepherd who is blindfolded or has eyes closed. The skipping is accompanied by the song: 'Little lambs of springtime, skipping all around, one among you in disguise, the lambs you will bring down'. This is sung three times while the shepherd in the centre cannot see. When a lamb is tagged by the secret wolf, they kneel down. At the end of the song, the group stops the skipping and stands in place to say, 'Shepherd did you see? Which one can it be?' The shepherd then opens eyes or takes off the blindfold and guesses which player is the wolf-in-disguise. After the guesses, a new shepherd and wolf is chosen.

> **AGE RANGE:** 7 years old
> **PLAY AREA:** Outdoor, small field, at least 20 x 20 paces
> **NUMBER OF PLAYERS:** 8+
> **EQUIPMENT:** Blindfold or handkerchief

Variations:

- This game can be played with a blindfold or by having the shepherd close their eyes.
- Number of guesses may increase depending on the size of the group.
- The game leader can add different movement challenges for the sheep (crawling, hopping, galloping, etc)
- The secret wolf may be given a different movement challenge for trying to tag the sheep (skipping along with them, running, hopping, etc.).

Hints to the leader:

- The wolf moves in the same direction as the sheep (for safety as well as staying incognito).

Skip in circle.

Wolf tags sheep.

Sheep then sit down on the spot they were tagged.

Shepherd blindfolded in the centre.

Lit - tle lambs of spring - time__skip-ping all a —round. ____

One a - mong you in dis-guise, the lambs you will bring down.

70. Sleepy Dragon
Created by Bonnie Bolz

There once was a village of children
who were very bold and brave.
They played with a fire-breathing dragon,
who lived inside a cave.
The dragon loved to chase them,
but he also loved to sleep!
The children tip-toed closer to the cave,
so dark and deep…

> **AGE RANGE:** 7–8
> **PLAY AREA:** Outdoor, 20 x 40 paces
> **NUMBER OF PLAYERS:** 8+
> **EQUIPMENT:** Cones to mark dragon's cave, long rope to mark villagers' line

The game leader chooses two players to begin as the 'Sleepy Dragons'. They begin by lying down in the 'cave' marked at one end of the field with a circle of low cones. The rest of the players are the villagers who begin back at the far edge of their village, on the opposite side of the field.

The villagers hold hands and step toward the dragon's cave as they chant the verse:

'Dragon, Dragon in the cave so deep – Are you awake? Or are you Asleep?' The villagers stop and listen – the dragons reply with snores or sounds of being asleep as they reply, 'Asleep'.

This repeats two more times (or until the villagers are close to the dragon's cave) and on the third time, the dragons leap to their feet and reply, 'Awake!' The dragons then chase the villagers back to their line, trying to tag as many villagers as they can before the villagers are safe across their village line. The villagers let go of each other's hands and run back home to safety, trying to avoid being tagged by the dragons. If a villager is tagged, they become another dragon, and join the others in the cave.

Variations:

- Can begin with two dragons.

- Dragons can add the element of surprise as to when they reply, 'Awake!'

- Game leader can limit the number of children that the dragon(s) can capture.

- The children who approach the dragon can do so by holding hands in a line, adding an element of camaraderie. When the dragons jump up to chase, children drop hands and run.

- Game leader can add a rhythm of clapping to help with the chant, helping the group stay together and to help them all to stop and listen for the dragon's response.

Hints to the leader:

- This game reveals the temperament of each villager – some are gung-ho, marching fearlessly toward the dragon's cave, while others take tiny, timid steps. Since the villagers are holding hands, this means some children may be pulling on others. Game leader can position themselves next to the more hesitant players.

villager   *dragon*

71. Bird, Tree, Flock
Contributed by Torsti Rovainen

The game leader divides the players into groups: trees and birds. For every bird, there are two trees. The trees hold their branches to form a circle together while the bird is safe inside the ring made by the trees. The game leader calls 'Birds!' – then the birds duck under their old trees and run to find a new set of trees to duck under and stand in. The game leader calls 'Trees!' – then the trees let go and find another partner to link branches with to form a new tree. The game leader calls 'Flock!' and all players run to find new places and people with which to form their roles. A good game to break up cliques.

Hints to the leader:

- Unless the group is evenly divisible by three, there will be one to two players without a tree/bird at the end of each call. These players can come to the middle, stand by the game leader, and call the next round's Bird, Tree, or Flock – then they may try to join whatever group was called, leaving one to two new stragglers to come to the middle.

AGE RANGE: 7–8 (can be done with older players too)

PLAY AREA: Indoor or outdoor, 20 x 20 paces or regular-sized room

NUMBER OF PLAYERS: 12+ (even more fun with fuller 'flocks' of 50 or more players!)

EQUIPMENT: None

72. Rattlesnake and Hunter

There is a blind hunter who uses other senses to catch her prey – she is known the world over for being able to catch rattlesnakes with her bare hands!

The game leader chooses one player to be the hunter and one player to be the rattlesnake. The player who is the rattlesnake holds an egg shaker or some rattling object. The other player is the hunter, and they are blindfolded by the game leader. The rest of the group forms a circle around the players and acts as a soft cushion to redirect if the blindfolded player starts to go out of bounds. When the game begins, the hunter tries to tag the rattlesnake who is trying to run away.

Hints to the leader:

- When blindfolding the hunter, the game leader may place a hand on their shoulder until the game

AGE RANGE: 7–9

PLAY AREA: Indoor, enough space to stand in a circle

NUMBER OF PLAYERS: 8+

EQUIPMENT: One rattle, one blindfold

begins and then again when the round is over. This helps to create a sense of security while in a vulnerable state. The putting on of the blindfold should be the final thing that is done before the game begins – don't leave the blindfolded player hanging while the rest of the group is still getting organised.

- Non-running players can still be an active part of holding the safe-space circle, even if they are seated.

73. Magic Knight
Created by Bonnie Bolz

Dragons have taken over the village, and the villagers are too frightened to leave their houses. One brave knight humbly steps forward to dare face the dragons – approaching at nightfall so as not to be spotted by the beasts! Though the knight cannot see, they wield a magic sword that has the power to transform the dragons into harmless house pets. How many dragons can the blind knight tame?

AGE RANGE: 7–9
PLAY AREA: Indoor or outdoor, 20 x 20 paces
NUMBER OF PLAYERS: 12+
EQUIPMENT: 4 x hula hoops, blindfold (optional)

The 'Magic Knight' stands in the middle of four caves (hula hoops) where the dragons lurk. The dragons all run round in the same direction. The Knight is blindfolded, as the dragons run at night. The leader and Knight chant, 'Dragons, Dragons run and hide, No longer may you here abide… ten–nine–eight–seven–six–five–four–three–two–one–**Freeze!**'

Then the Magic Knight points to the cave/corner where they think the most dragons are. All the dragons in this corner (or the closest corner to where the Knight is pointing) are 'Tamed' and come to sit at the feet of the Knight. The Knight gets three rounds to collect as many dragons as possible, and the new Knight is chosen from the tamed dragons.

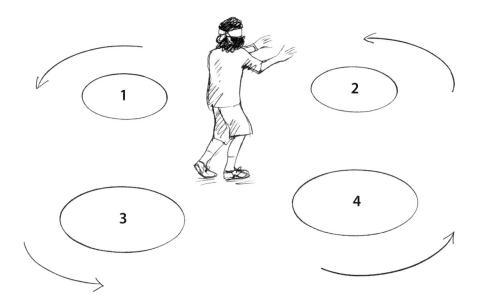

74. Lumberjacks and Wolves

Lumberjacks are using 'logs' to build a house. The Wolves are huffing and puffing and trying to blow their house down. The field is set up with hula hoops like a baseball diamond with hoops in the places of first, second, third, home base and the pitcher's mound. A bucket of 24 sticks (logs) is placed at the first-base hoop. Two wolves are chosen to begin in the wolves' den (pitcher's-mound hoop) – the rest of the group (lumberjacks) starts at the home-base hoop. The goal is for the lumberjacks to get all the sticks to the home hoop in a given amount of time. The wolves try to tag lumberjacks in between hoops. If tagged, a lumberjack goes to wolves' den. The lumberjacks in the wolves' den can be freed by a lumberjack who has run around the bases three times without being tagged. The lumberjacks may only take one stick at a time, one hoop at a time.

They may not take the same stick more than one hoop-distance – they must trade with another lumberjack. If the lumberjacks get all 24 sticks to the home hoop in the given amount of time, they win the day. If the wolves keep them from doing so, the Wolves win the day.

Variations:

- More objects can be added for variations (footballs, etc.) as well as flag belts for more challenging game.

Hints to the leader:

- Encourage the lumberjacks who have been tagged and are waiting in the wolves' den to form a line in the order they were tagged. That way, when a player comes to rescue a lumberjack, they know who is in the front of the rescue line.

AGE RANGE: 8–9

PLAY AREA: Outdoor, size of a small baseball diamond

NUMBER OF PLAYERS: 8+

EQUIPMENT: Bucket with 24 sticks, flag belts for all players, 5 hula hoops or bases

- To keep the players who have been tagged more physically active/engaged while they await rescue, there may be jump ropes placed in the wolves' den so they can use that time to practise their jump rope tricks. If adding this element, make sure the jump ropers are aware of the space around/behind them. Encourage them to spread out around the wolves' den, but they (or the game leader) must remember the order in which they were tagged so it's clear who gets freed first when a rescuer comes along.

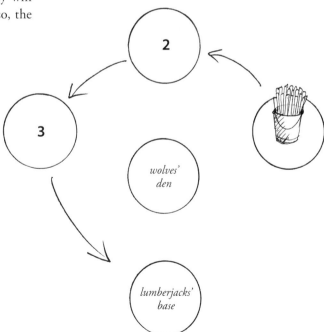

75. Wild Waterman
Created by a fourth-grade class with Susan Darcy

Once upon a time there was a village by the sea. At lunchtime every day the children in the village would gather on the sandy beach and play games. One day, they noticed an island not far off and thought what a delight it would be to go there and explore. So, they found a small rowboat, big enough for all of them to fit, and they rowed off to the island for their adventure.

When they reached the island, they all got out and began to explore their new surroundings. They spent all day in happy fun and adventure and did not notice when the sky began to grow dark. They did not notice when the waves on the beach began to crash more loudly and surge higher onto the sand. All of a sudden, they heard a crack and a rumble, a flash of light filled the sky and the rumble shook the sand under their feet. The rowboat that had gotten them to the island had been swept far out to sea, leaving them stranded as the waves grew higher and crashed louder. It was not too far from home for the older ones to be able to swim back but the younger children were not so confident. The bigger children agreed to stay close to the little ones and offer help if they needed it – together, they would help one another to swim to safety. Off they started and the sky was growing black and the wind was whipping the foam of the waves and spraying salty, stinging water into their eyes.

All at once something began to rise up out of the water. It grew over the heads of the children and seemed to reach the thick grey clouds. It was a man. A giant man with a beard of seaweed and shells, and fish were falling from it at great heights and flopping back into the water. Shells and crabs and barnacles clung to this man's beard. In a booming, gurgling voice he called out, 'I am the Wild Waterman, I catch who I can, swim if you dare.'

To make it home to safety, the children realised they would have to swim past this watery giant. So, they tried. Some of them were successful, but oh… some were not. For those who were touched by the wild waterman were magically transformed into giant clams that sank down to rest at the bottom of the sea. The children who had arrived safely back on the beach were terrified to

> **AGE RANGE:** 8–11
> **PLAY AREA:** Outdoor, 20 x 40 paces
> **NUMBER OF PLAYERS:** 8+
> **EQUIPMENT:** Rope or cones to mark the boundaries of the playing area; there must be two clearly defined safe zones on either ends of the playing area.

see their friends transformed and swam heroically back to save them, diving to the bottom and knocking on the clams to release their friends. But all was for naught. Nothing could be done and the wild waterman was beginning to hunt for these brave children who were trying to save their friends.

When it seemed that the wild waterman would catch a child, the clam would open, revealing a treasure that instantly protected the child and allowed them to escape from the wild waterman and return once again to the shore. Sometimes though, a clam would open and nothing would be inside. In these moments the child who was knocking on the clamshell would be transformed into a clam and the clam would revert back into a child! The child was then able to try to swim safely back to shore, trying to stay out of the reach of the wild waterman's grip.

The game leader chooses one child to be the wild waterman and the other children line up side-by-side on one end of the playing area. The wild waterman speaks to start the game:

'I am the Wild Waterman, I catch who I can, swim if you dare.'

The children run to the other side. If the wild waterman tags someone, they sink to the bottom of the sea (sit down) and become clams. The clams then have a choice: they can pick up a nearby stone (or other nature treasure) and put it in their hands or they can keep their hands empty.

The clams then put their hands together out in front of them in the shape of a clamshell – either hiding a treasure or empty. When the children run across, they have the option of knocking on the clamshell. If the clamshell opens and has a treasure, it gives the child a free walk to the other side. If the clamshell is empty, they switch places, giving the clamshell child a chance to join in the crossings again.

Once a predetermined number of clams are caught, the game leader ends that round and starts another by choosing a new wild waterman.

Variations:

- Adding additional sea creatures that have other functions different from the clams.
- Maybe the wild waterman has limitations of some kind.
- Maybe if four or five clams can hold hands, they become a giant squid that can move around the playing area and help or hinder the wild waterman.
- Ask your students to generate ideas. This will help them think critically and problem solve.

Hints to the leader:

- Tell the story of the game on the first day you introduce it, but you will not have to tell it again each time you play. Just stir their memory a bit: 'You may recall a certain beach, and a certain group of children who encountered a certain giant rising up out of the water…' They will have the imagery spring to mind sufficiently to let them enter into the spirit and joy of the game without more story time.
- Encourage (or require) children who have received a treasure to put their hands on their heads as they have their 'free walk' to the other side. This is a sign to the wild waterman not to chase them and to go after other players. If a player forgets to put their hands on their head and is touched by the wild waterman, that child must become a clam.
- The game leader can decide whether the wild waterman can or cannot tag players who are knocking on a clamshell or stand in wait while the clam negotiation is taking place. In different situations either of these might be good.

- The game leader can decide if a child may re-enter the playing area during a round if they have already made it across safely. Sometimes children who want to be chased and need more thrill and more challenge will come in and out of the safe zone and taunt the 'It'.
- Some children will want to be a clam and will happily sit there all day and not run around. Look for ways to balance out their participation and get them moving.
- The game leader can decide if the boundaries of the game are serious and if a player steps out they are automatically a clam, or if the boundaries are mere suggestions and don't really matter much. There are reasons, depending on the children in front of you, for either approach.

Chapter Two
Age 8–10

The Nine-Year Crisis

Around nine years of age the child experiences a transition from late infancy into 'middle childhood'. This is the start of the preparation for what lies ahead in puberty. At this time, children begin to experience their separateness from others, which can lead to a more conscious awareness of other people in relationship to themselves. Although most games have an aspect of winning and losing, it is of particular importance at this age that children learn how to accept both roles. At this age their emerging individuality is particularly vulnerable. Any game that could bring about 'pack-hunting' of victims must be very carefully handled. Playing highly competitive and individualistic sports too soon may lead children into an adult-type consciousness of winning at all costs. Children at this age still very much need to have their imaginations stimulated by pictures and rhymes within the game.

Many adolescent emotional disturbances can be traced back to unresolved traumas around the age of eight, nine or ten. Children at this age tend to be more open and impressionable. They should be encouraged to work through potential crises, which manifest themselves in various ways at this age. For instance, children often display their emotional difficulties and struggles by sabotaging games – see 'Breaking the Rules' (page xvii) for the different ways that this is done, and what the root cause could be.

This is a vital age, where many of the old structures that previously surrounded the child begin to be discarded. Adult instructions and guidance may start to be questioned. What is of great importance is that activities that build a new emotional structure and security are engaged in; games which give an outer expression to the inner changes are needed.

76. Elephants
as related by Martin Baker

One person is an elephant. She makes a trunk with one arm. She chases and tries to tag the other children. When someone is tagged, they are elephants too, and make a trunk, and chase the others.

Variation:

- Alternatively, (this makes the game last a little longer) when first tagged, the children begin to become elephants – they hold their nose with one hand. When tagged a second time, they grow an elephant's trunk, and can tag others.

This is another game that can effectively be presented through the images of a story: and can easily be adapted to any animal the children may be learning about: kangaroos, storks, frogs, etc.

The image of running hampered by something (in this game, the elephant's trunk) relates to the picture of the nine year old. No longer is the child as free from the constraints of the physical world – she is leaving the dreamy world of early childhood behind, and moving on into middle childhood.

77. Cat Trap

The players form a circle, with feet together and holding hands. This is the mouse's house. One child is the mouse and is in the centre of the circle. Another player is the cat, who is outside the circle and begins by saying:

Cat: *Mouse, mouse come out of your house,*
       And I will give you some cheese.

Mouse: *Not I.*

Cat: *Mouse, mouse come out of your house,*
       And I will give you some bacon.

Mouse: *Not I.*

Cat: *Mouse, mouse come out of your house,*
       Or I will scratch your eyes out.

Mouse: *You dare!*

Variations:

• To help the cat, the house can have a magic 'golden door'. This is a door that will open once for the cat. (Then a new golden door is chosen.) I choose the child who is the magic door by winking at him. The cat must go round the circle trying to catch the mouse. Suddenly a magic door opens when the cat runs by, and the cat can run into the house!

• A dog can be introduced. He chases the cat, who is chasing the mouse. The dog begins inside the house with the mouse.

The house always protects the weakest in a chase: so now the doors will open for the cat – but only when the dog is chasing him – as well as for the mouse.

Hints to the leader:

• It is **very important** that the children stand in the circle with their feet together at all times. Otherwise the poor cat who is trying to put its head through a door may be injured by a kick or a knee. Also, **never** let the cat try and climb over a door (the arms of the children forming the house) – he could easily fall and be tipped up onto his head, or injure his neck. I don't allow the cat (or dog) to charge at the house and forcefully break the grip of the players holding hands.

This game deals with inner and outer space: there is the space inside the circle (front space for the players forming the house, who face inwards) and there is the space outside the circle (back space). The players forming the house have to be aware of where the cat is, and where the mouse is – even when they are outside the circle; this means they must be 'awake' to their back space as well as to the space in front of them.

The children forming the house also have to be very quick to respond when a dog is introduced: they have to remember who is who, and who to let in (or out) so that the weaker animal is always protected. Lightning-quick thought is required!

This is one of the games I play to counteract bullying: here it is up to the group to protect the weakest: and the experience of being the dog, where the house is always acting against you no matter what you do, can be a powerful one.

78. Blind Lion
Inspired by Rudolf Kischnick

Once upon a time a mighty lion lived in the jungle. Every day he would go hunting for treasures, and because he was the king of the jungle, he slowly gathered all the treasures from the villages around him. But eventually the lion grew old. Although he did not lose his courage, he began to go blind. When the children of the villages outside the jungle heard this, they began to steal into the jungle, to try and fetch their treasures back. But the old lion could hear very well, and still kept some of his old strength in the magic power of his paws. So when he heard a child approaching his cave, he used this magic by pointing at the child, and put a spell on her. Then the child would have to return the treasure and go back to the village outside the jungle. The blind lion's magic was so strong that even in the villages he could hear the children if they made too much noise, and could make them return the treasure if he pointed his magic paws at them.

This game is played in complete silence. Choose one child to be the blind lion. She sits in the centre of the circle. Put the blindfold on the blind lion. Make sure her ears are not covered by the blindfold.

All the other children choose a treasure and hold it in their hands. They sit quietly in a large circle, about 10 paces from the blind lion.

As you are telling the story, collect the treasures from the children. Then place the treasures in a circle around the blind lion. Put the lit candle in

> **Equipment:** A lit candle and one 'treasure' for each child (I try to find beautiful objects such as crystals, shells, carved wooden objects etc.), a scarf to use as a blindfold.

front of the lion. The children must try to quietly steal their treasures back.

You must indicate who can begin to move towards the lion. No child may move until you have pointed at her. If the lion hears a child, he points to her and the child must go back to the circle line, until you tell her to start moving in again.

If the child manages to steal her treasure – but the lion points at her on her way back or when she is back in the circle, she must quietly walk back in and replace the treasure, then wait to be asked to try again.

To explain the rules, tell the children the story. The game ends when all the treasures have been taken back, and one child creeps in and blows out the candle.

Variations:

- The children can be asked to bring a treasure from home, or a treasure may be sought in the garden or environment nearby.

- Before the game begins the children can choose someone to exchange treasures with. They now try to rescue a treasure for someone else.

- 'The Lion and the Thorn Tree' can be played, basically in the same way. This is more a difficult version, in which the blind lion is sitting under an imaginary thorn tree. All the children are asked to remove one shoe and to place it in a circle around the lion. Sheets of newspaper are laid randomly within the circle. These are the thorns that prickle the children's feet and make a noise so the old lion can catch them out. The children must avoid the prickles.
- The game can be made even harder by placing each treasure directly on top of sheets of newspaper that are arranged in a circle around the lion, so that it has to be taken off with extreme care.

I play this game with nine or ten year olds, because this is when the children are beginning to realise that they are separate beings, that they can question the authority of teachers or parents. Blind Lion provides an image of how the teacher or leader of a group of children of this age may be feeling. Interestingly, it could also be seen as an image of the way the child feels. Without any need to address the issue directly, playing this game may help children feel more empathy towards the adult world; more importantly, though, it gives expression to a deep experience of loneliness and loss which they often now feel.

79. Witches

Once upon a time, in a country of many rivers, there lived an evil witch. Every day the people from the neighbouring village would go into the fields to care for their crops and herds, and the witch would lie and wait for them. As soon as they were in sight, she would chase them, hoping to catch one or two.

The people would run as fast as they could round the lakes towards the safety of their homes, with the witch hot on their heels. If the witch managed to catch someone, she put them into the closest river, until she could take them home to her cave in the mountains.

But the people were clever, they managed to salvage wood from the river; and they built bridges. When their friends and family were trying to escape from the witch, they were now able to cross the rivers using the bridges; but as everyone knows, witches can't cross water and the villagers were able to escape while the witch ran round the rivers.

One child is the witch. The others are the villagers. The benches are the rivers. The children who are tipped, form bridges by standing on the benches and putting their arms on one another's shoulders. The escaping villagers can run beneath the bridge's arms, using them as a short cut to escape from the witch who is chasing them. The witch is not allowed to cross the water by using one of the bridges, but she

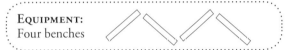

EQUIPMENT:
Four benches

may reach through to the other side in order to try and make a tip.

Both the villagers and the witch are free to run around the rivers (the benches). If low-standing, sturdy gym benches are not available, you can mark out rivers using chalk on the floor or playground. On the grass you can use cones or even jumpers placed at each end of the river (about four paces long).

80. Fleas
Also known as Dr Dooby

One person has fleas. She continually scratches them (e.g. on her head). She tries to tag the others, and to give them fleas too.

If someone is tagged, they must scratch the place where they were tagged. Then they can give others fleas. The game is over when all but one player has fleas.

Variation:

• To make this game last longer, you can introduce a 'Flea-catcher'. She can start freeing people from their fleas only when at least eight people are already scratching (out of a group of 20 children).

81. Sharks and Octopuses

One person is the shark. All the others start off as fishes. They stand at one end of the play area. The shark says:

'Come little fishes swim in my ocean'.

The fishes have to try to reach the other side without getting tagged by the shark. Once they leave the shore they have to continue to 'swim' to the other side. They may not run back to the safety of the bank they have just left behind. When they are at the other side of the sea they are safe. Each time the fishes wait until the shark says 'Come little fishes swim in my ocean'. (It is important that they all swim in the same direction.) They have to leave the shore as soon as the shark has finished speaking.

If they are tagged, they sit cross-legged where they were caught, and become octopuses. (If they sit cross-legged they cannot lunge, and there is less chance of someone tripping over their legs and injuring themselves.)

An octopus can try to tag the fishes that are swimming past, but has to stay seated. The fishes who are tagged by an octopus also turn into octopuses. The shark tries to turn all the fishes into octopuses.

Variations:

• You can introduce bits of 'wreckage' – a designated safe area. This may be a mat, a hoop or a tree, where three or so (decide on a number) fishes can shelter at one time from the shark. If more than the decided number of fishes shelter on the wreckage, the wreckage will sink.

> **PLAY AREA:** 25 paces long, 15 paces wide for 20 children

• The shark may change the call to 'Come little fishes hop in my ocean'. All the fish and the shark must now swim with a broken fin. This causes them to hop on one leg. Likewise she may substitute 'jump' or 'crawl' in her command rhyme.

Around the age of nine years, children become more aware that life is like a perilous journey, full of pitfalls and obstacles. At age seven, the children were presented with an obstacle outside themselves in the form of the swinging skipping rope – but that obstacle had a predictable rhythm, whereas the obstacles that are now perceived are less regular and far more chaotic. At this stage one can feel confident in introducing games that require more demanding dodging and twisting – movements that are required by the fishes in *Sharks and Octopuses* when they try to escape the waving arms of the hungry octopuses.

Chasing games like these are also a metaphor for the natural expansion and contraction processes which govern our lives (for instance in breathing). When a 'fish' in *Sharks and Octopuses* reaches the opposite shore and is safe, she will naturally feel relief. On the other hand, when being pursued, she feels an inner contraction and tension.

82. Dragon Tag
Plus Dragon's Teeth and Bear Tag

In a far-away country lived a fierce dragon, who loved to eat children. She would leave her cave, in search of food; and when she caught a child, she would eat it, and grow larger. With each child she ate, she got larger and larger, until she was so big that her body stretched right across the land.

Two players hold hands. They are the dragon. They secretly decide whom they will try to catch. The dragon catches a player by tipping – 'biting' her with its head (one end of the dragon), or by 'stinging' her with its tail (the other end).

When a player is caught, she joins the dragon by holding the hand of one of the players on the end of the chain. She is then allowed to choose the next victim.

The dragon must stay in one piece and not loosen her grip with the next person in the line. The game ends when everyone has joined the dragon or only one person remains uncaught.

Variations:

- **Dragon's Teeth**: Follow the rules for *Dragon Tag*. However, when the fourth person joins the dragon, it splits into two couples. (Or on the sixth tip, the dragon can split into two groups of three.)

- **Bear Tag**: The same rules apply: except instead of tipping a victim, the bear (-chain) must hold the victim in a bear hug for a count of three, without breaking.

Other Variations:

- Mark out areas where no-one may enter: e.g. swamps (see below). You can do this with hoops, ropes, gym equipment or even chalk marks on the floor.

- The runner may try to run 'between the bear's legs' (under the children's arms): but only when the bear is facing them. In this way children do not collide with each other because they may only run through in one direction. This will mean that the bear bunches up – which makes it harder for 'her' to tip.

- Instead of tipping or hugging, the dragon/bear must form a circle around the runner – who can try to escape through the closing gap in the circle.

This game again explores the dynamic between the group and the individual – as the dragon or bear gets larger and larger, the individual has less and less chance of escaping; but at the same time the dragon becomes more clumsy, and all its 'legs' need to cooperate with each other!

I developed the bear variation in order to encourage the children in a particular class to make physical contact with one another, without being silly because of a premature interest in sex. This variation helps children realise that touching can be fun and non-sexual, that they can touch each other in a relaxed way.

83. The Magic Jewels, the Fiery Dragons and the Stone Knights

One child is the queen (or king). She sits in her castle. Two children are the dragons. They have to try to stop the knights going into the lair and stealing the jewels. But the dragons have got so big that they cannot fit into the lair anymore, so have to stay outside the edge of their cave (outside the line of chalk).

The rest of the children are knights. They are in the castle. The game starts when the king or queen calls out, 'Knights, knights, rescue my jewels!' The knights charge towards the dragon's lair and try to capture the first jewel without getting tipped. Only one jewel can be taken at a time.

If the knight who has the jewel is tipped by a dragon on the way back to the castle, she gives the jewel to the dragon, who takes it back to her lair. The knight is now turned into stone.

When the first jewel has been successfully returned to the castle, the king or queen calls out: 'Stone Knights, Stone Knights, come back to me! The first jewel is rescued and you are free!' The knights are freed and return to the castle. Then the queen says again: 'Knights, knights, rescue my jewels!', and the process begins again. The game ends when the three jewels have been returned to the castle.

PLAY AREA: Mark out the queen's castle (a stone, a chair etc.) at one end of the play area; at the other end, mark out the dragon's lair, by drawing a semi-circle about five paces from the centre, where the jewels will be placed

EQUIPMENT: Three objects that can be used as 'jewels', e.g. crystals, shells, stones

Variations:

- When the first jewel is captured, the stone knights are not freed. This helps if the children are becoming reckless in their charging at the castle.
- The jewels can be rescued in any order. However, the knight who has a jewel can restore life to a knight who has been turned to stone.

84. Sluggabed
Inspired by Rudolf Kischnick

Draw a large circle (the 'room') on the ground, around the 'bed'. The circle should be about ten paces from the bed. On the bed 'Sleepy Head' lies sleeping with her eyes closed. She has a helper, who sits on the bed next to her.

The object of the game is to drag Sleepy Head's mattress out of the room without getting tagged. When Sleepy Head wakes up she is grumpy, and from her bed tries to tag whoever is trying to steal it. But she is too sleepy to stand up. However, her helper can run around and tag the other children.

The children wait in a large circle around the bed. As the verse is said they take one small step, heel to toe, for each line.

> Sleepy head
> Sleeps all day
> Steal her bed
> If you may!

On the last line they run in and try to drag the mattress to the line of the circle before getting tagged. The children are safe when they are not inside the 'room', but if they are tagged they have to sit out and wait for the next game. The game is over when either all the children are tagged or the bed is pulled over the line.

PLAY AREA: It is best to play this on a polished floor, so that the 'bed' can be safely and smoothly dragged

EQUIPMENT: Old mattress (or a strong woollen blanket, a carpet, a gym safety-mat; if you are using a blanket, tie 6 tennis balls around the edges, so that the children have some kind of handle to pull on) – this is the 'bed'

Variations:

- You can vary the number of 'helpers'.
- Or, limit the amount of children who can steal into the room each time the verse is said.

Around the ages of nine or ten, the children should begin to lose their dreaminess and wake up. *Sluggabed* is a metaphor for this waking process: the child on the bed has to be quick to tag the others, or else she will lose her bed.

85. Cat and Mouse House

Divide the children into pairs. Each child links arms with her partner. The pairs stand anywhere in the room or playground. These pairs are the 'mouse houses'.

Choose one child to be the cat, and another to be the mouse. The cat chases and tries to catch the mouse. The game begins with the cat saying:

Mouse, mouse run into your house
Or I will come in and eat you!

The mouse replies: 'Just try!' and runs away from the cat. If the cat chases and catches the mouse, then the mouse changes into the cat and the cat becomes the new mouse. In other words they change roles. But the mouse can take refuge in a 'house' by linking arms with one child standing in a pair.

But the house is too small for three people, so the child at the other end of the house becomes a cat, and the former cat miraculously turns into a mouse and has to run away as quickly as possible from the new cat.

Variations:

• Instead of standing, the pairs of players forming the mouse-houses lie down on the grass. This gives the new mouse more chance to get away from the new cat, who has to stand up when the old cat lies down next to her house-partner.

Hints to the leader:

• Girls and boys at this age might object to standing in mixed pairs, with linked arms. You can tell them instead to stand with their legs apart, only touching the other child with one foot.

• Another problem you may experience is that some children are never chosen to become the cat. Halfway through the game, ask the children who haven't had a turn to put their hands up: the mouse must only choose those houses to hide in.

• Boys and girls will sometimes not choose each other, so you can introduce the rule that an escaping boy mouse must choose a girl house to run into.

The intention of the game is to help children learn to stay within themselves in moments of change or of panic (i.e. when a cat becomes a mouse). At such a moment, the tendency is to take fright and lose one's centre, and the capacity to think or act clearly. Also, children at this age are often either too much out of themselves (tending towards aggression) or too much in themselves (passive, or introverted). For instance, Jane may start throwing herself around, verbally as well as physically, whereas Ruth will simply lie on her bed all day and read. This game will help balance such tendencies. If Jade is too aggressive, and concentrates too much on chasing and catching the mouse, she will not be able to quickly change into a mouse and escape when she has caught the old mouse. On the other hand, Ruth, the mouse, if she is too much in herself, will probably miss the opportunity to catch the new mouse when she changes into the cat.

These two tendencies are also related to our ability to plan ahead, to live into the future. To change roles so quickly requires a strong sense of self, which should be developing at this age. This game is also good for bullies and for children who lack a real sense of boundary, because it differentiates between your own and another's space. As a cat, your intention is to catch the mouse, and so you project yourself outwards, look out into the world. When you are a mouse, you tend to want to withdraw into yourself – and if you then have to change roles, you will probably take too long, in which case the new mouse will have run away.

The Nine-Year-Old Threshold

These games are examples of the **nine-year-old threshold** of leaving the dreamy world of early childhood and embarking on the path of middle childhood. Of course, this threshold is approached over a period of time – roughly two years – which may mean the child reaches it when she is older than nine. Yet all children experience this change. To the outsider (parent, teacher, friend) this may be indicated by an outward show of independence: for instance, if an adult now makes a mistake, the child notices and may well take great delight in teasing her about it. Or this change may be shown more inwardly – for example, with an expressed desire to achieve things without **any** help whatsoever.

The reaching and crossing of the threshold towards a more individual, independent state, is often a painful process. If this crisis in the child is met with sensitivity and understanding, she can grow tremendously. The nine year old requires obstacles to overcome in order to test and strengthen her emerging sense of self. But the adult who takes the child's show of independence as something that challenges authority, may respond with reactionary, self-protective gestures which both inhibit the child's passage and also distort it. Instead of a dictator, an absolute authority who bars the way, the nine year old needs a benevolent guardian who encourages her development towards selfhood.

This is something of a 'preview' of the role the adult will need to play when dealing with adolescents. In the twelve year old, for instance, barring the path towards independence can lead to a distorted independence in the late teens: no real independence at all, but a reliance on peer-group support (e.g. in gangs). During adolescence, however, the test is more orientated towards conditional versus unconditional love, unconditional love being an essential foundation-stone for building relationships with them. When adult caring is dispensed as a reward for the perceived good behaviour of a teenager, this can make her very insecure.

At nine years of age, learning through imitation is not as strong as it was before. Children start to learn more through observing.

The nine-year-old child begins to wake up to herself in a new way; then, in the following year, begins to test and try out her emerging powers. She starts to experience a confrontation with the forces which connect her to the physical world.

86. The Ghost Train

All the children in the village are asleep in their beds. The Ghost Queen comes to the village to steal the children, and to keep them as prisoners on her 'Ghost Train'.

The children kneel in a circle with their eyes closed. One person is the Ghost Queen or King. As the Ghost Queen silently walks around the outside of the circle of 'sleeping' children, she says or sings the following verse:

> The Ghost Queen walks and none can hear
> The midnight hour it strikes so clear
> Rise up, rise up – not slow, not fast,
> Be careful not to be the last.

She touches a child gently on the shoulder, who rises and joins the Ghost Train, by holding the hand of the last person on the 'Train' in perfect silence. The Ghost Queen keeps repeating the verse. Each child who joins the enchanted train also joins in singing the song. The last child in the train always wakes up the next one while the whole train proceeds and secretly winds around the houses of the village. And so it continues, with the verse repeated over and over again, until one child remains. If this child 'wakes up' (opens her eyes) before the Ghost Train has circled around her twice and is led out of the 'ghost door' (a prearranged place about 10 paces away), then all the children are freed from the train – and there is great rejoicing.

If she doesn't wake up in time, the Ghost Queen keeps all the children in her power, so this child, too, joins the train: the Ghost Queen has won the game.

However, if a sleeper feels that she may be the last person left and opens her eyes only to discover that she is not the last, (i.e. there are others who have not yet joined the train who are still sleeping in the circle) then she is also captured by the Ghost Queen and must now join the train.

87. Jack in the Box

Begin with two benches arranged in a T-shape. One child (player A) stands on bench A – she has the ball. The other children stand on bench B, all facing player A.

Player A throws the ball to player one, who throws it back to her. Player one then crouches down. Player A then throws the ball to player two, over player one's head. Player two throws it back and crouches down.

This continues until the last player in the line (say, player 14) catches the ball and throws it back. Then player one moves to bench A, and player A goes to the end of the line.

Variations:

• Divide the children into two teams. Now two 'T' shapes are formed with the benches. Each team has a ball and the procedure is followed again.

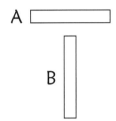

> **EQUIPMENT:** Two play balls, four benches

88. Canyons

The benches are placed parallel. One child (player A) stands on bench A – she has the ball. The other children stand on bench B, all facing player A.

Player A throws the ball to player one, who throws it back to her. Player one then crouches down. Player A then throws the ball to player two, over player one's head. Player ywo throws it back and crouches down.

This continues until the last player in the line (say, player 14) catches the ball and throws it back. Then player one moves to bench A, and player A goes to the end of the line.

Variations:

• Divide the children into two teams. Now two 'T' shapes are formed with the benches. Each team has a ball and the procedure is followed again.

Again player A throws to each of the players in turn. When the last player has caught and returned the ball, all the players hop off the bench and move it one foot (30cm) further away from bench A.

Then player one becomes player A, and the child

> **EQUIPMENT:** Two play balls, four benches

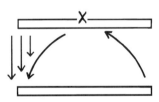

who was player A now goes to the end of the line.

This is such a simple and organised way to practise accurate throwing and catching! (Even though on paper it sounds so complicated.) The player on bench A has a chance to throw the ball over an increasing distance. To be able to do this means that the child needs to estimate the distance each time. The fact that players are standing on a bench means that there is little margin for error when the ball is thrown – if it is too far to the right or left the players will not be able to catch it.

89. River Bandits

There was once a man who lived in a faraway country. He decided one day that the time had come for him to go and seek his fortune. So he joined the rest of the travellers who were travelling towards the east. Eventually they came to a brown and fast-flowing river. Now, it was said that there were some boats on this river that were ferried by honest ferrymen, and others that were rowed by bandits. Some travellers had been caught by the bandits and made to serve them by robbing honest travellers.

It was said that the best time to cross the river was early in the morning before the bandits had woken up: for if you waited too long the noonday sun would shine, the river would rise, and the bandits would approach the bank in search of captives…

One person is a boat. A smaller person climbs on her back and is the bandit. The other children are travellers. They try to cross the river without getting tagged by the bandit or her boat.

The travellers start crossing only when the bandit says, 'Come and try to cross the river!' Once they have begun to cross the river, the travellers cannot turn back. If one gets tagged, they become a boat or a bandit, (depending on their size). They go to the side of the play area, and wait for a partner.

The bandits and boats cannot go beyond the banks of the river; but when the last traveller is left on the banks of the river, it floods, and the bandits on their boats can go beyond the river bank to catch the last traveller.

When the traveller is caught, or has successfully reached the village on the opposite bank, the river subsides, and the bandits return with the river to its original course. The bandits then call their challenge

> **PLAY AREA:** About 15 x 10 paces; mark out two 'river banks' across the width of the area, about 3 or 4 paces apart – this forms the river; it should divide the playing area in half.

again. The game ends when two or three travellers are left.

This game works primarily with images. The children at this age are awakening to a new consciousness; the new experience of being separate opens them to both positive and negative forces. But the negative forces now seem to threaten them from without – and are therefore terrifying in a new way. Such external forces cannot so easily be conquered or tamed: and the child can experience the confrontation with them in a very strong way. In *River Bandits*, we have a picture of this kind of experience. The rich image of the river, a symbol of change in both psychology and mythology, reflects the child's changing reality. The negative forces are symbolised by the image of the bandits on their boats, who chase the child while she tries to pass through a state of change. But these dark forces are encumbered and slow in movement, which enables the quick child to pass safely through their territory. But if a child is hesitant in taking on the challenge – if she hesitates too long before trying to cross the river – the dark forces are freed, and can engulf her. This can bring a realisation that life's dangerous course must be embarked upon, that delaying the journey does nothing to help conquer the dangers. If one acts too impulsively, though, one may also be caught.

90. Scarecrows

One person is the farmer. The farmer is trying to grow corn, but there is a flock of crows (the rest of the children) who keep on eating it. So the farmer chases the crows and tries to catch them.

If the crows get caught, they magically turn into scarecrows, and stand with their legs apart, arms outstretched. The scarecrows can be freed by any of the crows, who have to crawl between the scarecrow's legs.

While they are beneath the scarecrow, they are safe from the farmer. But as soon as the crow leaves the safety of the scarecrow, they are both in danger of being tipped.

Variations:

• Slowly add more farmers.

This is another traditional game which illustrates how the rules of play can be given to children in picture form. This is not just a more fanciful way of describing rules; in fact, developing the imagination has a great pedagogical task in child development. Through the imagination, children develop the ability to think and to reason – not in a dry, linear way, but creatively. Skills like problem-solving are nourished by developing imaginative thinking.

91. Shelter, Water, Food

Divide the group into two teams. One group will be 'nature'. The other group will be the 'animals'. The two groups go to the opposite end of the playing area. The 'animals' turn their backs away from 'nature' so they cannot see them. 'Nature' stays facing the 'animals'. Each player in both groups now chooses one of three signs to make with her hands.

1. **Shelter:** This is made by placing the finger tips of your hands together above your head. This shape resembles the sloping roof of a house.

2. **Water:** This is made by making a cup with your hands and holding them out in front of yourself.

> **PLAY AREA:** About 25 x 18 paces

3. **Food:** This is signalled by simply holding your stomach with both hands.

On a call given by the game leader all the 'animals' turn around. They must run and tig one of the 'nature' players who is making the same sign as themselves. The 'nature' player may only be tagged by one animal. If an animal is successful she takes the nature player back with her to where she started. The 'nature' player now becomes an 'animal'. If an 'animal' is not successful in being the first to tag a 'nature' making the same sign as herself, she joins the 'nature' group. This process is repeated over and over again until either one group has no players left or, after a set length of time, the game is stopped and the number of players on each side counted. The team with the most players wins.

92. Tunbridge World's Fair
Adapted by Torsti Rovainen

Welcome to the Tunbridge World's Fair! Such a popular place, that folks come from miles around to enjoy all the fun rides and delicious food – they even sell deep-fried pickles! Some local kids devised a sneaky game at this fair: go in and out of the crowd playing one-on-one tag! With so many people here, the Fair Marshal tells everyone that they cannot run! Walking only!

> **AGE RANGE:** Mixed age
> **PLAY AREA:** Indoor, small indoor space
> **NUMBER OF PLAYERS:** 10+ (very fun in large groups of 40+)
> **EQUIPMENT:** None

This is basically a tag game –but a walking one. Each player is paired up with a partner. Partners choose who will chase first and who will be chased first. At the 'go' signal, chasers chase by walking, and chasees run away by walking. When the chasers tag the chasees, they switch roles. This repeats over and over until the game leader calls an end. A fun and chaotic icebreaker game.

Variations:

- To enhance the sense of chaos, the players can be given a script: Chasees chant, 'I'm outta here, I'm outta here, I'm outta here…' over and over while chasers chant, 'Gonna getcha, Gonna getcha, Gonna getcha…' over and over. Note – this variation gets quite boisterous, and it's a lot of fun.

- The game leader (as the Fair Marshall) can add multiple signals, commands where every player must stop the chase and strike whatever previously-decided-upon pose or position that they've established, for example: 'Freeze!', or 'Everyone asleep!', or 'Cows', etc.

- The game can be done in silence, or with other chasing/running away chants (a great time to practise different languages, especially since people from all over the world come to the Tunbridge World's Fair!)

- The game leader as the Fair Marshal can call any player, along with their partner, who break the no-running rule to a designated area to 'serve their time' – either standing off to the side and counting to 25, and then going back in. Or, for more challenge, the game leader can add fitness challenges: e.g. hold a plank position and count to

20, or hold a wall-sit and count to 30, etc.

Hints to the leader:

- If there is an odd number, the game leader can either join in to make it even, or have the extra player be the Fair Marshal.

- This game can get very noisy if done with the chanting. For more sensitive players, try it in silence or with soft whispers.

- The game leader must always be on top of things to make sure players aren't getting hurt. While there will always be a few good-natured accidental bumps in this game, if the players are moving too quickly (even walking) or are out of control, the bumps could be more serious. While still allowing room for chaotic fun, take preventative steps to keep things from spiralling too far.

For children who may struggle to play this game:

- This game can bring the energy in the room to a high level, which some children experience as disorienting. To change the dynamic, try playing it slow-motion; the Fair Marshal is looking for which player has the smoothest, most fluid motion. This can include slow-motion sounding chanting as well, depending on the skill level of the players.

93. True For You
Adapted by Torsti Rovainen

An icebreaker game – good for large groups of people as a get-to-know-you game. The game leader can be the first person to begin or they may choose a person on the circle. They come to the centre of the circle and say something that is true for them (e.g. 'My name is _____, and I'd like to visit Europe someday'). Anyone on the circle for whom this is also true, walks through the centre of the circle to find a new place to stand on the circle.

Variations:

- Can add a rule that, as players walk through the middle of the circle, they find someone they do not know, shake hands and introduce themselves to one another, then find a new place on the circle to stand. At the end, there can be a name challenge – a player may try to name all the players on the circle. If they get stumped, a second person may take over where they left off.

- Can add any movement activity when the players are walking through the centre (high fives, back-to-back with linked elbows, try to sit and then stand, rock-paper-scissors, etc.).

AGE RANGE: Mixed age

PLAY AREA: Indoor or outdoor, any space

NUMBER OF PLAYERS: Most fun with large groups of 20+

EQUIPMENT: Cones to mark players' places – one fewer than the total number of players

Hints to the leader:

- Works best if you have clear markers on the circle to mark each person's place – cones or spots. Put out one fewer than the number in the group so that each time one person ends up in the middle.

- Watch out for intentional stragglers who want to be the one in the centre at the end, and may take too much time to find a new place on the circle. If there is more than one of these, the game can drag on can lose momentum. Remind the players that their goal is to get to another place quickly and safely. The game leader may want to call on players to come to the centre rather than leaving it to chance.

94. Circle Run Relay
Created by Will Crane

A good warm-up game! Count off numbers around the circle so that each half of the circle has a number. For example, if there is a group of 12 players, then the game leader would give numbers to the first six players (one to six), then the seventh player on the circle would be given the number one so that the second half of the circle is also given numbers one to six. To make sure that everyone has a number and knows their number, the game leader can call out the different numbers, having the players stand when their number is called. Each number ends up having two players with that same number, standing on opposite sides of the circle. At the start signal, players run anticlockwise one at a time in a circle as a relay, tagging the next person after they have run once around the circle.

Variations:

- The game leader may add any number of activities for players to do as they go around the circle (i.e. jump rope around the circle, crab-walks, cartwheels, walking backwards, balancing a bean-bag on your head, etc.).

Hints to the leader:

- All players stay seated/on their spot until it's their turn to run (skip, jump rope, etc.)
- In the case of an odd number of players, the game leader can stand in for a number or can choose one player to have two numbers, once at the beginning and once at the end, meaning that this player does one lap for one team, and one lap for the other.

> **AGE RANGE:** 8–10
> **PLAY AREA:** Indoor or outdoor, 20 x 20 paces
> **NUMBER OF PLAYERS:** 8+
> **EQUIPMENT:** None

For children who may struggle to play this game:

- Some children may get overly competitive to the point where they are no longer having fun or they are being hard on other players for not being fast enough. To turn the focus away from speed being the only thing that counts, the game leader can ask the players to count how many times they skip through their jump rope on their turn, or to see if they can pass their jump rope to the next person without dropping it, etc.).

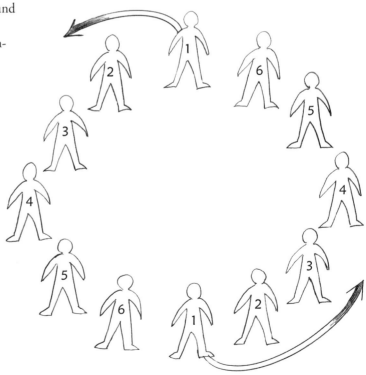

95. Star Gatherers
Created by Will Crane

How is it that some stars seem to stick in place, while others shoot through the sky? Ask the Star Gatherers!

This is a threshold-crossing game. If it's a large group (18–20+) the game leader chooses five players to be the Star Gatherers. They start in the centre (of the Milky Way) facing the rest of the players who are lined up on one side of the field (Shooting Stars.) The Star Gatherers make a right hand star as they call out to the Shooting Stars: *'Star Light, Star Bright, how many stars in the sky tonight?'* The Shooting Stars reply, *'None that you can catch!'*, and the Shooting Stars try to run to the other side of the field without getting tagged by the Star Gatherers. If they are tagged, they turn into a Fixed Stars (standing with feet and arms wide, right at the spot they were tagged.) The Fixed Stars have to stay in one spot on the field, but they can hop each turn to face the Shooting Stars. When the Shooting Stars 'fly across the sky', the Fixed Stars can tag them by leaning to the sides, and reaching their arms out, but the Fixed Stars must leave their feet in place on the ground. When the remaining Shooting Stars are the same (in number) as the original Star Gatherers, they become the new Star Gatherers and the game begins again. If they have been a Star Gatherer already they can choose someone who hasn't had a turn yet.

Variations:

- Rather than becoming a Fixed Star when tagged, players may join the Star Gatherer and become Star Gatherer helpers. This becomes much more challenging for the Shooting Stars.

- For smaller number of players, there can be just one or two Star Gatherers.

> **AGE RANGE:** 8–10
>
> **PLAY AREA:** Outdoor, large rectangular area, 20 x 40 paces
>
> **NUMBER OF PLAYERS:** 8+ (large numbers work well too)
>
> **EQUIPMENT:** Pinnies or coloured bands for the Star Gatherers, cones to mark the corners, cones or ropes to mark the back lines

Hints to the leader:

- Players will be tempted to run outside of the boundaries to avoid being tagged. The game leader can preview that, if a Shooting Star runs out of bounds, they 'fall out of the sky' and automatically become Fixed Stars at the edge of the field where they ran out – no tag needed.

For children who may struggle to play this game:

- If playing with a smaller group (with only one or two Star Gatherers), the game leader may choose to end the round when there are two or three Shooting Stars, rather than waiting until there is only one – safety in numbers, and less pressure on the sole surviving Shooting Star.

96. Spiders and Flies

'Won't you come into my parlour?' said the spider to the fly.
'Tis the prettiest parlour that ever you did spy.'

'The way into my parlour is up a winding stair, and I've many pretty things to show you when you are there.'

'Oh, no, no, no,' said the fly, 'to trick me is in vain,'

'For those who travel to your parlour are never seen again!'

The game leader divides the group into two teams: Spiders and Flies. There are 24 (or more) hoops laid out to create a path that leads to a centre hoop, and even number of hoops on each side, and making zigzag or 90-degree turns every three or four hoops. Players stand on opposite sides of the field, the team forms a line behind the first hoop of their team's path. At the start signal, the first player in each line hops with two feet in each hoop, trying to get as far as they can before coming face-to-face with the player from the opposite side. They then have a round of 'Rock, Paper, Scissors', to determine who wins that meeting. The player that loses the match exits the hoop path and runs to the back of their team line. The player that wins that match continues to hop forward to gain as much ground as possible before the second player hops out to meet them. These 'face-offs' continue, each team trying to gain ground toward the opponent's first hoop. If any player touches a hoop with their foot while hopping, they are immediately out and must exit the hoop path and run to the back of their team line.

The game is won when one side manages to make it all the way to the start of the opposite team's hoop path **and** wins the final Rock, Paper, Scissors round at that final hoop space. Teams then switch sides, mix up their line order, and another round begins.

AGE RANGE: 8–10

PLAY AREA: Indoor or outdoor, 30 x 30 paces

NUMBER OF PLAYERS: 6+

EQUIPMENT: 24 hula hoops

Variations:

- Any alternate version of Rock, Paper, Scissors will do. (Ro-Sham-Bo, Ready, Steady, Show!)

- For more challenge, the game leader can determine certain colour hoops to correspond to specific ways to move in that hoop. For example, all red hula hoops must be hopped into with right foot only, or all blue hula hoops must be hopped into with both feet, or all orange hula hoops must be jumped over and not touched at all, etc… This adds the element of quick thinking to the game and requires the game leader to keep a very close eye to call the 'outs'.

Hints to the leader:

- When playing with the above variation, an additional role may be added, 'Eagle-Eye'. One player from each side can be sent to watch the footing of the players from the opposite team, and send them to the back of the line when there is a 'foot fault'.

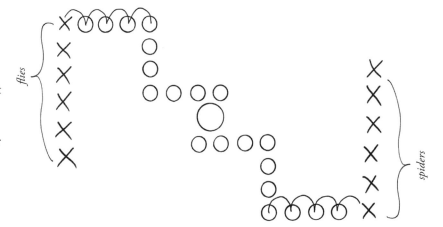

97. Wolves and Villagers
By Bonnie Bolz

A magical wolf pack surrounds a village. The wolves have the power to freeze the villagers into statues by touching them. The wolves' power lies in their tails… try to steal one, if you dare!

The game leader selects at least two players to start as wolves. For a group of 25, start with three to four wolves. The rest of the players are the villagers. The wolves try to tag the villagers to freeze them. When a villager is tagged, they stand frozen in place with their arms akimbo (hands on their hips, elbows out.) It takes two villagers to free the frozen villager by attaching arms and counting a full three seconds together to make the rescue complete. A villager helping to free a frozen person is safe from the wolves while linked arm in arm, even while they are waiting for another villager to link onto the other side. The villagers, if they dare, try to snatch the wolves tails without getting tagged. If they do, the wolf becomes a villager, and the villager becomes a wolf.

AGE RANGE: 8–10
PLAY AREA: Outdoor, 20 x 30 paces, open flat field
NUMBER OF PLAYERS: 10+
EQUIPMENT: Flag belts, cones to mark boundaries

98. The Runaround

Simple chasing game done in pairs. Each player stands at their own cone, set at least 10 paces apart from their opponent's cone. Players determine who will be the first to chase/be chased. At the signal, the chaser is trying to catch up to their opponent to tag them, and the path of the chase must always go in the same direction around each cone. If/when the first chaser catches up to their opponent and tags them, the players immediately switch roles and the run-around continues in the other direction.

AGE RANGE: 8+
PLAY AREA: Indoor or outdoor, large room or 20 x 20 paces open space
NUMBER OF PLAYERS: 6+
EQUIPMENT: One cone per player

Variations:

- Any mode of transport may be used: skipping, hopping on one foot, potato-sack race, etc.

tagger

taggee

Hints to the leader:

- This game quickly reveals which of the opponents is 'faster' when the mode of transport is running. The game leader may choose to make the bouts very short and switch out partners quickly and frequently. A little goes a long way, so this game should not drag on too long. It can be a fun alternative to boring old 'running warm-ups'.

99. Blue Sky/Grey Cloud
Created by Jeff Tunkey

Get ready for the weather to change quickly in this game: is it sunny and safe with blue skies all around, or are the thunderclouds rolling in, signalling a dangerous storm? Which way will the wind blow? Can you find your way to safety, whatever the weather?

The play area is set up so that there are multiple 'safe spaces' spread out around the area. (Folded up gym mats laid out flat work well for this game, especially if they are two different colours. Long jump ropes or hula hoops may also be used.) For a group of 10 players, there should be at least two of each colour 'safe space' – (i.e. at least two blue mats, at least two grey mats).

The game leader chooses at least two players to begin as the taggers. Taggers may not run onto a mat, but are trying to tag runners that are running between the mats.

Depending on the call by the game leader (the way the wind blows) runners are safe if they are standing on/in the safe space that is called by the game leader. Only two players can be on a safe space at a time. If there are more than two players on a safe space, none of them are safe and risk being tagged by the tagger.

If the game leader calls, 'Blue Sky', that means players are only safe on the blue mats. If the game leader calls 'Grey Cloud', players are only safe on the grey mats. If a player is tagged, they join the

> **AGE RANGE:** 8–10
>
> **PLAY AREA:** Indoor or outdoor, large room or 20 x 20 paces field
>
> **NUMBER OF PLAYERS:** 10+
>
> **EQUIPMENT:** If indoors, 6+ mats or rugs; outdoor, 6+ hula hoops or areas marked with large ropes

ranks of the taggers, so the game gets increasingly challenging as it goes on, with more and more taggers added to the mix. The round may end when the taggers have tagged all players, or when the game leader calls, 'New Round', at which point, all players (including those that were just taggers) run to a mat, new taggers are chosen, and the game begins again. A game of quick switches.

Variations:

- Game leaders who do not have access to gym mats, may use other things to mark safe spaces. Depending on what's available, the imagery of the game may change. If, for example, a game leader has hula hoops, the game leader may call 'Hot' or 'Cold' – runners are safe when no more than two of them are in a warm-colour/cool-colour hoop. Gym mats are nice but not necessary. Be creative!

82

100. Burn Ball

A bright, shining, fiery meteor is headed our way! Time is of the essence; put the fire out!

A lead-up to *Caterpillar Kickball*, *Burn Ball* can be played with one or two pitchers. One team is up to 'bat' – the other team is fielding. Player(s) kick the ball that is rolled to them by the pitchers. Kickers then run around the bases, making it as far as they can before the ball(s) are placed in the bucket(s). Players are out if they are caught between bases when both ball(s) are placed in the bucket(s).

Variations:

- Can be played with one or two pitchers/buckets – for smaller groups, use just one.
- Can be played where everyone on the team kicks prior to switching sides.
- Count outs as in baseball and switch sides keeping the same batting order.
- More challenging: add a rule that kickers must be joined at the hand as they run the bases.
- More challenging: add a rule that only one (or two) players may stop in a hoop – like forced runs in baseball.

Age range: 8–12

Play area: Outdoor, a small baseball diamond

Number of players: 10–30

Equipment: 1 or 2 playground balls, 4 hoops, 1 or 2 buckets

Hints to the leader:

- If playing with two pitchers, use different coloured balls – if red ball kicker's ball is caught, that kicker is out. The other runner continues until **both** balls are in the buckets.
- Players who are not able to run can choose a teammate to run on their behalf.
- The bucket may tip over if the ball is thrown into it, which does not count if the ball then rolls out of the bucket. If this happens, the runners may keep running. Encourage the fielding team to take care that the ball makes it into the bucket and stays there.

101. Beat Ball

Are you faster than a comet? Time is of the essence – can you beat the ball?

Beat Ball is played whereby the kicker either beats the ball in the path around the bases, or does not. Simple scoring – player either gets a home run or not. A smaller baseball diamond is placed inside the outer one. Fielding team has to work together to get the ball to go around the bases to players on first, second, third, and back to Pitcher/Bucket as the runner tries

Age range: 8–12

Play area: Outdoor, a small baseball diamond

Number of players: 10–30

Equipment: 1 or 2 playground balls, 4 bases/mats, 4 hoops, 1 or 2 buckets

for a home run. If the runner makes it to home base before the ball makes the rounds and back into the bucket, a point is scored.

102. Caterpillar Kickball
Adapted by Julianna Lichatz

For large groups, split the group into two teams – one 'at bat' and one in the outfield. The game leader (as the pitcher) rolls the ball to the first player 'at bat' over home base/hoop. That player kicks the ball into the air and tries to run as far as they can around the bases/hoops while the fielding team lines up and passes the ball down the line under (through their legs and hand to the next person) over (passed over their head to the next person) under, over, etc. down the line (simulating the movement of a caterpillar.).

Variations:

• This game can be simplified by finding one place on the playground or campus that the kicker must run to and back to be safe at home (rather than running around bases.)

• This game can be done with throwing rather than kicking.

• For smaller groups, all players serve on the fielding team (no lining up to bat), and the game leader calls players one at a time to kick.

• '*Snakeball*' – the fielding players that pass the ball down the line can pass across the right/left sides, alternating with each player. This encourages players to reach across the vertical midline of the body which helps with spatial orientation, primary reflex integration, and overall coordination.

> **AGE RANGE:** 8+
>
> **PLAY AREA:** Indoor or outdoor, large room or small baseball diamond (or an area 30 x 30 paces)
>
> **NUMBER OF PLAYERS:** 10+
>
> **EQUIPMENT:** one playground ball, 4 bases or hula hoops

Hints to the leader:

• When introducing this game, the game leader can be both the pitcher and the front of the caterpillar so that beginning players don't have to vie for the starting position of the ball passing.

• To make sure everyone has a chance to be the front of the caterpillar, the game leader can call out a player's name before the pitch so that the players know ahead of time who will be at the front of the caterpillar line.

103. S.P.U.D.

Players take hands in a circle. One person begins in the centre of the circle holding the ball in their hands. To begin the game, the person in the centre calls another player's name while throwing the ball straight up in the air. At that moment, all players on the circle (except for the player whose name was just called) run away from the circle and try to get as far away as possible from the ball.

The person whose name was called must then retrieve the ball and yell, '**Stop!**' All players must freeze right on the spot when they hear, '**Stop**'. Now, all players are frozen in place. The person holding the ball may take three steps toward any frozen player and then try to roll the ball in such a way that it will touch a player. If the ball rolls and touches a player, that person gets a letter: 'S' (Each time a player is touched by a rolling ball, they add another letter – to eventually spell S.P.U.D.)

The game continues as the player whose name was called becomes the player in the centre of the circle, ready to call a new name and throw the ball up. If a player collects all the letters of S.P.U.D., they are given a chance to clear the slate **if** they can manage the following feat. The whole group forms a line in front of that player and stands with their feet wide, creating a tunnel. If the player is able to roll the ball straight through the tunnel without the ball touching anyone's legs, they get a clean slate and erase all their letters and start over.

AGE RANGE: 8+

PLAY AREA: Indoor or outdoor, very large room/gym, or wide open field 40 x 40 paces

NUMBER OF PLAYERS: 8+

EQUIPMENT: One playground ball

Variations:

- The game leader may change the 'feat' that the player must perform if they get all letters S.P.U.D. to serve the needs of that particular player or the group in general.

Hints to the leader:

- Some guidelines can be helpful to encourage inclusion (i.e. boys call a girl's name, and vice versa, and no one may be called twice before everyone has been called once).

- Depending on the play area, the game leader can run to different parts of the campus and call out a count-down from ten to one; all players must run and make it to the circle before the count-down. This adds an additional challenge as well as the excitement of never knowing where the circle will be formed.

PART TWO

Beyond the Doorway

Chapter Three
Age 10–12

104. The Dog and His Bone

The players are hungry dogs, who want to get to the 'bone' (the stick or ball) as quickly as possible. Divide the players into two teams. Each team sits on a bench. Number the players on each team, e.g. Player one, Player two etc. The leader begins the game by calling out a number, say 'Five!' Players five from both teams race to pick up the bone.

The player who picks it up first, chases the other player with the stick and tries to tag him. If he is successful, the tagged player joins his team. The team with the most players at the end of a set time wins.

> **EQUIPMENT:** A short stick or a ball, two benches

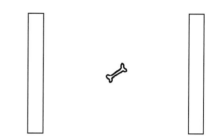

105. Shark's Jaws

The wooden staves are the jaws of the shark, and they open and shut. (They are moved together and apart by the kneeling pair.) The rest of the players have to brave the shark's jaws. They line up at one end of the play area, and approach the jaws. They must step in and out of them without being 'eaten'.

A second set of jaws can be introduced about one small pace away from the first set. Continue adding more and more jaws.

Variations:

- Two pairs sit facing each other with their staffs between them. Again, they open and shut the jaws. The players take it in turns to nimbly step in and out of the jaws, from one corner at a time.

> **EQUIPMENT:** Up to 18 wooden staves

The following verse is said:

> North, South, East, West
> Put your foot in, do your best.
> If the trap closes tight,
> You will scream all through the night!

This is a game requiring daring and courage. Ten year olds love a challenge and danger: *Shark's Jaws* is both! The players need agility more than strength to be successful.

106. Fire and Ice

In a far-away land lived two different peoples: those who had fire, and those who had ice. They wished to meet each other and share their fire and ice with one another, but between them lived a giant who didn't want them to work together. When he saw two travellers moving towards each other, he would step between them, and try to catch them by chasing one or the other. However, if the travellers managed to reach each other and touch, their magic was stronger than the giant, and they were free. The traveller who carried ice then went to the land of fire, and the traveller who carried fire went to the land of ice.

Divide the children into two teams: one represents fire, the other ice. The fire-group stands in a line on one side of the play area. The ice-group stands in a line on the opposite side.

One child is the giant. He stands in the centre and calls out:

> Fire and Ice, come to me!
> Fire and Ice, touch and be free!

Fire and ice try to touch each other without being tagged by the giant. If they are successful, ice joins the fire-group and fire goes to the ice-group.

If the giant manages to tag one of the runners (for instance ice), that runner becomes the new giant, and the other traveller (fire) returns to the group he came from. The old giant now joins the ice-group. If the giant fails to catch anyone after three goes, a new giant is chosen.

> **PLAY AREA:** Outdoor, playing field approximately 25 x 15 paces

Variations:

- Add the lands of earth and wind. Now there are four travellers coming from four directions. They try to meet – but if two are together and the giant chases them, they can split apart again in order to run faster.

This game focuses on the dynamic between the group (the different travellers) and the individual (represented by the giant). Many social situations are reflected while playing *Fire and Ice*: the lone individual working against others; the benefits of cooperation and social interaction. The giant represents the individual who is too selfish, who only wants to exist for himself and doesn't want anyone else to live in his environment. The fire- and ice-groups represent friendship; and it is interesting to watch which children try to help each other, and which are more like the giant – even when they are supposed to be working with a partner! This is also a game that is good for groups in which there is an element of bullying – being the lone giant in the centre of a huge space, while four other people work together to thwart you, is not so easy to bear!

107. MacPherson
By Graham Whiting

MacPherson is a game that requires children to keep listening and be attentive, no matter what else they are doing.

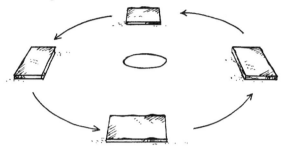

Near a small village once lived a fierce giant called MacPherson. He delighted in catching the village children when they were playing in the streets of their village.

So the villagers erected a wooden tower, and a guardian was hired to warn the children when the giant was approaching. But even though the children ran as quickly as they could into the safety of their homes, the giant always managed to catch the last and slowest child. He would put this child into his pot to cook him for supper. Sometimes the guardian would see if the children were listening out for him, and he would shout 'Mac... aroni' or 'Mac... Donald.' Then the children would laugh at him, but continue playing in the streets.

The children run round the outside of the houses in their village (the mats). The leader is the guardian who looks out for the giant's approach. When he sees him, he shouts out 'MacPherson!' Then all the children try to hide in the safety of a house. However, the last child who tries to run into a house is out. He is put into the 'pot' in the centre of the village.

Sometimes the guardian makes sure that the children are listening for his warning cry, and tests them by shouting out other words or names that sound like MacPherson such as 'Mac... aroni!' or 'Mac... Peersing!' If a child runs into a house then, he must also go into the giant's pot. The children are never allowed to run back – they must go into the house ahead of them.

> **PLAY AREA:** Lay out four mats, or draw four single bed-sized areas on the ground; these are houses; in the centre of the circle created by the mats is the giant's pot (another mat)

When there are fewer children left, the giant gets excited, and knocks down some of the houses. (Then I change one or two of the mats into jumps – by folding them in half. This means there are fewer houses in which to take refuge.) The children in the pot watch out to see which of the runners is last into a house.

Variations:

• While the children are running, they can try to tag whoever is in front of them. But at the same time they must make sure they take refuge in a house as quickly as possible when 'MacPherson!' is called.

• When the guard in the watch tower shouts 'Change!', all the children must change direction. (This is to give Amy, who always gets caught, a chance to catch Ben who is 'hot on her tail'.)

This is a variation of a very common form of running game, where there is a 'safe' area (e.g. in musical chairs). But in this chasing game, where the pursuer is invisible, the children are asked to move as quickly as possible when a certain word is said. In order to both run (chasing and being chased) and listen, the child must concentrate and be 'in' themselves, in a similar way to *Cat and Mouse House.*

108. Seven Stars

I discovered the following game in a rural village in Vietnam. It is a wonderfully simple, and very exciting game.

Divide the players into two teams. Team A builds a tower in the middle of the circle, using the seven tins – any shape or design they choose. Team A's aim is to prevent team B rebuilding the tower. Team B watches and notes exactly what the tower looks like (they will have to rebuild it in exactly the same design.) Team B's aim is to build the tower without being branded. Team B stands behind the line and one by one tries to knock down the tower with the ball.

If the whole team have a turn, but do not succeed in knocking down the tower, the teams swap over, and team A stands behind the throwing line and tries to knock down the tower they built, with the ball.

If more than three tins are knocked down, team B rushes forward and begins to rebuild the tower. Team A, however, tries to prevent them rebuilding the tower by branding them (team B) with the ball. Players on team A are allowed to pass the ball between them, but are not permitted to run with the ball.

When a member of team B is branded, he sits out. Children in team A must not hit the tower while trying to brand team B. If they do so, team B wins. If

> **Play area:** Draw a circle about 4 or 5 paces across; draw a line about 7 paces from the circle
>
> **Equipment:** 7 large tins and one soft playing ball; if necessary, use a tennis ball (see 'Equipment' in the Introduction)

the tower is rebuilt team B wins; but if all the players are out before they can rebuild it, then team A wins.

Then the teams swap over, and the game begins again.

Variations:

- An optional rule: players are only allowed to brand another player below the waist.

At this age, children have to strive to find the balance between their inner experience and what occurs in the world beyond them. For instance, in *Seven Stars*, Benny may be so inwardly absorbed with rebuilding the tower, that he forgets to dodge the ball – and is branded time and time again. The motif of creating and destroying is also emphasised in this game. The players find that it is easy to destroy the tower, but to rebuild it takes courage, perseverance, inner calmness and self-control in the face of adversity.

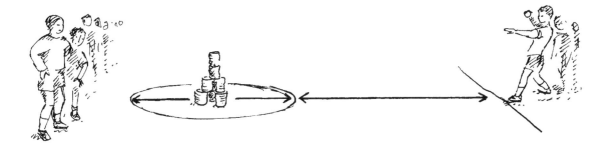

109. Alley Cat

One child is the cat. Another child is a mouse. The other players form the walls or pillars of alleyways by standing in four or more lines of three or more players (see picture, below). Each player must be able to touch fingertips with both people next to him, and, if they turn 90 degrees, also those two in front and behind them. Make sure the 'walls' are straight and aligned.

The mouse begins in the alley. The other players form the alleys by holding their arms outstretched. The cat begins by saying:

> Mouse, mouse come out of your house
> And I will give you some cheese.

Mouse: Not I.

Cat: Mouse, mouse come out of your house
And I will give you some bacon.

Mouse: Not I.

Cat: Mouse, mouse come out of your house
Or I will scratch out your eyes.

Mouse: You dare!.

Then the cat starts chasing the mouse down the alleys, trying to catch him. Neither the cat nor the mouse is allowed to go beneath the players' outstretched arms.

When the leader calls out 'Walls!' the players turn 90 degrees and form walls. Now the cat and mouse run in a new direction.

The leader can also call out 'Pillars!' The children who were walls or alleys now become pillars by dropping their arms to their sides. (This helps the cat to get nearer the mouse!)

To give the cat an even better chance, call out 'Stumps!' – the players now crouch down, and the cat can reach over them to tag the mouse.

It is also nice to have 'Towers' – the children stand with their arms raised vertically.

When the mouse is caught, (or you feel the cat needs a rest!) a new cat and mouse are chosen and the game begins again.

This is a good example of how the concept of one game (e.g. *Cat and Mouse House*) can be developed to meet the changing needs of growing children.

Instead of playing in a circle, the players now form straight rows. This means that they can no longer rely on the group (e.g. as part of a circle), but have to take individual responsibility for their place in the line. It is best if the leader encourages them to readjust their own walls or alleyways, so that they have the feeling that it's 'up to them'. If you allow children to put their hands on their neighbours' shoulders instead of touching with fingertips, this changes the game, and becomes more of a group activity again.

I have found it fascinating to observe that before the age of ten or so, children find it extremely difficult to consciously raise their arms horizontally. It would be more difficult for an eight or nine year old to move this horizontal plane through space (e.g. 90 degrees to the left). *Alley Cat* also introduces the element of geometry in games: this is picked up again in *Running the Gauntlet* (game 184) and *Coupe* (game 213).

110. Shipwrecks

One child is a shark. (Increase the number of sharks as you feel the need.) In the ocean, a ship has been blown up, and there are bits of wreckage floating around. The crew are swimming in the ocean (i.e. running between the pieces of gym equipment or logs etc.) But there is a shark who tries to catch them.

The swimmers are only safe if they are on a piece of wreckage – the shark will catch them if they leave any part of their body in the water (e.g. by the foot). If the shark catches a swimmer, then he becomes the new shark.

Variations:

- Only two swimmers at any time are allowed on each piece of wreckage – otherwise it will sink. When a third swimmer comes along, one of the others must dive into the ocean and make room for him. If there are more than two swimmers on a piece of wreckage, the shark can catch one or all of them.

- With more than one shark, swimmers are held prisoner in the sharks' lair. (I use a plastic hoop for the sharks' lair – the prisoners must, at all times have at least one foot in this hoop, until they are freed.)

- Swimmers are freed by being taken by the hand by a swimmer, who must be careful not to be tagged while doing so, and led back to the safety of one of the pieces of shipwreck. If either is tagged while doing this, both become prisoners.

- Only one prisoner can be freed at a time. The swimmer must return to a piece of wreckage before freeing another prisoner.

> **EQUIPMENT:** Six pieces of gym equipment – these are bits of the shipwreck, floating in the sea; for instance, box, mat, springboard, horse; or use furniture such as bench, table, bed, mattress, etc.; if playing outdoors, use logs, rocks, trees etc.; up to three different colours of vest, sash or headband to identify the 'shark(s)'; a plastic hoop

- It is good if one shark swims around catching swimmers in the ocean, while the other shark guards the prisoners from being freed.

- If you wish to control the rate of freeing, and slow it down, a rule can be introduced: a swimmer must, in life-saver fashion, let the prisoner cling to his back (a 'piggy-back' rescue) as she runs for safety.

Children love to play this game. Some children will not budge from the wreckage (the place of safety); often it will be the melancholic child who hardly ever gets caught because he waits and watches the shark, and then chooses the moment of greatest safety before running to the next wreckage. This may, of course, become slightly boring for him – but the game itself will allow him to be more courageous. If the leader forces such a child to take more risks, this can make him more cautious and timid; the impulse is coming from an external source. It is far better if he learns to modify his own behaviour through inner motivation, through a desire to enter into the game.

111. Hounds, Hares and Hunters [1]

One person has the ball (the gun). She is the hunter. The other children are hares, and run away from the hunter and her 'gun'.

The hunter shoots her gun (throws the ball) at the hares, but because her gun is too heavy, she cannot run with it. She has to 'shoot' from a standing position. If a hare is hit by the gun's bullet, he must sit cross-legged on the ground.

> **Equipment:** One soft ball

Once a hare is sitting down, he can help the hunter by catching and throwing the ball to her. (This means that the hunter is now freer to move closer to the hares she is chasing.) The game ends when the hunter has killed all but two of the hares.

112. Hunter and Hares [2]

One person has the ball (the gun). He is the hunter. The other children are hares, and run away from the hunter and his 'gun'.

The hunter shoots his gun at the hares, but cannot run with it. He can, however, throw the ball up into the air in the direction he wishes to go, and run to where he can catch it. He must do this by throwing the ball above his head, at least ten feet (three metres) in the air and catching it before it hits the ground. If a hare is hit by the gun, she must sit cross-legged on the ground. The game ends when

> **Equipment:** One soft ball

the hunter is too tired, or has injured most of the hares.

The sitting hares are freed if:
– a running hare catches the ball after the hunter throws it into the air, or
– a running hare can pick up the ball from the ground, and try to free the sitting hares by branding the hunter.

113. Hunters, Hares and Hounds [3]

Whoever has the ball (the gun) is the hunter. They start the game by throwing and trying to brand a hare. The hunter is not allowed to run with the gun at any time.

The other children are hares, and run away from the hunter and their 'gun'. If a hare is hit by the gun, he must sit cross-legged on the ground.

Any person may pick up the ball. He then becomes the new hunter. The person attempting to pick up the ball must do so cleanly, without fumbling it and dropping it on the ground.

A sitting hare can free himself by:
– reaching out and tagging a running hare. The running hare who was tagged must now sit down, and the sitting hare is free, or
– trying to brand a running hare, or
– catching the ball as it falls. Then the thrower becomes a sitting hare, and the catcher is free to run again.

> **Equipment:** One soft ball

A running hare can free the sitting hares by either:
– catching the ball on the full, when the hunter throws it into the air, or
– by picking up the ball from the ground, and branding the hunter.

The sitting hares can throw the ball amongst themselves if they wish.

Variations
• The hunter can pass the ball deliberately to a sitting hare, who must pass it back to the hunter. If he brands a hare on the next throw, the one he brands must sit down while the sitting hare who passed the ball back to him goes free.

114. Bandits

The field is set out with a crash-mat or a marked area of about 9 x 4 yards (8 x 3.5m), at either end of the space. These are the 'bandits' prison' and the 'village'. A river is laid or marked out, about two to three paces wide, floor mats across the whole width in the middle of the field of play. Place the three box-tops or mark out three bridges evenly spaced across the river.

Two to three bandits are chosen. They put on the coloured vests. To start with these bandits stand near the village. The rest of the players, the 'villagers', stand in the bandits' prison.

The aim of the game is for the bandits to try and capture all the villagers. The game leader then begins the game by releasing all the villagers from the prison. They will attempt to cross the river using the bridges, and get back to safety in their village. The bandits will try to prevent this by tagged as many of the villagers as they can.

If a villager is tagged, he must place his hands on his head and go straight to prison. He can be released from the prison if one of the free villagers rescues him by running over the bridge and up to

> **PLAY AREA:** 35 x 25 paces for a group of 25 players
> **EQUIPMENT:** 4–5 gym floor-mats, 2 crash-mats, 3 vaulting box-tops or similar (if none of this is available then improvise with other objects, even chalk marks on the floor will do); 2–3 coloured vests

the prison, taking him by the hand and leading him back to the bridge. If either is tagged by a bandit while doing this, then they both become prisoners. Once on a bridge, the escaping and the free villager may let go hands and try to get back to the village separately.

A free villager may only take one prisoner at a time. No-one may jump over the river. The bridge is the only way to cross.

The game ends when either all the villagers have been caught or after a set length of time the game is halted and the number of captured villagers is counted. If more are captured than are free, the bandits win. Or vice-versa.

bandits' prison   *village*

115. Dragon Fire
A version of Waking and Sleeping

Dragon Fire, like its sister *Waking and Sleeping*, is a game that requires self-confidence on the part of the leader – you need to have eyes everywhere when this game is being played; it has great potential for team strategy, but can also quickly spiral into chaos – especially if the leader is at all unfocused or has had a late night!
Divide the children into two teams.
Explain the rules using the following images:

There once lived a dragon in a cave. He was known as the Red Dragon, because of the colour of his scales. In order to keep alive, he had to have enough fire to eat. But he was lazy, so he got his dragon children to keep two fires tended outside his cave at all times. Sometimes the fires were small and weak, and then the dragon sent his children to steal fire from his brother, the Black Dragon, who lived on a neighbouring mountain. However, the brother also needed fire, and he sent his own dragon-children to steal the Red Dragon's fire, by roaring 'Dragon Fire!'

Now because the dragon children also needed fire to give them strength, they were not able to venture far or for long periods from the cave – the longer they stayed away from the cave, the weaker they became.

The basic rule of this game is: whoever runs into the field later than the opponent has 'more fire' and has the right to tag. Only two players are allowed on the field at any one time.

To start, one player from team A runs towards team B's fire when the leader calls 'Dragon Fire!' He either tries to steal a fire (e.g. the ball, or beanbag), or acts as a bait to player B, who has more 'fire' and so can tag him, because player B left his cave later than player A.

Player A can run back to the cave, and tag the next player in line – who now has more fire than player B, so player B must retreat.

If a player is tagged, he goes back to his own cave, and joins the back of the line. If he has a 'fire' in his possession when tagged, he first returns it to where he got it. A player who successfully tags another, carries on tagging.

The game is won when a team has stolen the fires of the other team.

EQUIPMENT: Two floor mats (or two marked areas, 3 x 5 paces): these are the dragons' caves; 4–6 balls (or beanbags): these are the fires

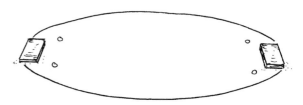

Variations:

- Instead of a player returning to the cave when tagged, tagged players can go out into prison. When all players in a team are imprisoned, the other team has won.

- When a player is successful and tags another player, he returns to the cave and is allowed another turn to go out and try to steal the fire. (But he is only allowed to go out three times in a row.)

Hints to the leader:

- For children who don't want to return to the cave, but who are never tagged, introduce the rule that after a count of 10 or 20 their fire is burnt out.

- To encourage quick changing of players, and to de-emphasise the chase, tell a player with more fire to leave the cave as soon as possible after the player on the opposite team (who has less fire) has left his cave.

- Position yourself at one end of the play area, so that you can see as much as possible of what's going on.

- If the game becomes 'bogged down' and no team is having much success in stealing the fire, place the fires, (the balls) progressively further away from the teams. This means it is easier to steal them.

Dragon Fire is a game of daring and courage. Children at this age love games that require them to go through a trial. Also, at this age, factions begin to show themselves: the children are reassessing friendships and loyalties. This game deals with the individual and the group.

116. Sticks and Stones
Created by Will Crane

Once upon a time, the world was whole, and all the people knew that they were one big family. But one day, a lightning bolt struck the earth, dividing it in two, and the great chasm between groups was created. Forgetting that they were one, the people began to believe that those who are not on their 'side' were strangers, not to be trusted. Each side believed that the other side has stolen their sticks – the powerful tools that gave each group its power. Thus, the groups proceeded to sneak into 'enemy territory' to get their power back!

This game is similar to *Capture the Flag* (game 118), but offers some interesting variations. The goal of the game is to run across the chasm, into the unsafe territory and bring the sticks back to your side. Each side starts with three sticks – they may place them in either of the two hoops that are on their side. The team that manages to get all six sticks on their side wins the round. Runners cannot be tagged while in a hoop. If you are tagged, you do not go to jail, but you 'turn to stone' (crouching down on your haunches with hands over your head in a little ball). You can be freed if someone from your side manages to jump over you without getting tagged. If this happens, you both put your hands on your heads for a free walk back.

opposing teams of six players each

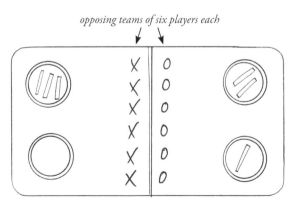

Age range: 10–12

Play area: Indoor or outdoor, rectangular field 20 x 40 paces

Number of players: 10+

Equipment: 4 hula hoops, 6 sticks, and ropes or cones to mark out the boundaries

Variations:

- Rather than crouching down and curling up into a ball when turned to stone, stones may go down on a knee instead. Rescuers can free them by clasping their hands and bringing them back to safety.

- Can add flag belts for a more challenging 'tag' option.

- Time limit option (i.e. the team with the most sticks after five minutes wins the round)

- A rule may be added that no team can win if they have any players as stones. This encourages rescues.

Hints to the leader:

- Some children rush into action without making a plan and spend much of their time as a stone (which can get boring!). Encourage those players to work with their teammates to make a plan. Also encourage players to notice their fellow stones and not forget about them when they are focused on stealing the sticks.

117. Giants, Knights and Farmers
Inspired by Rudolf Kischnick

Although the next game is ideal for 11 year olds, it can also be played with children of mixed ages, 7–16. I have played this game very successfully at a Michaelmas festival, with about 150 children, with the teachers acting as 'referees'. It was great fun. Remember to introduce a game like this in story form; at the Michaelmas festival, I emphasised the aspect of courage, of the community working together against the enemy, and of the harvest.

In a far-away land, it is harvest time. The farmers have worked hard all year to produce the golden grain, which they have just harvested. Not far away is a castle where a host of knights live. Although they are brave and courageous, they are no good at growing food. So they have reached an agreement with the farmers (children at this age love deals!): if the farmers give them grain, then the knights will protect their fields from the giants who roam the land.

So the farmers start dragging a big sack of grain from their village towards the knights' castle. But between the village and the castle is Giant Land. The giants are afraid of the knights on their flashy horses, and they know that the knights will starve if they don't get the grain from the farmers – then the giants would rule the land. So the giants try to stop the farmers taking grain to the knights, by catching them and clubbing them. To do this, a giant must 'club' a farmer twice in quick succession. When a farmer has been clubbed, he goes to

Age range: 10–11

Play area: Indoor or outdoor; a gym or grassy area is best as there is sometimes some falling over; at least 30 x 25 paces for a group of 25 children

Equipment: For the farmers, a sack filled with something heavy (pebbles or sand) not easy for the children to lift, but possible to drag; for the giants, 'clubs' made from loosely knotted veils or scarves; hats, one for each giant

the edge of Giant Land. The knights try to protect the farmers from the giants. They can capture a giant by pursuing him and pulling off his hat, which robs him of all power. The giant may now be taken back to the castle and held prisoner.

Divide the children into giants, farmers, knights and knights' horses. With a group of 25 players, five can be giants, eight farmers, six knights and six horses. The knights should be smaller children, the horses the larger ones. (If playing with mixed ages, the giants can be 13 or 14 year olds, the farmers 11–12 year olds, and the knights the 9–10 year olds.) The giants can wear knitted caps (made in the hand-work lesson), where all their power is stored. If the knights' horses get weary, they have to return to their castle to rest — that's where they are safe. The end of the game comes when everyone has collapsed in laughter, or better still,

when the grain has reached the castle! Alternatively, the game can end when half the farmers, or half the giants, have been killed or captured. This latter rule is especially useful when playing with large numbers.

At this age, the children are awakening to a new social awareness of the rights and strengths of the individual and of the group. They become aware that antisocial forces try to prevent justice happening (the giants); and that to be social (take grain to feed the knights) requires courage to face the risk of paying too high a price (being clubbed). For example, some children-farmers stick closely to a knight – they do not take any more risks than they have to, but at the same time limit their effectiveness; they are therefore putting personal safety above the social task – and this can go as far as an obsession with not being caught (but these tactics will never win the game).

On the other hand, some children-farmers sacrifice themselves too easily for the social task – they will try to distract the giants' attention away from the corn – but then the sack doesn't get moved at all! A similar pattern can be seen with the knights: some are brave and go out to get the giants – but forget to protect the corn (and the poor farmers). Sometimes a group of knights will surround the corn – which makes it impossible for the giants, and holds up the game. (In this case you can introduce a rule that only one knight can protect the grain.)

118. Capture the Flag – with Spies!

This is the same as normal *Capture the Flag*, except each team has a spy for the other team. Teams are selected by having players draw playing cards. There should be an even number of red/black cards, and the game leader pre-determines which card will be the 'Spy' card (seven works well, as in 007!) The game leader pre-arranges the deck for the number of players. For example, if you have 20 players, make sure there are 10 black cards and 10 red cards. Red number seven starts with the red team, but is really a spy for the black team.

During the game play, the spy has **one** chance to grab the flag and run it over to the other side. If they

AGE RANGE: 10–12

PLAY AREA: Rectangular area 20 x 40 paces

NUMBER OF PLAYERS: 10+

EQUIPMENT: Playing cards, one card per player

are caught, they are no longer a spy and must return to their proper side once freed from jail.

Hints to the leader:

• Observe how the teams interact when they **offer** to be a flag guard… usually the boring job.

119. Besieged
Contributed by Torsti Rovainen

Two kingdoms are vying for ultimate rule of the land. When the castle walls are knocked down, the kingdom is besieged.

Two teams are each trying to knock over the opponents' castle walls (three cones or pins placed upright at the back of each team's side.) Each team begins with at least three playground balls placed on the back boundary line. Players are trying to knock over their opponents' cones by rolling or throwing the balls at the cones. However, no player can ever be touched by a ball that is moving, regardless of who last touched the ball. If they are, they must exit the play area and count to 50 then join back in. The second time they are touched by a moving ball, they exit and count to 100. Third time, 200. Fourth time, they're out.

Players can defend the cones by standing in front of them, but if they are hit by a ball, they go out. Players can deflect balls headed toward their cones by throwing a ball at a ball that is headed for a cone, but they cannot pick up a moving ball that is in the play area. Players may not deflect a ball with a ball that they're holding in their hands; if this happens they are considered to have been hit by a moving ball, and are out. When balls roll out of bounds, only the players that are 'out' at the time are allowed to gather them and put them back into play. When they do this, they can gather balls from any out-of-bounds area, including the out-of-bounds area on their opponent's side.

> **AGE RANGE:** 10–12
>
> **PLAY AREA:** Flat, rectangular field about 20 x 40 paces
>
> **NUMBER OF PLAYERS:** 12+
>
> **EQUIPMENT:** : 6 cones, markers for boundaries on all sides, 10+ playground balls (or whatever other balls you have – the more the merrier!)

Variations:

- For more challenge, add the rule that players that are 'out', rather than standing on the side and counting, can stand on the opposite side of the field, behind their opponent's territory, and then try to knock over the cones from behind. This variation requires an extra line marker over which throwers may not step so that they don't get too close to the players/cones as they try to peg them from behind.

Hints to the leader:

- This game works best on a flat playing field or large indoor space. Make sure the balls are pumped up sufficiently enough to roll properly.

- When players attempt to put balls back into play that have rolled out of bounds, they must take care to do it in a way that does not get their own teammate out (watch out for 'friendly fire').

For children who may struggle to play this game:

- This game is a good lead-up game to dodge ball, since the balls are rolled on the ground rather than thrown in the air. For those that may struggle with this game, a special role can be created: 'ammunition collector', allowing a player to stay in motion but not need to stand in a place where they may be hit by the ball.

120. Walk the Plank or Join the Crew
Created by Will Crane

Pirates have snuck aboard the captain's ship with the hope of capturing the captain and their crew and forcing them all to sail out to a far distant land where it is said a giant treasure chest is buried! But the captain and their crew will not go down without a fight. The pirates would like the captain and their crew to join their ranks. If they refuse, the pirates will force them to walk the plank – and thus find themselves in a watery grave. The pirate calls to the crew, one by one, and gives them a choice: 'Walk the plank, or join the crew?'

The object of the game is for the crew to get to the other side of the shore without being captured by the pirate. One player starts as the pirate. They stand in the centre of the play area. The rest of the players are captured crew members, lined up at one end of the play area. The pirate addresses the crew one by one: '_____, walk the plank or join the crew?'

If the player answers, 'Join the crew', they then walk to one side of the field and may now help the pirate. If the player answers, 'Walk the plank', they then try to run across the field without being tagged by the pirate or any of the pirate-helper crew. If a player is able to make it across the field without being tagged by the pirate, then all crew members are set free – and the captain/crew have won the day.

Variations:
- Can add flag belts (tag becomes a flag-belt pull)
- Players may take on different roles: the pirate captain ('Arrrgh!'), who sometimes has a peg leg (has to hop on one foot) or sharks can be swimming in the water (one hand on top of your head). When tagged by a shark, you become one also.
- For more challenge and more of a rough and tumble element, there may be a few ruthless pirates that try not to let anybody escape (bear hug rather than a simple tag.)
- Add other elements to create movement options (crabs, seals, etc.) as ways to get back on the ship and keep more players in movement.

> **AGE RANGE:** 10–12
> **PLAY AREA:** Indoor or outdoor, 20 x 40 paces
> **NUMBER OF PLAYERS:** 10+
> **EQUIPMENT:** Cones/ropes to mark boundaries

Hints to the leader:
- If using flag belts, make a rule that pirates may not touch their own flag belt, and they may not stiff-arm any crew member who is trying to pull it. They may spin around but they may not touch their flag belt, and they may not touch any player who is trying to pull it.
- Flag belts sometimes come off or come undone when there is no one trying to pull it. To make the hands-off-your-flag-belt rule very clear, if a player's flag belt falls off, they must go out of the boundaries to put it back on. When their flag belt is back on and secured, they may come back in bounds.

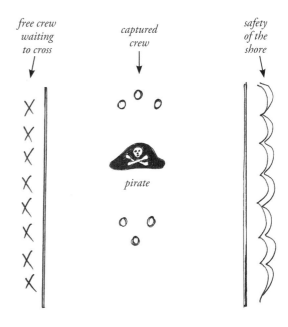

free crew waiting to cross

captured crew

safety of the shore

pirate

121. Doh, Doh, Doh!
Created by Will Crane

*Once upon a time, there were two lands separated by a wall of poisonous mist. On both sides of the poisonous mist, the people in the two lands lived happily, each not knowing the other was there. One day, someone got the idea to try to pass through the wall of poisonous mist and explore the other land and bring back some prisoners if they could. A daring explorer thought of an ingenious way to pass through without accidentally breathing the air on the other side. If a deep breath was taken and then he breathed only **out** – saying, 'Doh Doh Doh...' the whole time, and timed it just right to make it back to his land before he had to take another breath, it just might work...*

The game leader divides the class into two groups, each on different sides of a centre line, dividing the playing area in half. The game leader chooses one player at a time, alternating back and forth between teams, to be the explorer and to cross through the mist onto the other side. The explorer takes a big breath, crosses the line and runs trying to tag as many players as possible, all the while only breathing out saying, 'Doh Doh Doh...' as loudly as possible. If the explorer takes a breath before returning to their original side, they breathe the poisonous mist and are then forced to join that side. If they successfully return home, they may breathe normally and every player they were able to tag has to join the successful explorer's side.

Age range: 10–12

Play area: Indoor or outdoor, rectangular area 20 x 40 paces

Number of players: 8+

Equipment: Cones to mark clear boundaries, flag belts (one for each player), one long rope to mark divide the area in half

Variations:

- Can add flag-belt-pulls as alternatives to tagging.
- The game leader may call more than one explorer at a time from a side.
- The game leader may call an explorer from both sides at the same time.
- For more challenge: an additional rule may be added. An explorer may be waylaid by any child they tag in an effort to keep the explorer on that side until all their air is used up. Thus, the potential prisoners have a way to turn the tides.

Hints to the leader:

- Membership on each side will shift as the game goes on. The game leader should take advantage of the element of surprise, calling the players quickly and making quick switches.
- When playing with the waylaying variation, remind players that clothing may not be pulled, only hands, hugs, and/or firm grips on limbs and torso are allowed. This rough-housing rule can be very fun, but can also get out of hand, so the game leader must watch that no one gets hurt or embarrassed.

122. Life-Line
Created by Will Crane

This game has two teams, two goal lines, and a central object to steal. Each side has a goal line (the line they must get to with the given object) and a lifeline (the line they must touch before going for the object.) The game leader gives each player a number that corresponds with a player on the opposite team, meaning each player has an opponent with their same number.

To begin the game, each team is lined up on the sideline boundaries closest to their goal line and furthest away from their lifeline. The game leader places the object in the centre of the field and then calls one of the numbers. If their number is called, the person on each side runs first to their lifeline to touch it with their fingertips, then they run to the central object (beanbag, football, tennis ball, playground ball, etc.) The goal is to grab the object and run it across the goal line without being tagged by a player from the opposite team. A player can only be tagged if they are holding the object. If a player is tagged, the play is dead – the object is placed back in the centre of the field and the players go back to their sides. If a player is able to run the object across their goal line, they get one point for their team.

AGE RANGE: 10–12

PLAY AREA: Indoor or outdoor, rectangular area 20 x 40 paces

NUMBER OF PLAYERS: 8+

EQUIPMENT: Cones to mark corners, ropes to mark back lines, one ball/beanbag

Variations:

- The game leader can use maths problems, whereby the answer to the problem is the number that runs.
- Flag belts may be added rather than a tag.
- The game leader may call more than one number at a time, allowing for players to pass the object between them.

Hints to the leader:

- Watch out for head collisions when players are coming from opposite directions to pick up the object.
- Be sure to keep track of which numbers you have called so that there is a fair rotation of the action.

For children who may struggle to play this game:

- Matching the players up adequately with their opponents is the best way to minimise the struggle that some children might experience in this game. Don't start too young. Fourth graders love this.

123. Revolving Door

A line of players forms at the shooting line under a basketball hoop. The first two players in the line each hold a basketball. At the start of the play, the first player attempts to make a basket. If they do, they bounce pass to the next person in the line that does not have a ball. If they do not, they keep trying to do so while the second person in the line tries to beat them by making a basket first. If the second person in line makes a basket before the person in front of them, they are sent out the Revolving Door (this can be a stationary place on the sidelines or some kind of fun obstacle course to keep them moving). The

AGE RANGE: 10–12

PLAY AREA: Indoor or outdoor, flat surface around a basketball hoop, 20 x 20 paces

NUMBER OF PLAYERS: 2+

EQUIPMENT: Two basketballs

Revolving Door can only hold two people. If a third gets sent to the Revolving door, the first gets sent back into the line. In this game, being sent out is only temporary, ensuring that the less-skilled players get a chance to practise.

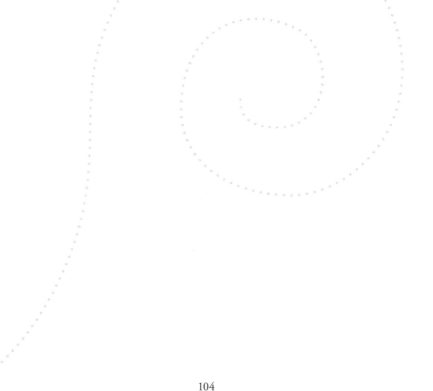

124. Baseball-Basketball
Created by Will Crane

Two teams. One team plays outfield, other team is up to 'bat.' The first player to 'bat' throws the basketball into the playing area and runs as far as they can before the fielding team makes a basket. If the player makes it home before fielding team makes a basket, they score a point.

After everyone has a turn, teams switch sides.

Variations:

Easier:

- Give a point for every base touched before a basket is scored.
- Make sure you have several rebounders who can put the ball back up quickly.

More challenging:

- First innings – lay-ups
- Second innings – foul shots
- Third innings – three-pointers.

AGE RANGE: 10–12

PLAY AREA: Indoor or outdoor; field set-up requires one basketball hoop, and a small baseball diamond beneath it

NUMBER OF PLAYERS: 8+

EQUIPMENT: One basketball, 4 bases

Hints to the leader:

- It's helpful to practise shooting hoops before the game begins. Depending on the skill level of the group, the game leader may add a rule that no fielding player may shoot a second hoop until all players on the fielding team have shot once. This may slow down the game, but it ensures that the action is spread evenly rather than only one or two players making all the hoops for their team.

- Once a fielding team member scores a basket they may only assist (rebound, or pass to another player until everyone on the team has scored.) This keeps the game from being dominated by skilful individuals.

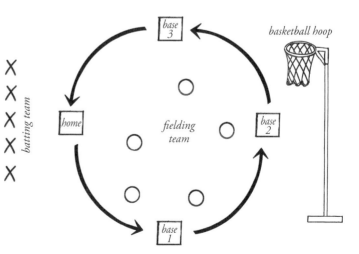

125. Wizard/Elf/Giant
Developed by Torsti Rovainen

In a far-off land, there lived three creatures with special powers: great big Giants that could overpower the Elves, clever Elves that could confound the Wizards, and magical Wizards that could cast spells on the Giants.

Have the full group practise postures for each creature: for example, Giants (arms up, grimacing giant-faces), Elves (hunker down and look sneaky), or Wizards (casting spells with arms). Once the full group has practised these moves, divide the group into two teams. Each team goes to their 'home base' about 40 paces apart. Each team then huddles to decide whether they will be Wizards, Elves, or Giants. Groups should determine both a first and a second choice, in case there's a tie.

Game then begins as both groups simultaneously advance to the middle of the field, halfway between each team's home base; once they're there, both teams say '**Giants, Elves, Wizards,** (pose)' and after '**Wizards,**' either just show, or both say and show the motion their group came up with (to the rhythm of 'Rock, Paper, Scissors, Shoot!') Winning group then tries to tag the other group as that group flees to their base. For example, if one team is 'Giants' and the other 'Elves', the Giants chase the Elves towards the Elves' base. Once the runners have crossed their home base line, chasers cannot follow them.

Anyone tagged goes to the other side and is joyfully welcomed to that team.

If there's a tie, say 'Giants Elves Wizards (pose)' again and do the team's second choice. If there's a second tie, both teams re-huddle, and enjoy the speculation both groups share as to how to outwit the other team.

AGE RANGE: Multi-age (even adults)

PLAY AREA: Outdoor, 20 x 40 paces, open field

NUMBER OF PLAYERS: 6+

EQUIPMENT: Corner cones or ropes to mark 'home base' for each team

Variations:

- Players can make up three groups of their own choosing, each with its own pose (i.e. Salmon, Bear, Mosquito: Salmon eats the Mosquitos, Bears eat the Salmon, Mosquitos bite the Bears).

Hints to the leader:

- Game leader can be big and dramatic when showing these to increase both the fun as well as the commitment to the moves. If the group shows them and they're half-hearted, say 'I wouldn't be scared by that Giant! 'Let's see a real Giant!'

- For younger students or people just learning the game, stick with just one choice. In the case of a tie, groups switch sides and start over.

- Game leader can help facilitate/bring consensus to the group.

126. Bears and Lions Ball
Created by Jeff Tunkey

Got some old tennis balls around that have lost their bounce? Brooms that have seen better days? How about some old refrigerator boxes? Don't put them in the trash – turn them into treasure!

The object of the game is to be the team that gets the most balls into its tall box. Game leader begins by giving equal amounts of tennis balls to each team. Two teams stand on opposite sides of a gym-size playing field behind each team's throwing line. Each side is given their box (placed in the middle of the playing area), 20–30 tennis balls and a 'Retriever'. The Retriever's job is to shuffle the balls back to their side using a broom or a hockey stick. Throwers may

AGE RANGE: 10–12

PLAY AREA: Indoors or outdoors, 40 x 20 paces (distance adjusted for age)

NUMBER OF PLAYERS: 8–30 (or more)

EQUIPMENT: Two large boxes (such as refrigerator boxes or tall garbage cans), 40–60 tennis balls, two brooms or hockey sticks, playing field with marked throwing lines

not come out from behind the throwing line because one player on a rotating basis from each team will be given the job of Retriever.

Variations:

• Throwers have to bounce the balls into the boxes.

• Instead of throwing all at once, the throwers throw in the order of the line. If it's a miss, the Retriever can pass it back to the last person in line and in a chain-like fashion, each person passes the ball to the next person at the front of the line. If it's an overthrow, the opposite side's Retriever shuffles it to the first person in the opposing team's line and the game continues back and forth.

• Increase the distance between the boxes and the throwing line for more advanced players.

Hints to the leader:

• Caution players that sticks or brooms may not be drawn back or swung above waist level.

• It enhances the fun of the game if every so often the game leader calls a stop, peers into the two teams' boxes, gives a knowing look, but does not announce the score-in-progress. This game can seem like complete chaos as it ensues, and neither team can really know which team is ahead.
This makes the reveal at the end a dramatic and satisfying event.

127. Castle Ball
Created by Jeff Tunkey

Two sides have a home mat at the back end of the other side's playing area. The sides are clearly marked by a centre line down the middle. Begin with one receiver on each mat. Anyone who successfully throws across to their receiver(s) get to join the receiver on their mat. First team to have all players on their mat wins. Each team tries to intercept the throw before the receiver can catch it. If intercepted, that person tries to throw the ball to their receiver. Players may **not** touch the back mat or blanket. If they do, the penalty is that the result of the play is a catch, whether caught or not, and so the thrower (from the other team) gets to join their team on the mat.

> **Age range:** 10–12
> **Play area:** Indoor or outdoor, 40 x 20 paces
> **Number of players:** 10+
> **Equipment:** 2 mats or blankets, 1 volleyball

Variations:

- Type of ball can vary depending on age/skill level. Can start with a Gator-foam ball, move to a firmer handball, then to a tennis ball for more challenge.
- A volleyball can be added, players serve the ball underhand to the other side.

128. Twin Tag/Three-Deep

Welcome to the Land of Twins: two's company, three's a crowd!

Players spread out around the area and stand next to another player (their twin partner) side by side with their elbows linked. One player is chosen to be the first 'Chaser' and another player is chosen to be the first 'Chasee'. At the start signal, the chaser runs after the chasee and tries to tag them. At any time, the chasee may be safe by linking elbows to a twin, making the opposite side's twin the new person to be chased.

> **Age range:** 10–12
> **Play area:** Indoor or outdoor, 20 x 20 paces, size adjusted to number of players
> **Number of players:** 10+
> **Equipment:** None

Variations:

- Three Deep: Same concept but partners stand one in front of the other. Two players begin as 'Chaser' and 'Chased.' At any time, the chasee can stand behind a set of partners. The person in front of the Three-Deep becomes the new 'Chaser'.

129. Rescue Tag

Red-tailed hawks are circling above the playful meadow creatures below. How many creatures will they stun? Can the meadow creatures work together to save themselves from the hawks?

The game leader chooses two or three players to be the red-tailed hawks. They wear pinnies or coloured bands. The rest of the players are the meadow creatures (can be any animal they want.) If tagged by a red-tailed hawk, the player lies down on their backs with all four limbs in the air. Other players can rescue them in the following ways:

Variations:

- One player tapping all four limbs (hand, hand, foot, foot).
- Four players each holding on to a limb.
- Four players lifting the 'dead animal' and carrying them to safety – a blanket or mat on each side of the field.

Hints to the leader:

- The game leader should have the players practise the rescue before the game begins, especially if playing with the carrying variation of the rescue. Encourage players to use both hands on each limb, and to take hold at the wrist (both the rescuers

> **Age range:** 10–12
>
> **Play area:** Indoor or outdoor, 20 x 20 paces, size adjusted to number of players
>
> **Number of players:** 7+
>
> **Equipment:** Pinnies or coloured bands/sashes for red-tailed hawks, at least two mats or blankets on each size of the play area, cones or markers for boundaries

and the one being rescued), not just the hands. The player being rescued should pull themself up a bit while being carried so that they are not dead weight.

- The most dangerous point of the rescue is when the player being rescued gets lowered onto the blanket or mat. Encourage players to work together to lower the player gently – no drops!

130. Heads or Tails?

Flip a coin... or two... or twenty!

The game leader asks each player to (secretly) choose either Heads or Tails. This will be the team that they will be on when the game begins. At the signal, each player shows their choice by either placing their hand on their head, or their hand on their waist. All Heads are chasing the Tails, if they tag them they 'flip' them to Heads. All Tails are chasing Heads, trying to tag them to 'flip' them to Tails. The round is over when all players are on the same team.

Variations:

- Same as above, but with 'Thumbs Up/Thumbs Down'.
- Players may wish to create their own 'duo duel' – using two opposing gestures. Encourage the poses to be distinct and well-balanced so that neither team has an advantage due to one of the poses being an easier one to maintain.

> **AGE RANGE:** 10–12
>
> **PLAY AREA:** Indoor or outdoor, large room or space at least 30 x 30 paces
>
> **NUMBER OF PLAYERS:** 10+ (fun with large groups of people)
>
> **EQUIPMENT:** None

Hints to the leader:

- This is a fast-paced, somewhat chaotic game. Many players will have simultaneous tags. In this case, players can do Rock-Paper-Scissors to determine the outcome. The loser is then the one that 'flips'.
- This is a fun game for multi-age – adults too!

131. Hot Dog Tag

Teenagers love to hate this one – as it requires core strength and getting up and down swiftly!

The game leader chooses a 'Chaser'. The Chaser tries to tag anyone in the group. If tagged, player lays down on their back. They can be freed if two other players lie next to them, and all together they lift their arms and legs off the floor (pike position) and say 'Bun, Bun, Bun' – Then all three get up and join in the game again.

Variations:

- The game leader can call out multiple switches of the 'Chaser' at any time in the game. Quick switches can be fun once the group gets the hang of the game.

Age range: 12+

Play area: Indoor or outdoor, regular room or contained area (20 x 20 paces – not too big)

Number of players: 10+

Equipment: None

Hints to the leader:

- The game leader may decide how strict to be on what does or does not constitute a 'rescue'. Some players will try to get away with just lying there flat without raising their head and feet (lazy dogs!)
- Watch out for players running near people's heads as they are lying down awaiting rescue. (No squashed dogs!)

132. Wish Ball

Lead-up game to *Space Ball*. The rules are the same as for *Space Ball* except:

When a team has a ball, they must throw it to a teammate who is standing in a hoop, thus giving a physical and visual image of personal space. Having fewer than half the number of hoops encourages players to move to a hoop rather than staying put in a hoop.

Age range: 10–12

Play area: Indoor or outdoor, 20 x 40 paces (size adjusts to number of players)

Number of players: 8+

Equipment: Hula hoops (enough for almost half the players) and a soft volleyball or rubber ball

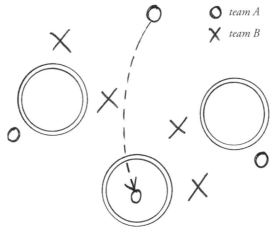

O *team A*
X *team B*

133. Tic-Tac-Toe Relay aka Hash-Tag

You think you're too old for Tic-Tac-Toe? Think again!

The game leader places nine hula hoops or four long ropes to create a tic-tac-toe board, placed on the ground a good running distance from the starting line where the players line up. Each team is given three beanbags of the same colour. Each team is racing to see which team can get three of their bean-bags in a row first. Action plays out in the form of a relay. On the signal, the first player from each team runs to the 'board' and places their bean-bag in one of the nine 'squares' and then runs back to tag the next person on their team. This continues in relay fashion until one team gets their three beanbags in one row.

As happens in the on-paper version of Tic-Tac-Toe, all three beanbags from each team may be placed on the board without either team winning (a tie) – when/if this happens, the game does not stop. Players (who are now out of beanbags) continue with the relay, but they are not adding any more beanbags to the game. The players are then allowed to move one of their beanbags to another spot, and then continue to run back and tag the next player. This continues until a true three-in-a row victory.

AGE RANGE: 10+

PLAY AREA: Indoor or outdoor, large room or open area 20 x 20 paces

NUMBER OF PLAYERS: 6+

EQUIPMENT: 9 hula hoops to create one tic-tac-toe board; long ropes may also be used to make the 'hash-tag'; 6 bean-bags (3 of the same colour for each team)

Variations:

- Non-running players can be the judges – standing over the tic-tac-toe board and watching for stray beanbag placements, etc.

- Alternative moves to running are also fun: skipping, galloping, walking backward, etc.

Hints to the leader:

- Watch out for players running into the hoops/ropes in the excitement of the game. Players should be encouraged to place their beanbags in the spaces rather than throwing them.

- Make a plan for the beanbags to be reset after each round so that players don't waste too much time. This game is most fun when the rounds are quick in succession. The game leader may add a visual signal to start the relay – this ensures that players will be watching/focused and ready and the game leader does not have to shout.

or...

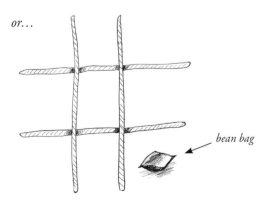

bean bag

134. Curtain Ball
Created by Jeff Tunkey

When it rains, it pours! All Hail is breaking loose! Looks like it's curtains for us all!

Two teams of even numbers stand on each side of a volleyball net. Each player begins holding one soft-skinned ball. At the start of the game, players must throw the ball up and over the net, trying to catch a ball that is thrown from the other side. If a player is able to catch a ball 'on the fly' (before it hits the ground), that player then has only ten seconds in which they are allowed to run out of bounds to the other side, and try to peg a player on the other side with the ball that they caught. If at any time, any player is pegged by a ball or if they are touched by a ball from above but not able to catch it, that player must switch teams and play from the other side. Balls that roll out of bounds can only be retrieved by players on that side.

Variations:

- Depending on the space, the game leader may add a 'three-step rule' for side pegs, meaning if a player catches a ball on the fly, that player may only take three steps from where they caught the ball, to then try to peg a player on the other side. The number of steps may vary depending on the size of the playing area.

- Additional roles may be added:

    - *Rain Catcher*: Each team may designate one of their players to be the 'Rain Catcher'. This player is then the only one who is allowed to collect balls that have rolled out of bounds. Rain catchers may then run those balls back and roll them to the players on their side.

    - *Referee*: Each team may designate one of their players to stand out of bounds on the opponents' side. The referee calls the 'switches' when players are hit by a ball. Only recommended for more mature players/groups.

> **AGE RANGE:** 10+
> **PLAY AREA:** Indoor or outdoor, room with high ceilings or area size of volleyball court
> **NUMBER OF PLAYERS:** 10+
> **EQUIPMENT:** Volleyball net; large curtain/sheet draped over the net; 10+ soft-skinned balls

- *Fun Run*: Once per round, a player that catches a ball on the fly may take one 'Fun Run' which allows them to run all the way around the outside boundary of the opposing side, and try to peg players on the opposite side. On a Fun Run, however, a player may not stop their running motion. They must make their shot on the run. If they stop their motion, they must join the other side.

For children who may struggle to play this game:

- This game can be overwhelming for some players. When learning the game, begin by using only four balls. Add more balls as the players become more comfortable with the game.

The next three games can be played as a preparation for volleyball.

135. First Aid or Apothecary
As related by Rob Sim

On a battlefield some of the warriors have been injured by a mighty Captain who is their enemy. They are unable to walk. The warriors' friends see this and go to their rescue. They do this by carrying the wounded back to a tent where they are healed and may again go out to challenge the mighty Captain. However, the mighty Captain will try to stop the warrior reaching the tent by chasing away any helpers. If he catches any of them, they too will be wounded and fall to the ground, where they will have to await rescue.

Choose one or two mighty Captains who wear the vests. Spread the mats, blankets or chalk marks around the playing area. These are the healing tents. The game begins with all the warriors asleep lying on the ground. A bell rings or a drum beats to wake up the warriors to tell them that the mighty Captain has come into their land. They are powerless to fight him and must wake up and run away, trying to avoid being tipped by him.

If they are tagged they fall to the ground. Other warriors who are not yet wounded may try to rescue the wounded by carrying them to the mat. If, in doing so, any of the carriers are caught by the Captain, then

> **AGE RANGE:** 10–12
> **PLAY AREA:** Indoor or outdoor, 25 x 20 paces for 25 players
> **NUMBER OF PLAYERS:** 10+
> **EQUIPMENT:** 5–6 floor mats or blankets, 1–2 coloured vests, drum or bell

they too must fall down. If they succeed in reaching the mat then the wounded warrior may re-enter the battle.

The game ends when:

– the mighty Captain has caught and wounded all the warriors and no-one is left to make any rescues

– or a prearranged number of warriors (perhaps 12) have been caught and healed.

A warrior can only be healed once. If she is wounded again she must leave the playing area and wait until the next game. In this way the game is played until only one warrior is left. She is made the next mighty Captain or may be given an extra life the next time this game is played.

The following games are aimed more at players of **11 years and older**.

136. Newcombe

Divide the players into two teams, one team on either side of the net. The ball is thrown over the net by team A. Team B try to catch the ball on the full, and throw it back. The ball is allowed to touch the net as long as it lands in the opposing court. If the ball is thrown out of the court or into the net, or dropped, a point is awarded to the opposing team, and they get to 'serve' (throw) the ball over to restart the game. A team may win a point regardless of whether they

> **AGE RANGE:** 11+
> **PLAY AREA:** Indoor, a volleyball court and low-set net – or a badminton court and net
> **EQUIPMENT:** A slightly deflated volleyball

served or not (unlike real volleyball). The first team to reach 10 points wins.

137. Blanket Ball

Each player takes hold of the edge of the blanket and stretches it tight. The volleyball is placed in the middle. The players toss the ball into the air by slackening and tightening the tension of the blanket, and moving their arms upward. The players try to get the ball into the air as many times as possible without it touching the ground.

> **AGE RANGE:** 11+
> **PLAY AREA:** Indoor or outdoor
> **NUMBER OF PLAYERS:** 10–15
> **EQUIPMENT:** A volleyball; a double woollen blanket

Variations:

- There are two blankets and two teams. Give the teams three minutes to see how many throws and catches to themselves they can do.

- The teams try to throw and catch the ball between the two blankets as many times as possible.

- The two teams stand either side of the volleyball net and see if they can throw the ball, using the blanket, over to the other side, where the other team will try to catch it.

Rounders

Games 138–143 on the following three pages are all variants of the game rounders. The most successful way to introduce rounders to ten to eleven year olds is to call on the children's imagination, using a theme and images. In preparatory games for rounders, I use the image of trains and stations; I have found that when I don't use a pictorial introduction, the children often become agitated, argumentative and sullen.

Working with images, however, offers a way for all ability groups to enter fully into the spirit of rounders – which demands courage, timing and quick thinking.

138. Clocks

Divide the group into two teams. Team A form a clock by standing in a large circle. Team B line up next to the clock. They take it in turns to run around the outside of the clock as quickly as possible. When they have circled the clock once they tip the next runner.

Team A have the ball. They throw the ball from one player to the next in the circle as quickly as possible. The leader counts how many 'ticks' (catches) the clock makes, until the last runner reaches the end of their run. Then the teams swap over. The team with the least 'ticks' against them wins.

AGE RANGE: 11+

EQUIPMENT: 1 ball, as for rounders

139. Trains and Stations

The bases are four stations. These are guarded by four 'stationmasters'. 'Railway workers' (the fielders) will try to help the stationmasters. The 'trains' (batters, or in this case, throwers) run between the stations, starting in the 'goods yard'. 'The grand stationmaster' (leader) guides the trains, but helps the stationmaster and railway workers.

To start, divide the children into two teams – give each team a set of coloured bibs. The trains go to the goods yard, and stand in a line. The railway workers spread themselves out over the diamond. The stationmasters each go to their station (base). The ball is given to the first train. He throws it somewhere in the area between the first and the third station (see illustration).

Then he runs to the first station, or if there's time, to the second, third or even home (fourth) station. However, once the train stops at a station, it cannot start again until the ball is thrown by the next train.

If the ball is caught on the full by a railway worker or stationmaster, the train who threw it is 'derailed' (out). When a train is derailed, he must return to the goods yard, and join the back of the line.

The railway workers and the stationmasters are not allowed to run with the ball (initially you might wish to allow the railway workers to run rather than pass the ball. Running with the ball gives the railway workers an advantage, particularly if they are not old

AGE RANGE: 11+

PLAY AREA: 4 bases placed (or marked) in a diamond shape: 12–20 paces apart

EQUIPMENT: A slightly deflated mini play-ball is ideal (this is about the size of a large grapefruit); 1 hula hoop; 4 bases or bags, plus 4 x 8-foot (2.5 metre) high poles, with a rag tied on the end (like a thin flagpole) – the pole is then firmly knocked into the ground to make a highly-visible base; coloured bibs or sashes for team identification

enough to throw the ball properly.)

The railway workers must field the ball as quickly as possible and either:

– throw it to the stationmaster, who touches the ball on the base before the train arrives at the station. For example, Emilio is the first train. He throws the ball, and runs towards the first station. Sasha picks up the ball and throws it to the stationmaster, who touches the first base with the ball.

– throw the ball to the grand stationmaster who will be standing in the Central Station (the hula hoop), checking to see if any trains are still travelling towards any of the stations. If any train is not in a station it is derailed. (Or you can play that only the most advanced train, e.g. running to third base, say, is derailed.)

If the railway workers manage to do either of these, then the train is out and returns to the goods yard. A train does not have reverse gear – it may not go back to a station having left it. When a train reaches the goods yard without being out, the train's team gets one point.

The last train has to try to run past all the stations and into the goods yard without being out: the last train is 'express'. (Or, once the last train has run as far as it can without being derailed, the grand stationmaster can have a turn to throw the ball, in order to give the last trains a chance to run to the final station. The grand stationmaster doesn't leave the station after throwing the ball.)

When each train has had a turn at throwing the ball, the points are added up, and the teams swap over.

Variations:

- When you begin with *Trains and Stations*, it may be good not to limit the number of trains allowed in any station at a time. Gradually limit the number to three, then to two – and finally to only one train per station; so that if the train at Station one begins running toward Station two, the train at Station two must run to Station three: so the trains are 'shunted' to the next station.

140. Carriages

There are no stationmasters, instead all the fielders are railway workers. Again, they are not allowed to run with the ball.

When the ball is thrown, the railway workers line up where the ball was retrieved, all facing the same direction. They stand with legs apart, forming a tunnel. The ball is passed through the tunnel as quickly as possible. When each worker has passed the ball, the last one holds it up. The train who throws the ball runs to a station, trying to reach it before the ball is held up.

141. Express Trains

This is played exactly in the same way as *Carriages*, except that the train who threw the ball tries to run through as many stations as possible, before the ball is held up. He then returns to the goods yard. He gets a point for each station he reaches before the ball is through the 'leg tunnel'.

142. Basket Trains

Railway workers are allowed to run with the ball if they are outside the diamond created by the bases. This time there is no grand stationmaster. Instead, the ball must be thrown into the basket at the Central Station (without bouncing out!). If a train is not in a station, it is out.

Or a railway worker outside the diamond can run with the ball to the station – if he arrives there before the train who is travelling towards it, the train is out and must return to the goods yard. (You can, alternatively, have a basket at each station as well as at the Central Station.)

Equipment: A basket – preferably one without a handle that could obstruct the ball (a cardboard box could be used instead) – this is placed in the centre of the diamond of 'stations'

143. Swedish Rounders or Derailed

This time, the play ball is hit off the tee with the fist; or thrown (if a child prefers to do this). Another version involves the batter or 'train' kicking the ball when it is slowly rolled towards him by the stationmaster.

To get a train out, the railway workers must brand him, or touch him with the ball – before he gets to the station. Railway workers are not, however, allowed to run with the ball unless they have to retrieve the ball from beyond the borders of the diamond.

The train is allowed to dodge the ball, provided he is still within one pace either side of the line which forms the side of the diamond. If the train 'punches' the ball off the tee, and it is caught on the full, the train is out and returns to the goods yard. If there are other trains on the stations, they remain in (or return to) the station where they were at the time of the punch.

Hints to the leader:

- The grand stationmaster role may be dropped as the children improve at the game, but it helps the timid children to enter the game initially. (They tend to stay close to the leader when fielding.)
- Ask the trains to raise one arm when they reach a station and decide to stay there – this makes it easier to judge whether a train is safely in the station or not.

Rounders is a game that requires fair play and acceptance of the leader's judgment. This is very challenging to some children. To encourage children to play fairly and accept the leader's judgment, various methods may be tried:

- At the end of the game, award bonus 'homers' (a point for a train who has successfully travelled through all four stations) for the teams that have encouraged each other and worked well together.
- As a consequence for any negative comments or criticism towards any player, or inappropriate questioning of the leader's decisions, a train can be asked to drop back one place in the throwing order. Or more seriously, be sent to the back of the line. If a fielder behaves in this way, you can allow a train to advance to the next station.

> **AGE RANGE:** 11+
>
> **EQUIPMENT:** One play ball, one tee, available at sports stores (a simple version can be made by driving a garden stake into the ground so that the top of it is at waist-height for the hitter)

These options place the onus on the players themselves and create positive peer pressure. It is, however, important to clearly state the consequences for positive and negative behaviour in advance, before the game begins.

Rounders games can easily be dominated by a few of the more physically gifted children. Whilst wanting to encourage the strong, it can result in the weaker, more reserved children feeling left out and so withdrawing from the game. *Carriages* and *Express Trains* are rounders games that involve, by necessity, all fielders at all times and are very exciting to the batters or throwers who are watching.

Trains and Stations and *Carriages* can both be developed into bat-and-ball games instead of throwing. Follow the same rules, but instead of throwing the ball, the train hits it with a bat.

A good way to begin to use the bat is to hit the ball with a tee (tees can be bought through most sports stores or made in the way previously described).

Begin by using a large grapefruit-size ball if possible, and a standard rounders bat. As the players' skills develop, a smaller, harder ball can be introduced.

At the very beginning, learning to use a bat can be frustrating for the batter if he cannot hit the ball very far. It also becomes boring for the fielders as they have little to do. One solution is to use a tennis racket and tennis ball. It is easier to hit and the ball travels further, giving the fielders a chance to run.

Chapter Four

Rediscovering the Playground

Many children today have forgotten how to play games. How often do you see children in school playgrounds, or on the streets, skipping, playing marbles, or playing traditional games? The wealth of verses, rules, and ideas for games that need no referee and no specialised equipment are rapidly being lost. At some schools I have visited, I have seen children playing a few playground games; but these were just the impoverished remains of what was once a rich cultural tapestry. Children very seldom still invent their own particular rules; they tend to just follow the basic structure, the skeleton of the game. How much more alive are games which also take account of specific, individual conditions and circumstances – such as involving the tree that stands in the play area, or inventing a rule to help a certain child with a differing physical ability.

The oral tradition of verses (which often deal with social issues) has also faded. The rhythms of such words and rhymes can be highly beneficial to children's development. Playground games help children build up their motor skills, their social skills (e.g. in negotiation, tact and assertiveness); they can also help them develop their identity, their sense of themselves in relation to the world.

In the schools where I have visited or worked, I always spend much time in the playground 'reintroducing' games like hopscotch, clappies, four square, and a number of playground games I have either seen being played around the world – where television and videos are still not the norm – or ones that I remember from my own childhood.

The children take up these games with great delight; and supervision of the play area also becomes much more relaxing for the adults! There will be a noticeable difference in the number of bullying attacks – not that this does not occur in games, but the structure of a game, its rules etc., help the children to interact in a more social manner. Parents, too, may find that their children complain less about being bored, or are less interested in screen time. In fact you may find that you have an empty house to yourself for an entire afternoon!

144. Moon, Moon

One child is the sun. The other children are the moons. The sun tries to catch the moons. The moons go to the inside of the circle.

The sun stays on the outside. He may not cross over into the circle but must try to tag the moons who are inside. The sun may reach over the line, provided his toes do not cross over. He may even place one hand on the ground inside the circle to extend his range.

The game ends when either a player is tagged and then becomes the new sun, or all players are caught except one.

PLAY AREA: With chalk, a stone, or water, draw a circle on the ground about 5 paces across, as shown below – the circle can be altered according to the number of players

NUMBER OF PLAYERS: 5–10

Variations:

• The circle can be divided into a half or quarter moon. This is done by drawing lines across the middle of the circle. The sun can now run along these line to catch the moons.

145. Wall Tennis

The players hit the ball to one another with their hands, so that the ball bounces on the wall and the ground before it is returned.

NUMBER OF PLAYERS: 2
EQUIPMENT: One tennis ball per pair

Variations:

• *Variation 1*
A line is drawn on the wall (one metre off the ground). The ball must be hit above this line.

• *Variation 2*
A line is drawn on the ground approximately one metre from the wall. The ball must bounce on the players' side of the line.

146. Clappies

The first player begins with the ball. She tries to complete all the parts (given below), and then the variations, without dropping the ball. If this happens, the ball is given to the next player, who begins again with Part one, and then adds the variations, beginning with Variation one.

When all players have had a turn, the ball is returned to Player 1, who begins at Part 1 again. The winner is the child who successfully completes the most variations.

Part one

The player throws the ball straight up in the air, and catches it.

Part two

The player throws the ball, lets it bounce once on the ground, and then catches it.

Part three

The player throws the ball up, lets it bounce on the ground, then 'bounces' or 'pats' it with her hand into the air, and lastly catches it.

Part four

As in Part 3, but this time she pats it twice: once with the fingers of her hand pointing away from her body, then with the fingers pointing towards her.

Part five

The player throws the ball up in the air, then claps her hands first behind her back, then in front of her body, and lastly catches the ball.

> **EQUIPMENT:** One tennis ball

Variations:

- All the variations are added any time between throwing the ball and catching it (between the beginning and end of a part.)

- *Variation one*
  The player completes parts one to five with the following addition: *Twiddles* – The player makes a circular motion with both hands. This is done by placing a palm of one hand on the back of the other. Fingers pointing sideways, thumbs near solar plexus. The hands now rapidly circle each other.

- *Variation two*
  Parts one to five, adding *Shoulders* – The player touches her shoulders with both hands at some point between throwing and catching the ball.

- *Variation three*
  Elbows – The player touches her elbows.

- *Variation four*
  Knees – The player touches both her knees – but her feet must be off the floor when she does.

- *Variation five*
  Touch the Ground – The player touches the ground.

- *Variation six*
  Turn Around – The player turns 360 degrees.

147. Nest and Eggs

Variations:

- One player is the mother bird. She must protect her eggs from being stolen. The other players are crows who wish to steal the eggs. When one player says, '**Guard your eggs!**', the game begins.

- The mother bird is blindfolded. One player is assigned to be her 'guide dog', and to prevent her from being harmed. The other players move the nest to a new place, and sit round it, trying to keep quiet. The mother bird tries to find her nest.

- The mother bird stands in the centre of the circle with one of the eggs in her hand. The other players stand with their toes on the circle, and the mother says the following rhyme:

  > Mother bird has lost her way.
  > Finds another if she may.

PLAY AREA: A circle, with stones in the centre

EQUIPMENT: Stones, or some other objects, to represent eggs; a scarf or rag to use as blindfold

Some of the players who are standing on the circle have an egg in their hands. In a small circle of, say, nine players, there will be three eggs. The mother bird tries to tag the players who have an egg. These players may not move. She has three guesses.

When one is tagged who has the egg, she is the next mother bird. If she uses up her three guesses without finding an egg, she chooses a new mother bird and the game begins again.

148. Finding the Fire

One person is the fire-seeker. They must find the fire stick and tag the other players with it. They close their eyes while the other players hide the stick somewhere in the play area. They look for the stick, while the other players give them hints by saying '**Colder, colder**' if they are walking away from the stick, and '**Hotter, hotter**' when they are walking towards it. When they find it, they shout '**Fire's burning! Fire's burning!**' and begin chasing the other players with the stick in their hand.

PLAY AREA: A designated tree or post or 'water' (a safe area)

EQUIPMENT: 1 stick

A player tagged by the player carrying the fire stick is out. A player can take refuge at the 'water' but for no longer than 10 seconds (or any other agreed period).

149. Wolf and Sheep

One child is the wolf. He must try to catch the 'smallest' sheep. One child is the shepherd. He stands in the front of the line. The sheep line up behind him, with their arms around the waist of the person in front.

The 'smallest' sheep is the one at the end of the line. If the line breaks, the person who wasn't able to hold on becomes the new wolf. The old wolf becomes the shepherd.

150. Humpo Bumpo

A game of physical skills and balance! Two players bump against each other within the circle. They hold one of their legs in one hand, and

the other arm behind their back.

The winner is the one who manages to stay on one leg within the circle while bumping the other player out!

151. Four Square

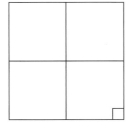

The next game is so popular that I usually recommend that the court be painted onto a tar or concrete surface – for endless use! Introduce the first version to the younger children (it prevents more aggressive playing). The older children will get bored and want to play the 'straight' version.

The aim of the game is to reach the highest square and remain there as long as possible (to remain as Ace). The squares are graded: the serving square (indicated by a small square on the outer corner) is 'Jack', the lowest in rank; the second square is 'Queen'; the third 'King' and the fourth and highest is 'Ace'.

The Jack serves the ball by hitting it into any of the other squares. The receiving occupant of a square hits it into another square. The hitting of the ball is done with an open hand. The hand therefore performs the same task as a tennis racket would in tennis. If the ball lands on the outer lines of a square it is considered to be in. If the ball lands on the inner lines it can be played again, or play can continue.

A player is out when:

– he catches or throws the ball.

– he fails to return the ball.

– he hits the ball so that it bounces in his own square (This rule does not apply to *Down Ball*, see below)

PLAY AREA: A square divided into four equal boxes; each side of the square is about 4 yards (3.6 metres)

NUMBER OF PLAYERS: 4 at one time

EQUIPMENT: A play ball

– he hits the ball too hard and it lands outside the court.

When a player is out, he goes to the back of the queue of those waiting to play. (Or, if only four are playing, he becomes Jack.) The rest of the players are then 'promoted': if the King went out, then the Queen becomes King, Jack becomes Queen and a new server (Jack) enters the game. To score: the Ace gets a point every time a player goes out (either Jack, Queen, or King).

Variations:

152. Down Ball

The players must hit the ball so that it first bounces in their own square before going into another square.

153. Carry If You Can

The players divide into two teams of four to eight players. One player from each team stands on line AB and tries to throw his stone so that it lands on line CD. The player whose stone lands on or closest to the line is the winner, and his team has won the right to play first.

Step 1: Team A stand behind line AB, and Team B put their stones on line CD. Team A try, one at a time, to throw their stones on top of Team B's stones on line CD.

If a player fails to hit one of Team B's stones, then it is Team B's turn. If all the players in Team A are successful, then they go on to Step 2.

Step 2: Team A stand behind line AB, and Team B put their stones on line CD as in Step 1. Team A throw their stones, one at a time, a one-hop distance from where they are standing.

Each player then hops so that he lands on his stone with his foot. He then lifts up his foot, balancing on his heel, picks up his stone and tries to hit one of Team B's stones.

If a player fails to land on his stone, or falls over, or misses one of Team B's stones, then Team B is allowed to try. If all the players of Team A or Team B are successful, they go on to Step 3.

Step 3: Instead of throwing the stone a one-hop distance, it is thrown a two-hops distance, and the same sequence repeated as in Step 2.

Step 4: The same again, but this time three-hops distance.

Step 5: Team A balance their stones on top of the arch of one of their feet, and from line AB they hop towards Team B's stones on line CD. When they get there, they try to drop their stone on one of Team B's. The stone must not fall off the foot at any other time.

Step 6: Step 5 is repeated, but the players put the stones between their two feet.

Step 7: The same, but the stone is held between the knees.

Step 8: The stone is held between the thighs.

PLAY AREA: Draw 2 lines on the ground, 4–5m apart
EQUIPMENT: Each player must have a stone (about 7–8cm in diameter, 2cm thick)

A ——————————————— B

C ——————————————— D

Step 9: The players bend over backwards in order to balance their stones on their chests as they walk toward line CD.

Step 10: The stones are put on the left shoulder of the players.

Step 11: Then they are put on the right shoulder.

Step 12: The players put their stones between the chin and the neck and walk towards CD, without bending.

Step 13: Again, the players hold the stone between their feet, but this time they hop backwards.

Step 14: Hopping backwards, the stone is held between the knees.

Step 15: The players hold the stone between their thighs, and hop backwards towards CD.

Step 16: The players bend forwards this time, and balance their stones on their backs. Walking forwards to CD, they let their stones fall over their heads to hit the stones on CD.

Step 17: As in Step 16, but walking backwards.

Step 18: As in Step 16, but walking forwards with the stone balanced on the players' heads.

If a player fails, then their whole team lose their turn; and when they are able to play again, they replay the step they were trying to complete. The first team to complete all eighteen steps are the winners.

154. Tree Tag

The children stand in the middle of the play area. At a signal, they all run to one of the trees. The child who wasn't able to reach a tree stands in the middle of the play area and when the others change places, tries to reach an unoccupied tree.

> **PLAY AREA:** Designated 'safe areas', e.g. trees – one less than the number of players

155. Maze Race

Team A's aim is to reach the outer limit of the spiral, while Team B tries to reach the centre. One player from each team starts at a given signal. They run round the spiral: Player A from the centre outwards, and Player B from the outside inwards. When they meet, they have a 'contest' (see below) to determine who will be able to continue.

If Player A wins, he continues to run towards Team B, but now a new Player B has begun to run round the spiral towards him. When they meet, they have another contest. The loser of the contest drops out of the game.

When a member of a team, let's say Player A, reaches Team B's home,

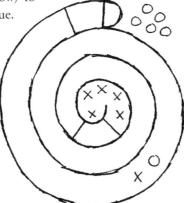

another Player A begins running from the centre of the spiral towards Home B. The team that succeeds in getting one of their players into their opponents' starting area, wins.

Variations:

- If a player loses a contest, he does not drop out but returns to his team's starting area while the winner runs on to meet the next challenger.

  Using this method the game ends when all the players from one team have managed to get to the starting area of their opponents.

156. Paper, Scissors, Stone

This is a hand contest used in the *Maze Race*. Two players stand facing each other, with their hands behind their backs. They count: '**One, two, three!**' On '**three!**' they each bring one hand forward, making the shape that represents either paper, stone or scissors.

Paper beats stone: it can cover the stone.
Scissors beats paper: it can cut the paper.
Stone beats scissors: it can blunt the scissors.
If the hands are the same, then the players count again.

157. Thumb Wrestling

The aim is to hold your opponent's thumb down with your thumb for a count of three. Two players face each other and link hands. The following verse is said:

One, two, three, four
I declare a thumb war. Bow…
    (they make their thumbs bow)

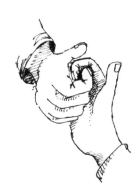

And then the fight ensues! The winner is the one who holds down his opponent's thumb while saying:

One, two, three
I declare VICTORY!

Reflex Games

158. Crocodile Jaws

Two players face each other with their hands together, touching each other's hands with the tips of their fingers.

One player starts. They try to 'catch' their opponent's hands between their hands, in their 'crocodile jaws', before the other takes their hands away. They are successful if they touch their opponent's hands, thus

'biting' them. If successful, they try to catch him again. If he misses, it is the other's turn.

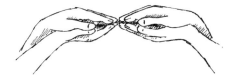

159. Knuckles

As above, except opponents place their fists together and take it in turns to try and hit each others' knuckles with their clenched fists. (Watch out for bruising!)

160. Flip Overs

One player holds their hands palm up (they will be the 'striker'). The other player places their hands palm down on their opponent's. The striker must very quickly withdraw her hand from underneath, and touch the back of the opponent's hand before the latter withdraws it. No feints or dummies are allowed.

The players change over when the striker is unsuccessful; the 'striker' always has palms facing upwards.

The next game is similar to *Running the Gauntlet*

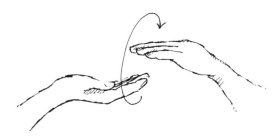

(game 184). *Barges and Banks, Locks and Barges* and *Shooting the Rapids* are all very similar, but have small variations.

161. Barges and Banks

Divide the players into two teams: bargemen and pirates. The bargemen try to reach line A and return to line B without being caught.

The pirates (in our example, Team A) stand on the four corners of the court. One of the pirates gives the signal for the game to begin.

The bargemen try to run across the river without being caught by the pirates. The pirates can either run along bank A or bank B, or they can swim to the middle of the river. However, they can only chase one bargeman: if they do not succeed in catching this one, they must return to their corner before trying to catch another.

A bargeman is safe if he stands on one of the 'safe' banks of the river. If a bargeman is caught, the teams swap over: Team A become the bargemen, and Team B become the pirates.

However, if a bargeman succeeds in crossing bank A

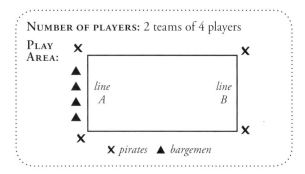

and then back to bank B without getting caught, his team scores 1 point, and can try to reach bank A again. The winning team is the one which scores the most.

Locks and Barges is very similar to *Barges and Banks*. Make sure that the size of the play area is carefully measured – the dimensions are quite crucial!

162. Locks and Barges

The aim is for the bargeman to pass across the locks and back without being caught. The lock-keepers must keep two feet on their lines at all times. The lock-keepers each stand on one of the lines which cross the court (locks A, B, C or D on the diagram above). They are not allowed to move to any other lock, except for the lock-keeper on lock A, who can move down the centre lock at any time.

The game begins when one of the bargemen touches hands with Lock-keeper A (on lock A). The bargemen try to dodge lock-keepers A, B, C and D to reach lock D and then return to cross lock A without being tagged.

The bargemen **must** stay within the lines of the court – if not, they lose their turn and become the lock-keepers.

If any bargeman is tagged, the teams swap over and the game begins again. If a bargeman crosses D and A without being tagged, his team gets a point; and all of the bargemen return to begin again behind lock A. The team with the most points wins.

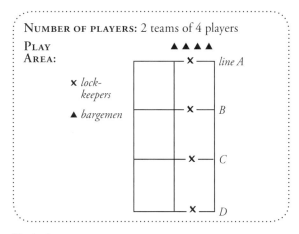

Variations:

• Instead of having one lock-keeper per line, I sometimes use three on lock A, two on lock B, and one on lock C. Then players score one point if they cross lock B, two points if they cross lock C without being tagged, and three points if they cross lock D. If two or three bargemen run at the same time, they can work together to distract the lock-keepers.

The next game works wonderfully on a sandy beach; it is easy to dig the trenches (the rapids), and the sand is harmless to fall on. It is a variation of *Locks and Barges* and *Barges and Banks* that originally came from Bangladesh.

163. Shooting the Rapids

Divide the players into two teams: canoeists and pirates. The canoeists stand on Bank A. Their aim is to try to cross all nine rapids and then return to Bank A.

The pirates each stand in a rapid. They are only allowed to move within their own rapid, except for the defender in Rapid 1 who is allowed to move down the central rapid, in the first part of the game; and the pirate in Rapid 9 who can move down the central rapid in the second part.

The game begins when the pirate in Rapid 1 gives the signal. Then the canoeists try to reach Bank B without being tagged. If one gets tagged, the teams

NUMBER OF PLAYERS: 2 teams of 9 players
PLAY AREA: See below

swap over and the game begins again. But if the canoeists are successful, they wait behind Bank B until all the canoeists have arrived safely.

The second part of the game begins with a signal from the pirate in Rapid 9. If a canoeist reaches Bank A without being caught, he scores one point for his team. The teams then swap over and begin with part one again.

The team with the most points wins.

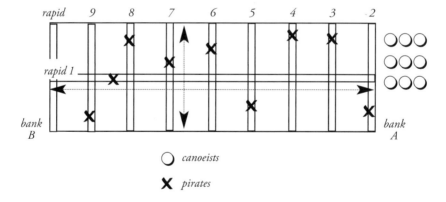

canoeists

pirates

The next game is derived from another game from Bangladesh, and has the unusual feature of a 'goal' which moves closer and closer to the team that wishes to score.

164. Base Camp

The players divide into two teams: the home forces (Army A) and the enemy (Army B). One player from Army A is the Commander and stands in the circle (see diagram). The rest of Army A form a chain from the commander towards the border.

Army B move onto the court from behind the border to begin the game. Army A's chain tries to catch Army B's soldiers until the commander gives a signal.

At the signal, the chain breaks loose and soldiers A try to cross the border without being killed (tagged) by Army B, who are now the chasers. Army B are not allowed to home guard the base camp.

If a soldier from Army A is tagged, they are 'dead' and sit out of the game. The first soldier to cross the border wins a medal for bravery. He helps the commander by standing in the base camp and jumping as far as he can towards the border. The base camp is moved to this spot. (The place where the brave soldier landed is the new camp's centre.) The brave soldier then joins Army A again and the game continues.

When the base camp reaches the border, Army A has scored a point, and the game begins again with the same team.

The commander can also score a goal, by leaving the base camp and running to cross the border. If he scores, he returns to the base camp and the game begins again. However, if the commander gets tagged when trying to run towards the starting line, the teams swap over, and the game begins again.

When the commander leaves the base camp, a player from Army B can step into the base camp; and if the teams change, he will be the new commander. The team with the most points wins.

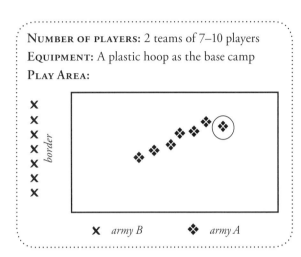

NUMBER OF PLAYERS: 2 teams of 7–10 players
EQUIPMENT: A plastic hoop as the base camp
PLAY AREA:

border

✗ *army B*   ❖ *army A*

Marbles

165. Snooker

This is probably the most common and popular of all the marbles games. It needs to be played on a smooth surface. It is a two-person game but can easily be adapted for more players.

Complete a *Liner* (game 171) to see who goes first.

This is a traditional 'knuckles down' style of shooting game where one knuckle on the shooting hand must touch the ground. The thumb then flicks the marble. The shooting hand must be no further than a couple of inches (5cm) away from the shooting line. The shooting hand is not allowed to cross the line. In other words the marble has to be flicked not thrown.

1. Draw a circle about 10 feet (3 metres) across.

2. In the centre of the circle, 12 marbles are placed either in a tight pack or in a cross.

3. The first player shoots and tries to knock one of the marbles out of the ring.

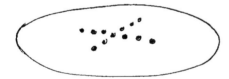

4. After this shot the following things can happen:

    i.   If none of the marbles are shot out of the ring, you lose your turn. If your shooter ends up in the circle, you leave it there. That is where you will shoot from the next time it is your turn. If your shooter goes outside the ring, then you pick it up and shoot from the edge next time.

    ii. If you shoot and hit another marble or more than one marble out of the ring, but your own shooter also ends up outside the ring, you get to keep the marbles you knocked out. Your turn is over and you shoot from the outside next time.

    iii. The best outcome is this: you shoot and knock one or more marbles out of the ring, but your shooter remains inside the ring. In this case you get to have another go, shooting from where your shooter stopped rolling. This can be repeated over and over until either of the first two options occur.

The winner of the game is the first to knock out six marbles. If this is done consecutively, without a break, then the winner keeps all twelve marbles.

166. Dead Eye or Cannons

This is a simpler version of *Snooker*. In this game your shooter has to end up outside the ring in order to claim any of the marbles you may have knocked out. A smooth, flat playing area is needed. Four to eight players can play at a time.

1. A ring of about six to seven paces across is drawn. Each player places five marbles in the middle of the ring. The marbles are tightly clustered together.

2. Complete a liner to see who goes first. The first shooter breaks the marble-pack with the aim of knocking out as many marbles as possible, while

endeavouring to end up with their own marble outside the ring. If their marble does not end up outside the ring, then they must replace the marbles they knocked out, putting them back into the middle of the ring. If they are successful in knocking out some marbles and ending with her shooter outside the ring, they get to keep the others she knocked out.

3. Each shooter may only have one turn at a time, regardless of the outcome. The shooters take it in turns. The game is over when all the marbles have been knocked out.

167. Jacks

This is a game where the rewards and losses are high. A flat smooth surface is needed.

1. The players play a counting-out game to decide who will be Jack. In another variation, only those who want to be Jacks submit themselves to the counting game. The others wait.

2. If you are the Jack you place a marble on the ground and walk back about twelve paces. A shooting line is drawn. All players line up and take it in turns to shoot.

3. The aim is to hit the Jack marble. If you do, then you become the new Jack and collect all the marbles shot so far. If you miss, then the Jack player will collect and keeps yours and everybody else's marbles, once each player has shot three marbles.

4. Another version of this game is as follows: if you hit the Jack marble then you collect it and all the others that have been shot; but the Jack player must also give you as many marbles again as were on the field at the time you made the hit.

168. Noughts and Crosses

This game is good for the pavement (sidewalk) although it can be played on earthy ground. It can only be played with two players.

1. Draw a Noughts-and-Crosses square on the pavement.

2. Draw a shooting line about four paces back (in another version you draw a circle around the squares at about the same distance back, and shoot from anywhere outside it.)

3. The aim of the game is to complete a diagonal or straight line of three marbles in three of the boxes. Taking it in turns the players may either try to place a marble in a box or knock the opponent's out.

4. There are two versions of what may count as a win:

   i. Only one marble is allowed in a box at a time. This legal marble is either the one that was there first or one that manages to knock another cleanly out of a box, **or**

   ii. There is no limit to the number of marbles in any one box. The first to make a 'three of a kind' wins.

169. Sailor's Boot

This is an old favourite and can still be seen in many playgrounds. You'll need a smooth flat surface. Usually between two and five players can join in.

1. One of the players takes off a shoe and places it in the middle of the playing area.

2. Draw a circle of about four to five paces across.

3. Every players puts in five target marbles around the 'boot'.

4. The first player shoots in knuckle-down style.

He tries to knock one of the target marbles so that it hits the boot. If he can do so he keeps the target marble and gets another turn, shooting from the outside of the ring each time. The game ends when all the target marbles have been captured.

170. Leap Frogs

You can play this game on a rough or smooth surface, usually about ten players at a time.

1. Player one throws a marble about ten paces away. This is called the Jack.

2. Each player in turn tries to underhand throw a marble as close as possible to the target. Anyone who gets within a hand span of the Jack wins. The game stops as soon as someone has done this.

3. If you are playing for keeps, the winner may claim the Jack. In another, tougher version the winner may claim all the marbles that were thrown.

4. If no-one gets within a hand span of the target then a step is measured away from the Jack. Anyone who has thrown within that step gets to try an eye-dropper. The closest marble tries first. This is done by standing over the Jack and dropping your marble from eye level, trying to hit the target. If you are successful you claim the Jack as you would have done if you had been within a hand span.

171. Liners

This is a very traditional way to begin a game, to see who will go first.

1. Draw two lines about a foot (30cm) apart and then walk back about eight to ten paces. Now draw another line where you are standing. This is called the throwing line.

2. No-one must cross the throwing line. Each player now has a turn to try and throw a marble as near as possible to the closest of the two lines. If a marble rolls over the back line then it is automatically out.

3. The player with the marble closest to the line wins the right to be the first to shoot in the next game.

172. Gaga Ball

A great addition to any playground. Simple rules: All players stand inside the pit. The goal is to get the ball to touch another player (knee or below) to get them 'out'. Players may only use their hands to hit the ball. If a player hits a ball out of the pit, they (or the last person to have touched the ball before it goes out) are 'out'. Players may only hit the ball once before the ball hits another surface (either the wall or another player) before they are allowed to hit the ball again. This is considered a 'double-hit' and it means that the player has gotten themselves out (a self-out.) Players may also accidentally hit the ball in a way that it hits them (knee or below), and this is also considered a 'self-out'.

Variations:

- Elimination round: This is the simple version where the goal is to be the final player in the pit. This means that, one by one, players are eliminated, exiting the pit so that in the end there is one final victor.

- Revenge round: In this version, players have a chance to get back in after they've gotten out. Players can get back in the game if the person who got them out gets out. In the case of a 'self-out', a move in which a player hits the ball in such a way that it strikes them below the knee, they step out of the game and get back in when the next player that has a 'self-out' gets out.

AGE RANGE: 9+

PLAY AREA: Outdoor, octagonal 'pit' with walls about 2–3 feet high, about 8 x 8 or 10 x 10 feet

NUMBER OF PLAYERS: 10+

EQUIPMENT: One gaga ball (lightweight playground ball works fine)

Chapter Five
Age 11
The Greek Olympics – Beauty, Truth, Strength

Equipment

Javelin

I use lightweight javelins of up to 400 grams in weight. As these are quite expensive, a couple can be bought every year, so that the school accumulates them over time. Otherwise, they can also be made from (straight!) saplings or bamboo with wound string handles and sharpened points.

For bamboo javelins, insert a dowel and sharpen one end. The dowel will also give a bit of weight. (I have also seen metal points used with bamboo.)

The handle should be positioned so that when you balance the javelin at the handle-end nearest the tip, it does not tilt back or forward. In this way the javelin will be slightly weighted towards the sharpened end. This will allow it to stick into the ground.

A wooden javelin can be decorated and carved, with a dedication to the gods running vertically down the shaft; children who make their own often regard them as real treasures.

Use hula hoops or old tennis balls for targets.

Discus

Making a discus is also a worthwhile thing to do. Select a close grained heavy wood; a block measuring about 9 inches across and 2 inches deep (23 x 5cm) should be used. Cut, whittle, and chisel the block down to a disc shape. Model it on a 0.75 kilogram discus. Soak or immerse it in oil for at least a couple of weeks (months is better) to prevent cracking and to add extra weight. Then carve and burn the dedication to the gods in Greek writing either in a circle or a spiral. I usually use a small soldering iron to go back over the carved inscription to make it a little clearer.

Weights (for running weight jumps)

I make simple weights out of plastic-lined cloth bags. Sew a long tube with one end sewn together. Put enough sand in a plastic bag and place this inside the tube. Tie a knot immediately above the sand, and then one approximately 20–30 cm above it (this forms the handle). The weights should weigh about 1.5 kg (3 lbs) each. Alternatively, small weight-lifting dumbbells can be used.

For the High Jump

Use two javelins stuck in the ground with an elastic 'practise high-jump band' between them. (This is an elastic rope covered with 1 foot (30cm) long, thin foam rectangles. These are easily made or can be bought as 'practise high-jump bars' from most sports suppliers)

$$-8 \quad -6 \quad -4 \quad -2 \quad 0 \quad +2 \quad +4 \quad +6 \quad +8$$

A measuring arrow: This will be needed in the high-jump event. Use an arrow or 2–3 feet (60–90cm) length of thin dowelling. Mark it every inch along its shaft from the bottom to the top. About half way up the shaft make a mark that is distinct from all others. This will be the 'zero' or starting measure. On one side of this mark write +1, +2, +3 and so on until you have come to the end. On the other side of the zero mark, write -1, -2, -3, and so on.

Golden Cloth

This is used instead of the starting 'shot' of a gun. The Ancient Greeks began their events by holding a golden cloth over one arm, and letting it fall. The signal that the runners can start the race is given by dropping the cloth to the ground.

Tunics

The children enjoy making the day as authentic as possible, so dressing up is always a feature – not only for the athletes, but also the judges, teachers, parents and other helpers!

The athletes wear short white tunics or togas, made from old sheets, over a white t-shirt and shorts. These can be decorated with their city's colours (see 'Olympic Camp'). An old white sheet is all that is needed. Cut it into a rectangle 8–10 feet long and 1–2 feet across (2.5–3m by 30–60cm), depending on the height and shoulder width of the athlete. Cut a hole in the middle so that it may be slipped over the head. A belt should be tied around the waist. The tunic should be about three inches above the knees.

The athletes also sometimes like to make their own laurel wreaths. These are worn at the Opening and Closing Ceremonies. Similarly, the judges (Gods and Goddesses) can wear long tunics, with gold-sprayed wreaths if desired!

Scrolls

These also help make the event more 'authentic'. Scrolls are carried in the Marathon, used in the Relay Race, and used to keep scores.

Make a simple scroll with some paper and a dowel. For the athletes, the following words can be inscribed: 'Beauty, Truth, Strength – Let the Games begin!'

Medals

Simple but beautiful medals made from clay and baked can be given to each athlete. A silk ribbon may be attached to hang it around the neck. Or a simple wooden stand made so that the medal can sit on a shelf when it is taken home.

Preparation of the Arena

The Olympic Arena (a playing field) must be prepared before the children arrive for the Olympic Camp.

Below is a suggested layout for the events. These are marked out with chalk or paint, ropes and flags.

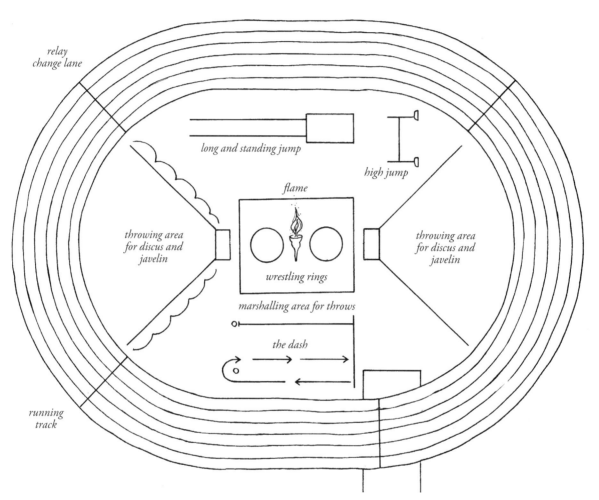

Practice

The children enjoy the practice leading up to the games almost as much as the day of the event itself. In a world so full of instant gratification, to get pleasure from practising seems to me a healthy thing.

It is important to practise two or three times a week, for an hour, over several months. In this way, the children build up competence in all events and can choose their favourite events for the day.

A day or two before the Olympics, the newly-formed city teams (see 'The Olympic Camp') have several practice sessions. The athletes, in city teams, move around all events with their city leader or Counsellor (a teacher or parent).

All athletes participate in all events during the practice, but at the end of the day they choose which events they would like to enter at the Olympics. (Normally they choose 2 or 3, although if practically possible it is ideal for all athletes to participate in all events.)

The Events

The events are described in the order they are played at the Games. Practice exercises as well as the final technique are described. (In Javelin, for example, there are two kinds of throw: an introductory, practice throw, and the throw that is used on the day.)

Running

173. The Marathon

This is a one mile cross-country-style run. On the day, the athletes each carry a scroll. Stewards are placed along the route to direct the runners.

Begin training the athletes with a half-mile run, gradually building up to a one-mile distance. Not all children will be able to run one mile; I usually design the course in a figure of eight, so that those who aren't able to complete the whole course can finish halfway.

Encourage the children to run beautifully by imagining that they are carrying a laurel wreath on their heads; by letting their arms swing freely; and by making sure that their legs are doing the work.

The Greeks worked with this threefold principle as well: they saw it in terms of body (the power and strength of the legs and arms), trunk (a relaxed chest and back), and spirit (a free and 'carried' head). So in running, the athlete's posture should be upright, and she should run with a sense of lightness. It may sound obvious, but to run with both strength and beauty is one of the hardest things to do, particularly if one is tired!

On the day of the Olympics, the first and last lap of the Marathon is around the Arena.

174. The Dash

This is a 100m sprint: 50m to a pole, around it, and 50m back to the finishing line. This reflects the ancient Greeks' less goal-orientated concept of running: that you do not only run towards, but also away from something. They felt that becoming aware of the dynamic between these two polarities of 'back and front space', enabled the runner to be more 'present' – instead of focusing only on striving to reach the finishing line. Again, remind the athlete to run beautifully and let her legs do the work!

On the day, no more than four runners can run a race at one time (otherwise there will be too many collisions when they run round the pole!).

175. The Mini Marathon

This is a 300–400 metre race around the track. Use a staggered start. But once the race begins, the runners do not have to keep in lane.

176. The Relay Race

This usually takes place at the end of the Games, as it is one of the most exciting events. The athletes should practise receiving the baton (scroll) while already moving. This enables them to get off to a 'flying start'.

Originally, the relay race was run by passing a lit torch from runner to runner; but I usually use a scroll! This is a 4 x 75m or 4 x 100m relay race, depending on the size of your track.

Each city has a scroll which will be passed from runner to runner. At each station on the track (see diagram of layout of Arena) stands one runner from each city.

The runners have a staggered start: the runner in the outside track must be four paces ahead of the runner next to her, etc. Runners must stay in their tracks.

As in a conventional relay race, the scroll is passed from runner to runner, and the team with the fastest and most beautiful runners wins.

This is a very exciting event. It also offers the opportunity for children who may be shy of performing on their own, to participate without feeling exposed. It is a good idea to have the fastest runner run last.

Jumping

177. The Running Jump

Step 1: Running for speed

When teaching children to long-jump, I use the image of the four elements to help them. Begin by letting each child in turn run and jump – to get a feel of the ground, and of the sand when landing. Then let them run again, this time 'building up the fire' as they approach the sand pit – running faster and faster (at top speed by the time she reaches the sand pit). Encourage the children to run in a free and healthy way: relaxed shoulders, head not too far forward or too far back, arms swinging freely from the shoulders, back straight. In order to help them run smoothly and gracefully, tell them to 'run like water'.

Step 2: Leaving the ground

A successful long-jumper makes use of gravity when she leaves the ground at the start of her jump. Weight helps achieve a lengthy jump. When the child reaches the sand pit, she should use the 'weight of earth' to give her the strength to leap into the air.

Step 3: Flying in the air

The longer the jumper can stay in the air, the more successful (and aesthetic) her jump will be. Encourage the children to use the element of air: to enjoy the feeling of flying.

Step 4: Landing on the earth

Tell the children that their jump will be measured from where they leave the ground to the closest mark their body makes on the sand (e.g. not necessarily where the feet land).

Remind them that the Greeks placed as much value on the quality and grace of the jumper as on the length of the jump. So how the jumper lands is also important – which is where the fluidity of water comes in.

I prefer the children to discover for themselves where they feel the various 'moments' are. The way I have described it is the conclusion they usually come to – but it sometimes varies. The children can make a good case for the run-up stage being like water, getting faster and more powerful; the take off being like a fiery explosion; the air moment seldom differs; but the landing comes when we return to earth.

The length of the jump can be measured from the board (or sand wall) – the last place your foot touches before you leap – in adult 'feet'-lengths. Prepare this before the event.

178. Weight Jump

The Ancient Greeks included weight jumps (with hand weights) in their Olympics. It is thought that this method enabled them to jump as far as in the running jump, perhaps even further. The children often won't be able to jump quite as far, but this activity is important because it helps them experience gravity, and its uses.

The jumper takes a weight in each hand. He stands facing the direction in which he will jump, with his feet together.

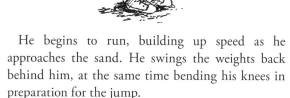

He begins to run, building up speed as he approaches the sand. He swings the weights back behind him, at the same time bending his knees in preparation for the jump.

As he swings the weights forward, he jumps – kicking his legs forward. Just before landing on the earth, he swings the weights behind himself again, and releases them.

179. High Jump

The Greeks didn't have high jump as we know it; apparently the only similar event was an ancient type of pole-vaulting (over live horses). It is believed that this could have been derived from the Cretan tradition of acrobatic bull-leaping.

Outside Athens is a site where, it is believed, high jump was practised – where the athlete landed on stone. This was, some think, so that athletes learned to land gracefully on their feet, truly meeting the earth.

In our Olympics, therefore, we don't have any mats; the two jumps used (the athlete can choose) are hurdle jumps and scissor jumps (see below).

Hurdle jump

This jump is done by approaching the rope directly – front on – and leaping over it, much as one would a hurdle.

Scissor jump

The run-up is the essentially different thing here. A large arc is run so that the rope is approached side on and the leading leg is kicked up and over, while the other leg quickly follows in a scissor action.

The height of the jump is not measured in the conventional way, but, instead, against the height of the child. This allows the smaller athletes (who conventionally would have no chance in this event)

to take part on an even basis with the taller athletes. After the athlete has successfully completed her jump, ask her to come and stand with her back to the rope that is at the height she just cleared.

Place the middle, or '0' point, of the measuring arrow on the sacrum of the athlete: more or less at the waist band of the shorts, or about three adult fingers above the top of the coccyx. Count the number of notches above or below the '0' mark on the arrow. In this way a short athlete clearing a certain height may have the score +3, but a tall athlete who has jumped and cleared the same height may only have the score of -1. The taller athlete will have to clear a much greater height in order to obtain a +3 score.

hurdle jump

scissor jump

180. Wrestling

The wrestling that the children do is modified: for even in Ancient Greece, particularly towards Greco-Roman times, this event was quite brutal. In order to make the competition more fair, I divide the children into weight groups.

The hands should be held at chest height, and a circle, a 'magic ring', is formed by the arms of the two wrestlers when they join hands. The key to this type of wrestling is to keep this ring as round as possible. The athletes must not use heads or shoulders to push, which would mean breaking the ring. The legs should do all the work, and the head should be kept clear and relaxed. Wrestling is a good way to teach children to make use of their body's weight and strength while keeping a 'clear head.'

If an athlete touches the line of the wrestling ring, or is pushed out of it, she loses one point. If she breaks the 'magic' arm-ring by using her shoulder, head, or chest to push, without quickly moving to re-establish it, then she also loses a point. She may absorb and move out of the path of a strong push but she must not pull against her opponent or deliberately release hands. If this occurs, one point is lost.

181. Discus

The Greeks called the discus the 'Truth Sayer', because the way it flies through the air reflects the inner gesture of the athlete. The Greeks saw the discus as a way of sending messages to the gods. The discus was not thrown, but released. One needs to be very open and wide in the area of the ribcage in order to release it successfully. When teaching children to throw the discus, 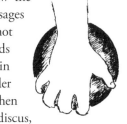 I use various preparatory exercises to build up the skills needed. Before you start, make sure the children realise that the weight of the discus means that it can hurt someone badly. Do not allow the children to throw it unless or until you indicate that it is safe to do so.

Step 1: Swinging the discus

With the arm loosely resting next to the body, the discus is held in a vertical position, with the fingers spread apart, and the tips of the fingers curling around the edge of the discus.

Swing the discus in an arc (not higher than the shoulder) making sure it always remains vertical. Do this with both right and left arms, emphasising the weight of the swing at the bottom of the arc and lightness or levity at the top.

Step 2: Bowling

The children stand facing a partner. They are an arm's length away from each other. If you have left-handed children, make sure they choose a left-handed partner.

They roll their discus into their partner's empty hand, making sure that the discus rolls away from them. The last finger to leave the discus will be the index finger. The discus is held vertically.

Next, tell the children to put one discus down. Then the partners move away from each other, so that they are about ten paces apart.

The child with the discus starts. She 'bowls' the discus along the ground to her partner by swinging the discus (as in Step 1) and then releasing it.

If the discus goes in a straight line, then the child had it vertical when she released it – but if it curves she did not! The elbow and wrist must remain relaxed throughout the release of the discus. Encourage the children to use the weight of the discus, as in Step 1. If you feel confident, the next step could be to repeat the 'bowling' of the discus, but this time throwing it into the air; it must still remain vertical.

Step 3: The cloak

Each child has a discus and works alone. Begin by holding the discus in the throwing hand, as described in Step 1.

The child holds her other hand (the helping, or non-throwing hand) horizontally in front of her, pointing in the direction of her aim. The palm should face upwards. While the arm is being lifted, a small step is taken towards the direction of the aim. The helping arm then wraps an imaginary cloak around the child's body (see picture above). The child follows this arm, bending the knees and twisting the torso.

As the arm goes round the body, the child pivots on her toes, keeping the knees directly over the feet. At this point, the discus can be swung back and forth (see Step 1), so that the weight of it is experienced. Then, slowly, the non-throwing arm unfolds the cloak a gain, and the body follows the movement back – but this time, the throwing arm comes forward. The children must not release the discus yet. When unfurling the 'cloak', it is important that the 'albatross' position is reached (see next picture), in which the chest is forward and the arms – like the wings of a bird – are extended backwards. This is the position in which the discus will eventually be released.

Step 4: Releasing the discus

Line the children up along the edge of the field, facing the way they will throw. Tell the (right-handed) child, who is standing at the end of the line, and holding the discus in her hand on the side where no-one else stands, that she is the 'anchor'. Tell the child on the other end of the line to take four or five steps forward, and the others to make a straight line between the two of them. This is so that if a discus is released early it will not hit another child.

An image that I find helps the children release, as opposed to throwing the discus, is to liken the gesture to that of skimming stones across water.

Follow Step 3: except now the discus is released. Remind the children to release the discus so that the last finger it touches is the index finger, as in the Bowling exercise. The difference is that the discus is now bowled horizontally.

There must be two distinct arm movements.

The first (i.e. the non-throwing or cloak hand/arm) should first swing as far as it can freely; only then should the throwing arm move. This is the throw used on the day of the actual Olympic Games: but then one child does it at a time.

182. Javelin

Hints to the leader:

- It is important to keep the athletes disciplined about the use of such apparatus as javelins – which can obviously harm others. Most accidents occur when good organisation is not enforced.

Following these guidelines should prevent accidents from occurring:

- Delineate a clear throwing line.

- The athletes must not move from behind the throwing line – except when the leader has called '**Collect!**'

- Avoid lines or queues, particularly when sharing javelins. If a queue must be formed, a clear second line can be drawn at least five paces behind the thrower. (Few accidents happen with the sharp point of the javelin, but more often with the opposite end, behind the thrower.)

- Never allow children of this age to run with a javelin.

- Carry the javelin vertically when walking.

- When picking up the javelin after a throw, place one hand on the end of the shaft, and twist and pull. Run your hand down the javelin to the handle as you bring it to the vertical.

To form a correct holding position:

With the non-throwing hand placed below the handle, hold the javelin upright, point down.

Then form a circle using the thumb and forefinger of the throwing hand. Run the throwing hand down the javelin until the thumb and forefinger touch the handle. The other fingers then close on the handle.

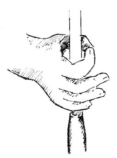

The throw of the hunter

This is an ideal throw for the beginner. The athletes stand in a line. The left-handed athletes should stand together, to the left of the other children. (It is best if they can work together in a group.)

Divide the number of athletes by the number of javelins (i.e. 20 athletes, five javelins makes four groups). Do not allow the athletes to stand in lines or queues – they may be hurt if they stand behind a javelin thrower. See above for how they can stand instead. A rope can mark the throwing line. Give each athlete in each group a number.

To begin, all number ones stand with the javelin's point touching the ground, keeping it as vertical as possible. This is the **Ready** position.

It is important that all the athletes, as well as the javelins, are standing straight and upright! The athletes hold the **Ready** position. The non-throwing hand points at a target on the ground approximately seven paces from the throwing line.

Drawing an arc in air, lift the javelin above the head, not above the shoulder. This is called **Draw**.

Extend the arm backward a little more. This is called **Reach**.

Make sure the tip of the javelin is pointing towards the ground and not horizontally or up to the sky.

Release the javelin with a smooth and directed throw. This is called **Throw**.

All the athletes **Wait** while the leader checks that everyone has thrown their javelin. The leader calls clearly 'Wait!'

Only when the leader calls out '**Collect!**' are the athletes allowed to go over the throwing line and retrieve their javelins, using the technique mentioned above (see 'Hints to the leader' opposite).

Variation

- At '**Reach!**', bring the non-throwing hand to meet the throwing hand: the javelin is now being held in two hands. The point of the javelin must point down.

By bending the knees (but not the back), and reaching back with the arms, the athlete prepares to throw the javelin forward. Continue with **Throw**, **Wait** and **Collect**.

The throw of the warrior

This is the throw used at the Games. The athlete aims to throw the javelin in a beautiful arcing flight, in this more recognisably classical throw.

The athletes stand in the **Ready** position. Now the **Reach** position is slightly different: instead of holding the javelin slightly behind the head, the throwing hand is extended further back, so that the arms form a 45-degree angle to the ground.

The javelin is then released – **Throw**, **Wait** and **Collect** follow.

Variation

- At the **Reach** stage, put the back end of the javelin into the ground so that a small resistance is provided before throw.

Or, a partner can hold the end of the javelin near the ground – but great care must then be taken not to harm the partner.

The Olympic Camp

It is wonderful when other schools or groups all work towards an Olympic Day and meet together. (For instance, at the 1995 Olympics in Sussex, UK, we had 200 children taking part.) This is best done by the schools all meeting together before the Olympic Day, at the chosen location.

Divide the children into city teams (e.g. Athens, Thebes, Corinth and Sparta), taking an equal number of children from each school group to make up a city (e.g. five children from every school in each team).

The first day is spent practising the events (see 'Practice'). After supper the children can paint or draw their city's colours onto their tunics (see 'Equipment').

We then have great fun playing a massive game night together. (For example, *Storm the Castle*, game 194, works wonderfully with so many players – we call it '*Storm the Acropolis*' for this occasion!)

The children can camp in city or class groups.

Note:
Parents are normally very pleased to help with catering and extra supervision, and get a great deal of pleasure from being part of this event, despite a rather sleepless night.

The Olympic Day

The Opening Ceremony
The athletes, dressed up and lined up in their city states, march towards the Olympic Flame to the rhythm of a drum beat, and perhaps some flute players play. Practice the day before will ensure beautifully choreographed movements that have been specially designed for the ceremony.

Each city state is headed by a torchbearer. The torches may be lit from the campfires of the cities or classes. (Simple torches can be made by wrapping a cloth around a wooden handle, and dipping this in kerosene. Obviously extreme care needs to be taken when doing this.) Then a special story and a verse may be recited, invoking the gods to give the athletes strength and grace.

Next the Eternal Flame is lit by the torchbearers. (We make the Eternal Flame with a paraffin-soaked Hessian bag in a big metal container, specially shaped. The container is placed on a raised dais.) This is the sign that the Games have begun.

Scoring
As well as strength, skill and the physical beauty of the athletes, their inner qualities – such as determination and effort – are also prized at these Olympic Games. There are many ways this can be judged. The athletes' performance is assessed on various levels.

A consideration for strength may relate to how fast they run, how high they jump etc., but also to how determined they were in achieving their goal. For example, the first runner back in the Marathon may score well for strength; but the third runner back may also score well because she ran with great determination.

The style is also considered. This evaluates the truth and grace of the athlete's movement. Truth and grace show, for instance, in how upright the athlete's posture is, and in the degree of ease and beauty with which she moves. The javelin might only have been thrown two javelin-lengths by Joan of Corinth, but the arc of its flight and the angle it landed at was excellent, and the throw itself was poised and graceful. Longer throws may rely on brute strength and score less on style.

These two aspects are considered together to give an overall evaluation.

The judges or the *Archon* as they were known in ancient Greece, keep a careful note of each participant's efforts, and at the end of the day every participant is awarded a medal.

The medal could be awarded for winning an event, or for a quality that one athlete in particular demonstrated. (For example, 'John of Thebes, for Determination in the Marathon', or 'Sophie of Corinth for City Spirit in the Relay Race'.)

A simpler version is for the judging to be done by each City Leader/Counsellor watching her athletes train and perform and making note of a particular quality they display in a particular event.

I should also mention that no award is given for the City who won the most events: and surprisingly, this is hardly ever asked for either.

The Events

The events occur in the order described. In keeping with the Olympic tradition I have had live pipe or wooden flute music, played by a white-garbed and garlanded parent while the throwing, jumping and wrestling events are taking place. This has a remarkably calming and centring effect and also keeps activities such as wrestling from becoming too brutish. It amazes me how difficult it is to become aggressive when such beautiful music is being played!

The Feast

A feast is held at some time during the day. It is made possible by all the athletes' parents donating a plate of food, which of course is laid out on tables in a banqueting style. Music may be played and the Counsellor and helpers or trainers (known in Greece as the *Paidotribes*) from each city play host to the athletes. The feast may take place in the middle of the day, so that the events continue afterwards; or it may take place a little later in the afternoon, after all

the events have finished. If it comes later, this gives the Counsellors and *Paidotribes* time to compile a list of awards, without the athletes becoming restless.

Poetry Reading

In keeping with ancient tradition there may be an offering of poetry, composed and read by the athletes. They are encouraged to speak with a strong, clear yet musical voice. This is one of the most demanding of all the Olympic events and often produces very moving and beautiful works.

Closing Ceremony

The medals are ceremoniously given to the athletes. They are called by name and city and their outstanding quality is announced for all to hear. The *Paidotribes* and Counsellors award the medal. If it is a large gathering you may wish to divide the athletes into their separate cities – although around a central point such as the flame – and conduct the giving of the medals separately.

A verse is read, vowing the cities' friendship. (In Ancient Greece at the time of the Olympics a truce would be called between warring cities.) A story may be told: for instance, in Greece, when an Olympic winner returned home, his father would hammer a new doorway out of the wall, through which the athlete entered his house; after this it would be bricked up again so that no-one could step over the same threshold again.

Children at this age are naturally upright and graceful. Activities such as throwing the javelin and discus, running and long jump, make use of the athletes' present abilities; they can have the sense that now, for the first time, they are competing as individuals, that they are striving for beauty and excellence of movement, as well as physical prowess.

Coaching the athletes can draw upon the qualities of the four elements: earth (using weight and gravity), air (levity, flight and uprightness), water (grace and powerfully flowing movements), and fire (speed, effort, explosiveness) to help them improve and deepen their movements. For instance, I might say to Joe, 'A bit more fire in your run to the long jump would help you jump further' or 'Lovely air-element, Sarah!' when she throws the javelin in a beautiful arc.

Children at this age seem to have a natural relationship to this kind of guidance. The whole preparation, and then the actual day of the Olympics, is a part of their lives that they long remember and cherish. It forms a strong basis that can sustain and harmonise both their subsequent sporting activities and their approach to life itself.

The five Greek exercises prepare children for the 'sixth' exercise – that of the game and its modern expression, sport. They experience an archetypal way of moving and being, which can later help guide them in the difficult years of adolescence that lie ahead. The ability to be able to perceive and appreciate such qualities as truth, beauty and strength, and their shadow – untruth, ugliness and weakness of intent – will later metamorphose into an ability to make morally guided judgments in the teenage years and beyond. It is truly a Golden Age!

Chapter Six
Age 11–12
Twilight and Dawn

At around the age of 11–12, children frequently enter a brief golden age of balance and harmony – within themselves and also with those around them.

As childhood begins to fade, the first dawning light of adolescence rises on the horizon; but for a while yet, the scales are equally balanced. Often at this age one can notice children developing a sense of justice and fairness – of democracy with one another. Whereas adults may previously often have been needed to intervene in a difficult group-situation, the children now become more capable of sorting things out themselves. A feeling of fellowship often develops between classmates; the bonds and friendships they form at this nodal point – tinged with a dawning individuality of emotion, yet still embedded in the group-consciousness of the child – often remain important to them for many years to come.

By now children will have come fully into their bodies, but are not yet subject to the strong pull of gravity of adolescence. They inhabit the body in a harmonious, integrated way. It is worth savouring this moment. The pressures to 'grow up' are strong, but children at this age will actually feel relieved if their parents and teachers help and encourage them to stay children a little longer.

Over the years I've developed many games to meet the needs of the 11–12 year old. These are universally popular in whichever country they have been introduced. Children who have already received over-formalised sports coaching respond particularly well, often visibly relaxing and enjoying the game.

183. Clay Pigeons

Divide the children into two teams: the hunters and the pigeons. The hunters have the ball. They stand behind the line and try to hit the pigeons as many times as possible.

The pigeons take it in turns to run along the wall, touching the far end before returning and tipping the next pigeon. While running they try to dodge the hunter's ball. They must keep going forward, and are not allowed to stand still.

If the hunters hit a pigeon, they get one point.

PLAY AREA: This game needs to be played near a wall, against which the ball can be bounced – draw a line on the ground about 8–10 paces from the wall

EQUIPMENT: A practice volleyball/punctured tennis ball

When all the pigeons have had a turn to run, then the teams swap over (the hunters become the pigeons, and the pigeons become the hunters). The team with the most points wins.

pigeons

hunters

184. Running the Gauntlet
A variation of Clay Pigeons

Divide the children into two teams (nations, or armies). Team A stand scattered across the play area (battlefield) between the two lines.

Team B line up along one of the lines, the first player holding the gauntlet in her hand. She is given the ball, and starts the game by throwing it anywhere in the field that she wishes. She then runs across the battlefield, to touch the opposite wall and return, while at the same time dodging the ball, which Team A are trying to hit her with.

Runners are not allowed to move backwards or stop still at any time. When player one returns to the home wall, she gives the gauntlet to the next member of Team B, and stands at the end of the line. Team A use the ball to try to hit the players of Team B as many times as possible. The members of Team A are not allowed to run with the ball but they are allowed to pass it among themselves.

Team A can hit the player 'running the gauntlet' as many times as they wish (or can!) – but they are not allowed to obstruct her path. Team A's hits are accumulated and remembered while each member of Team B takes a turn to 'run the gauntlet'.

When all the players of Team B have had a turn at running, the score is noted down, and Team B change places with Team A. The team with the highest number of hits wins.

Variations:

- Each player can decide whether she will run back immediately after touching the opposite wall, or wait. If she waits, she can only run once the ball has been thrown by the next player on Team B. (This is different from the game above, where only the first player throws the ball.)

  Or she can wait until the next, or the next etc. player throws the ball. (But she has to run when the last player throws the ball.)

  The players get one point if they run to the opposite wall, wait, and then to the home wall without getting hit; or two points if they manage

> **PLAY AREA:** Draw two lines at either end of the play area of about 30 x 25 paces for 20 players, or else use a confined space, e.g. a gymnasium or a hall, or a fenced-off tennis court
>
> **EQUIPMENT:** One practice volleyball or foam playball (or a punctured tennis ball if desperate); one glove, or beanbag, or coloured cloth (the gauntlet)

to return without resting at the opposite wall. If a player is hit, she must return to the back of the line along the home wall.

- Instead of a gauntlet you may give the runner a 'sword' made of foam (a 2 feet, or 60cm, length of foam pipe-insulation, or a cloth with a loose knot tied in the end.) The runner may now try to hit any of the throwing team with the sword, but she is not allowed to run backwards. Any of the throwing team hit by the sword arc out and must leave the battlefield, only rejoining when it is their turn to run the gauntlet.

Around the age of 12, most children begin demanding precision – both of themselves and of others. In *Running the Gauntlet*, the players have to realise that they must throw in front of the runner and accurately in order to hit a moving target! When they were younger, they were not able to grasp the principle of throwing in anticipation of a moving object – but now, with their increasing ability for geometry, they can do this. Similarly in *Coupe* (game 213) they are putting into practice the intersection of lines in a geometrical way.

Running the Gauntlet has a David and Goliath aspect: a small, solitary individual facing a daunting and strong adversary. To do this requires courage. This is a wonderful game to play with groups that are involved with bullying – the bully will experience what it is like to be a victim when she runs through the 'battlefield' alone and defenceless under attack from a group of others. Running the Gauntlet is one of the most popular games that I play with 11–12 year olds; it releases many helpful social impulses, in spite of its bloodthirsty appearance.

185. Space Ball
As developed by Jaimen McMillan

This is another of the most popular games that I use. Although the instructions for playing it seem rather complicated when read, *Space Ball* is a game that uses many of the rules of modern ball sports. So persist – you will be well rewarded! Be aware, though, that to referee this game requires your full attention, as the game moves very quickly, and disputes can easily arise.

Divide the group into two teams. The aim of the game is to throw the ball ten times uninterrupted between team members.

The referee counts the successful throws, starting at one again every time the throws are interrupted, or the ball dropped. Each time this happens, the ball is handed over to the opposition team.

Some rules:

- No running with the ball.
- When a player has the ball, she can pivot round, using one foot as an anchor.
- Space rule: No physical contact with the other players. Players should keep at arm's length away from the others, or at double arm's length. (Decide on this before beginning the game.) A player can prove that someone is 'in her space' in the following way. If Joan of Team A has the ball, and can touch Alex of Team B while holding the ball in two hands and not moving her feet, Team A gets an extra point.
- A penalty point can be awarded if any physical contact occurs.
- Deliberate bounce passing is allowed.
- All passes must be more than a double arm's length.
- Pass back rule: A player cannot pass back to the person who threw to her.
- If a throw is deflected, but is caught without it dropping to the ground, play continues. (See optional rules.)

Equipment: One volleyball

- A 'space foul' can be committed if an opposition player intrudes on another by cutting across her space (two arm lengths) in order to intercept the ball.
- The ball is awarded to the opposite team when:
  - it is dropped
  - it is knocked to the ground
  - it is caught by a member of the opposite team

Optional rules:

- Boys can only throw to girls, girls only to boys.
- 'Hot potato' rule: Players can only hold the ball for a maximum of three seconds.
- If a player of the defending team catches a deflected ball, the defending team 'inherits' the other team's total, which is called 'capturing the points'. For instance, Team A has six counts, but on the seventh throw the ball is deflected and caught by Jamal of Team B. Jamal now throws the ball to another person from Team B, and this is Team B's count of seven. Team A will have to start at one again, unless they can catch a deflected throw.

You may find that students playing *Space Ball* tend to bunch up rather than spreading out over the whole playing area. To work with this, you can award double or triple points for a long pass; or divide the area into sections, and indicate who from each team must remain within these areas.

186. Hoop Ball

Each team is designated two hoops. Two players from Team A and two from Team B each stand in a hoop. Follow the rules as for *Space Ball* – but to score a full ten points, the teams have to throw at least two successful passes to their respective team-mates in the hoops during the ten passes. The two members of either team standing in a hoop can pass to one another if they wish.

Variations:

- The four players in the hoops are 'neutral', but in order to score ten, each hoop player must catch the ball.

> **EQUIPMENT:** Four hoops

187. Bench Ball

Each team is designated a bench. One player from each team stands on their team's bench. The other players must try to throw the ball to the bench person – if successful, then the team gets a point. Each team tries to prevent the ball reaching the bench person of the opposite team.

If the bench person falls off the bench when catching the ball, no point is awarded. When a point is awarded, the other team is given the ball. The team with the most points wins.

Adapt the rules from *Space Ball* freely to suit this game – for instance, no physical contact, the other team is awarded the ball if it is dropped, etc.

Bench Ball specifically prepares the children for playing basketball. In this game, however, instead of throwing the ball into the basket, the players throw it to their bench-player. When the player who wishes to shoot sees a defending player in front of the bench, the only way to score is to throw the ball in an arc over the defending player's head. The only

> **PLAY AREA:** Two benches are set one at either end of the hall or playground
> **EQUIPMENT:** Two benches and a play ball

way a defending player can prevent the opposite team scoring is by jumping up and intercepting the ball – since the player on the bench is so much higher.

When the children begin to get used to playing this, you will find that they inevitably place taller players on the bench and also use them for guarding the opposite team's bench. This means that the smaller players have more playing time with the ball; which, if you launch straight into basketball would never happen; the taller players would tend to dominate the game. I try, as far as possible, to let the children discover their own strategies for winning (e.g. to put a tall player on the bench) – it gives them satisfaction and confidence in their own abilities.

188. Mat Ball

Follow the rules and layout for *Bench Ball*, except now the players representing the 'baskets' stand on crash-mats instead of benches.

> **EQUIPMENT:** Two crash-mats – placed at either end of the play area

189. Hot Ball
Related by Rob Sim

Follow the rules for *Space Ball*. However, to score, the ball has to be 'hot'. A player can make the ball 'hot' for her team by catching it with two hands, while she has one foot flat against the wall.

Once the ball is made 'hot' by a team, this team can try and score. To score in this game, the 'hot' ball must be bounced onto a mat, and then caught by another member of the same team. As soon as a 'hot' ball is intercepted, caught or touched by the opposite team, it is no longer 'hot', and must be made 'hot' again.

No one is allowed to touch the mats. Once a point is scored, the ball is given to the other team, who must try and make it 'hot' before scoring.

When teaching games, it is often difficult to prevent the players forming a cluster around the ball. Hot Ball is a version of *Space Ball* which encourages players to spread themselves across the play area.

PLAY AREA: 4 floor-mats/blankets/square marked areas – 3 x 6 paces

EQUIPMENT: A ball that can bounce well on the mats – e.g. a volleyball

190. Wall Ball

In *Wall Ball*, points are awarded to the team which touches the ball against their wall. Adapt the basic rules of *Space Ball* to suit this game.

Begin with the two teams standing on the side of the play area. Number each player (for this example, I will assume eight children in each team).

Place the ball on the floor in the centre of the play area. Call out four numbers, e.g. 1, 3, 5, 7! Players 1, 3, 5 and 7 from each team run first to their wall, and touch it, and then to the ball which I roll first to one side, then to another, so that the players do not collide in an attempt to be the first to reach it. From then on the usual rules of *Space Ball* apply – but now, to score a point, a player must stand with two feet on the ground, both hands on the ball, and touch the ball against their wall.

When a point is scored, the players return to their team, and the leader places the ball in the centre of the area, and calls another four numbers.

Variations:

• Calling out numbers is just one way of limiting the number of players on the court, which is particularly useful when a group is learning to play such a game, and it helps weaker players to participate. However, there are many other ways of doing this – invent your own!

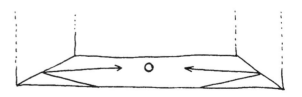

191. Target Ball

Target Ball, another variation of *Space Ball*, is also a preparatory game for basketball. It encourages all children to try to shoot at the basket, and dribbling can be introduced. To encourage the players to include weaker members of their teams, I have a rule that, for instance, Johnny on Team A, and Gemma on Team B are 'doublers' – if they score anything, their points are doubled. However, only a doubler can mark a doubler (otherwise poor Johnny will be swamped by the hefty and/or agile opposition!).

Follow the rules for *Space Ball*, but the throws and catches are not counted up. Instead, the scoring depends on how accurately the teams shoot at the basketball ring:

- one point for hitting the back board
- two points for hitting the black square
- three points for hitting the ring
- four points for making a basket

Allow the players to bounce the ball three times (basketball dribbling). As long as the ball is within the player's own space, no intercepting is allowed.

PLAY AREA: A basketball court – alternatively, anywhere where there are two basketball hoops and backboards

EQUIPMENT: A practice volleyball – when the children are stronger, you can introduce a real basketball

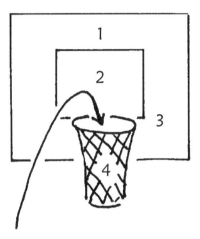

At this age I choose teams to prevent exclusion and favouritism. *Space Ball* is a useful game for 12 year olds; they no longer want to play nursery games, nor are they old enough for conventional sports. At this time, competitive sports are premature; the 12 year old has not developed enough as an individual to be able to handle the stresses involved. *Space Ball* is an intermediate team game which draws on and develops the children's present physical abilities and spatial awareness. This game (and its variations) will prepare them for other sports.

Year after year I have been astounded at the flowering of unblemished physical beauty in children of this age. The heaviness and self-consciousness of

puberty have, for the most part, not arrived; yet the children are now strong enough to run, jump and throw. Also, boys and girls are still able to compete equally.

At this age it is particularly important to instil a sense of beauty in the students: beauty of spirit as well as body. They want, of course, to measure their physical abilities; but if encouraged, will also come to realise and appreciate the importance of inner qualities. This is why, at this age, I have encouraged an 'Olympic Day' at the schools where I have taught, modelled on the Ancient Greek games.

I also invite other groups of children from neighbouring schools to come and participate.

192. Storm the Castle

Once there were two kingdoms, side by side, separated only by a fast-flowing river. Both kingdoms had powerful and rich rulers, who governed their people from the stronghold of their castles. Now for many years these two kingdoms had been at war with each other – as both kings were greedy and wished to rule both kingdoms as one.

Day after day the soldiers would face each other over the fast flowing river – and occasionally the braver of the soldiers would show their courage by venturing over it and into enemy territory, in an attempt to storm the castle and capture the enemy's flag. Sometimes they would be made prisoner by the enemy, and thrown into the prison; but at other times they managed to break through the enemy's ranks and – with the help of their fellow soldiers who distracted the enemy forces – would storm the castle, and capture the flag. But alas, on the journey back through the enemy's land, they rarely failed to escape the enemy – then the flag was returned and the brave soldiers were sentenced to prison. But sometimes the most courageous and swift of the soldiers would manage to get back across the river without the enemy noticing – and then the enemy kingdom was conquered!

- Divide the players into two teams: The Blue Army and the Orange Army for example.

- One or two soldiers from each team are the guards, and stand in front of their team's castle, protecting the flag from attack. No more than two guards are allowed.

- The rest of the army line up on their side of the river (the centre line), facing the enemy.

- Any soldier can venture over the river – or the enemy can try to drag her over the water by issuing a challenge to join hands and have a human 'tug of war'. If they succeed, then they send her to prison.

- Any player pulled over or tagged must immediately place her hands on her head while crossing the battlefield, so as to be identified as already caught.

> **PLAY AREA:** About the size of a small soccer pitch for 30–35 players; this game works best on a large field – you can mark out the areas with rope
>
> **EQUIPMENT:** Two hoops; two 'flags' – in different colours; bibs/vests or sashes to distinguish the teams

- If more than one soldier is made prisoner, they start to form a chain from the prison towards their home kingdom, with the first prisoner closest to home, and the most recently captured prisoner closest to the prison.

- A soldier can only be freed from prison when a member of her own army manages to get across the river and into enemy territory without being tagged, takes the imprisoned soldier by the hand and runs back to her own side.

- If they are caught then both become prisoners and go to the back of the chain.

- A team may appoint only one prison guard. This guard can only attempt to recapture a prisoner by starting from the sentry box – which is a hoop ten paces away from the prison. This gives the prisoners a fair chance to escape.

- Any number of soldiers can enter enemy territory at any time.

- Once inside the enemy's castle a soldier may stay there for as long as she likes and is safe from being tagged; but once she leaves the castle and tries to make a run back to her own castle, she is not allowed to return to the enemy's castle to avoid being tagged.

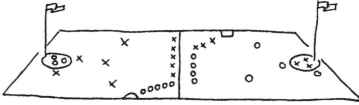

- Any number of soldiers are allowed in the enemy's castle at one time. In fact this is a good tactic because the castle guard is then unsure who will try to make a break for freedom.

- The runner who has the flag may not try to conceal it as she tries to run back to her own castle.

- If she succeeds in carrying the flag back, the opposing players who may have been successful in getting into her castle, may not run out and tag her as she approaches. If this were to happen the game would seldom come to a conclusion.

- Opposing players who are giving chase to the flag carrier may invade the opposition's side, but then have the power only to tag the flag carrier, not any of the opposition soldiers.

- The opposition soldiers may tag any invading attacker who has come over the river in pursuit of the flag carrier, hence protecting the flag carrier and helping her to get back to her own castle.

The aim is to capture the flag by storming the castle, and to take the flag back safely to one's own kingdom. The army who manages this first, wins. When the children are 11 and turning 12, they are ready for games in which two teams face each other. The players are strong enough in themselves to face the enemy, and will enjoy this new way of playing. It is also good at this age to introduce games which require more 'formation'.

193. Skittle Prisoner

This a major variation which can be adapted from any of the volleyball games such as *Newcombe* (game 139), and *Air Raid* (game 191).

For example, you may play a game with the rules identical to those in *Newcombe*); but each player places a skittle on the ground. If her skittle is hit by a ball or knocked over by one of her teammates, she is out. This involves not only catching the ball but also being aware of where you are treading.

I developed this game when I visited an inner city school, which only had a ball and a long rope (and a lot of social problems!). When I visited again two years later, *Volley Prisoner* was played passionately by the 10, 11, 12 and 13 year olds, in every available space. In fact, the children had invented the 'revenge' rule (Variation nine). The school still had no sports equipment; but I suspect the social problems had been helped in a small way!

In most games the children with less ability are isolated, or go out: this is when you see 'practical' Darwinism in the worst sense. This is not healthy or helpful for either the skilled or the less skilled players – it gives both groups an antisocial experience. Including less skilled players in a team does not

mean that one does not strive for excellence – each individual in the team should still strive to play to the best of her own ability; no-one needs to feel inhibited.

In the game described above, the best players almost invariably go out first – the ball is often thrown not towards, but away from them. The less skilled and less involved players tend to spend the most time on the court, often being left to defend the team's honour! If they succeed in saving the game by winning a prisoner, this prisoner is usually one of the stronger players – and they'll get a real cheer for this. If they don't succeed, then the game ends, and everyone gets to be back on the court for the beginning of a new game.

However, the less able players have had a lot of practice (something they don't usually get in many games) and have tried with all their strength to protect their team. I have seldom heard anything but unaccustomed praise for the less able at the end of this game.

194. Double Trouble

You can mark out the play area with a long rope, or with anything handy – clothing or whatever. If you don't have a net, a rope strung between two poles (or trees, drain-pipes etc.) can be used.

Level One – Divide the group into two teams. Team A starts with the ball. A player throws it over the net and wins a point if the other team lets it fall to the ground. Then Team B throw the ball, and the same scoring applies. However, the ball must not go out of the lines, or into the net. If this happens, then the opposite team (i.e. the team that was to receive the ball) is awarded a point. Any member of either team can throw or catch the ball – but players must not pass the ball to one another. Players are not allowed to move from where they caught the ball. Play continues until one team reaches 20.

Level Two – Introduce a second ball: so that at any one time there are two balls being thrown or caught. This speeds the game up considerably!

Hints to the leader:

- You will have to exercise your perfect peripheral vision to keep score in this game when two balls are being used! (I usually stand at the net and listen carefully for the ball hitting the floor.)

PLAY AREA: Net and lines as for a volleyball court: 18 x 9 paces

EQUIPMENT: Two practice volleyballs or soft foam balls

Not only does this game provide the children with a fun way to practise throwing and catching; it also requires quick footwork. When the ball is approaching, the feet have to move quickly in response. This is another game that is preparatory for sports such as netball and basketball, and yet does not 'overshoot' into premature competitive sport.

195. Over the Garden Wall

Follow the rules for *Double Trouble* but this time you begin the game with every player holding a ball. On the signal to start, the players throw the balls over the net onto the other side of the court. In this case it does not matter if they go in or out, as long as the players get them over.

The player who has just thrown their ball then retrieves another ball and throws it over. Meanwhile the other team will have done the same thing. This is repeated over and over again. The teams try to clear their court of as many balls as possible by throwing them back over

PLAY AREA: Volleyball court, 18 x 9m

EQUIPMENT: Volleyball net; many play balls and volleyballs – at least one each

on to the other team's court. No-one may hold a ball for more than three seconds (hot-potato rule).

At the end of a set period of time, perhaps two minutes, the leader calls '**Stop!**' No more balls may be thrown. The leader then counts the number of balls on each side. The team with the fewest balls on its side wins.

196. Volley Prisoner

Play this game using a net and court lines as for volleyball. Somewhere in the centre of each side of the net (depending on how far the weakest child in the group can throw the ball to get it over the net) make a chalk cross to mark the place the children must serve from. If you're playing outdoors, you can use a rope to form the lines.

Divide the players into two teams. Player one from Team A throws the ball from the serving place. Before the ball goes over the net, she calls the name of one of the players on Team B, in a loud voice.

If the ball is caught by any member of Team B, she throws it back and calls the name of one of the players of Team A. Continue in this way until the ball is either:
– dropped by a member of the catching team. If this happens, the named player is out, not the player who drops the ball. The named player becomes a 'prisoner' and stands to the side of the court (see illustration for where the prisoners stand).
– the ball is thrown into the net or outside the boundary lines. If this happens, the thrower becomes a prisoner and stands on the side of the court.

It is important that the prisoners stand (or sit) in a line, so that it is clear who became a prisoner first. (The prisoner who has been in her team's prison longest is always the first to be released.) In order to release prisoner one from Team B (i.e. the first prisoner in Team B's prisoner line, her team must throw the ball over the net and call loudly 'Prisoner!' (instead of the name of one of Team A's players). If the ball is dropped or hits the ground inside the boundary lines then the prisoner first in line can re-enter the game.

If a prisoner is released and re-enters the game, her name may not immediately be called until another of her team has become a 'prisoner'. This is to prevent one player spending all her time as a prisoner.

A team may not call 'prisoner' twice in a row in a rally. In other words the children must alternate their calls between naming a player on the other side and calling 'prisoner'. If they do call 'prisoner' twice, the player who called out the second 'prisoner' is out and herself becomes a prisoner. This is an important rule as it helps bring about a resolution in the game, and makes it more exciting. The game is won by either:
- making all the opposing team go to prison.
- setting a time limit after which the leader counts

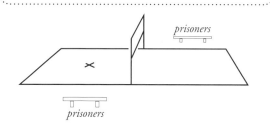

EQUIPMENT: A volleyball

prisoners

prisoners

up prisoners. Whichever team has captured the most prisoners wins.

Variations:
• Allow two passes amongst team members each time the ball comes over to their side.
• The ball must be 'set' over the net in volleyball style. This is best done by allowing two passes. The receiver of the second pass throws the ball high in the air so that a teammate can 'set' or 'volley' the ball over the net.
• The ball may be 'dug' by any player – especially when a ball is first received from the opposing team: i.e. one player digs, next player catches and throws, third player sets over the net.
• You may even allow a bounce dig. This is good as it takes away the danger of hurting arms.
• A player can 'catch-set'.
• The teams have a row of players near the net who catch-set, and a back row who catch-dig.
• Have a 'hot-potato' rule – no player can hold the ball for more than three seconds at any time.
• Instead of calling names, a score is kept. (This is a more advanced version of this game.)
• The 'revenge' rule: if a player has just become a prisoner, before she leaves the court she is allowed one more throw from the serving line. If she succeeds in getting someone out on the other side then she may stay on court. If she does not then she must leave the court and become a prisoner.
• If only two players are left on a team, they can release one of their prisoners by catching the ball successfully three times.
• As fewer and fewer players are left on the court, you can 'shrink' the area of play.

197. Blind Prisoner

This is also a very fast game – children receive some fitness training by engaging in it, and it also requires very quick thinking. It gives expression to the children's increasing capacity for sharpened thinking and reflexes, which becomes noticeable at this age.

Divide the children into two teams. Follow the rules for *Volley Prisoner*. The difference is that the children now have to remember who is left on the other team, for the screen prevents them seeing. Make sure that the children who are prisoners are not visible to the opposing team. (They can sit at the back line of the court.)

Two rules which you can use at your own discretion:

- Players are not allowed to pass the ball to another person in their own team once they have caught a throw.

> **PLAY AREA:** A volleyball court with net – either use crash-mats leaning against the net, or blankets pinned to the net, so that the teams cannot see each other; make sure blankets touch the ground, to prevent the teams peeking underneath!
>
> **EQUIPMENT:** A volleyball; crash-mats or blankets and pins

- Players are not allowed to try to disguise their voices.

198. Air Raid
As related by Rob Sim

This is a variation of *Blind Prisoner* – so use the same equipment. However a cloth-covered ball is especially good as it cannot be heard when it hits the ground.

Follow the rules for *Blind Prisoner*, except no names are called out. The teams thus wait in silence for the 'air raid'. I use this metaphor to describe how a person goes out: when a 'bomb' (the ball) hits the ground, it explodes and kills the nearest person (who then sits out for the rest of the game). No player may dive out of the way of an incoming bomb; she must try to catch it. The game ends when one team has no more players left on the court.

These two games never fail to appeal to children. They seem to love playing 'blind'. This is an awakening game for 12 year olds: the dreamy children will probably have a struggle to catch the ball successfully, but the effort of trying not to dream will help them. *Air Raid* is characterised by outer stillness (the

children will not be running around very much) and by inner activity (each person on the team has to be awake and concentrating – otherwise they will not be able to catch the 'bomb'!). Quick reflex action is a help, but not usually enough – the children must be really present and attentive. I suppose this game could be described as a type of human computer game with its unpredictable 'bombs'; but instead of using finger reflexes only, *Air Raid* requires a more holistic state of awareness and wakefulness – the players have to be ready with their whole body to move and catch the ball. They also have to be inwardly ready to respond to something they are not able to see in advance. They do not know how or when the bomb will appear. In a sense this is a picture of how they are feeling: at 12 they are on the threshold of puberty. They know change is coming, but they have no clear picture of what this will be like, or when it will come.

You will be well rewarded if you persevere with the following game, *Go Tag*. In spite of its apparent complication on paper, it is actually a very simple game, and passes the 'acid test' with flying colours (which for me is whether the children want to play it for hours). Basically, the game involves one team trying to cross from one side of the play area to the other without getting tagged by the other team's members.

199. Go Tag
As related by Martin Baker

Draw a line across the centre of the play area, and one either side of this line, about three paces away from the centre.

Divide the players into two teams – Team A (the running team) and Team B (the chasing team). Team A line up on the far end of the play area. Team B line up along the centre line, the first player facing Team A, the second player with her back to Team A, the third facing, etc. so that each player faces alternate directions.

The leader starts the game by walking on the far side of Team B, and touches a player on the shoulder who is facing Team A. This player is the first tagger.

The first tagger tries to catch players from Team A, who run around the side of the line formed by Team B, to the opposite court (Court C), while trying to avoid getting caught.

Team A are safe from the chaser once they're in Court C. Once they reach Court C, they run back to Court D, trying not to get tagged.

The tagger is not allowed to cross the centre line. So when a tagger (Amy) facing Court D has chased all of Team A into Court C, she then touches the back of another player of Team B (who is facing Court C). This player now runs forward to try and tag Team A. Amy takes this new tagger's place along the centre line, this time facing Court C. When a player is tagged, she must sit out.

A running player who crosses the middle line safely must run at least five paces away from the middle line before she can again cross back to the other side. You may wish to mark this line with chalk. Otherwise a player could simply hop from one side to the other and never get caught.

Another rule that will prevent hopping backward

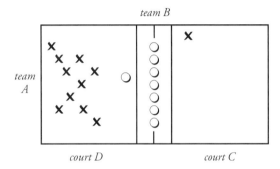

PLAY AREA: 25 x 20 paces for 25 players

team B

team A

court D   *court C*

and forward is that if you run around one side of the line to escape, you must go to the other side the next time you swap sides.

When all the running team's players are out, the teams swap over (in our example, Team A will now line up alternately along the centre line).

To make this game even more exciting, you can time how long it takes each team to tag all the players of the running team.

This is a game that requires a clear formation: a team are only likely to succeed if they keep a good formation and applies thought or strategy. I will sometimes send the teams off to plan their strategy – and I am always surprised how involved they get in discussing tactics. The conversation may begin with some simple remark like 'Well, I think we should all run as fast as we can!', which will lead to more complicated planning. Also, this provides an opportunity for Annie to complain 'I never get the chance to tag!' – and the others may well give her more turns.

200. Bird in a Cage

One person starts off as the bird. She stands in the centre of the circle. The other players form the circle, by standing and holding their staves upright, resting their fingers lightly on the top of the staff. They should stand so that there is about one foot (30cm) between each staff. The staves form the bird's cage.

At a signal, each person moves to the next staff without letting it fall. If a staff falls, the bird tries to escape by trying to touch the fallen staff. If she succeeds, then the person who failed to catch the staff becomes the new bird, and the old bird takes her place.

Equipment: Wooden staves – one for each player

Variations:

- You have to miss out one staff and catch the next one.

- If someone fails to catch a staff successfully, and the bird escapes, the person who left the staff behind her is the next bird, not the person who dropped it.

201. Paper Boats

The aim of the game is to throw the balls at the bigger ball, hitting it and knocking it over the opposing side's line.

Place the heavy ball, the 'boat', in the middle of the playing area, the 'pond'. Divide up the players into two teams.

Each team takes six to eight paces back from the boat. They are now standing on the edge of the pond. Draw a chalk line at the edge of the pond for each team. Draw another across the middle of the pond. Give each player a ball, the 'stone'. On the call '**Paper boats!**', the players throw their stone and try to hit the boat and knock it to the edge of the opposing team's side of the pond (the line). They may retrieve

Equipment: One playball per player; one big heavy ball – a lightweight medicine ball is ideal, or a semi-deflated basketball will do

any ball on their side of the pond and try over and over again to hit the boat over to the other side.

No player can step over the line marking the edge of the pond to throw their ball. A player may go into the pond on her team's side to retrieve a stone that is stuck. But she must then return to the edge to throw it. No player may touch the boat with her hand to prevent it crossing the line. The game is over when the boat touches the line marking the edge of either team's pond.

202. Waking and Sleeping

The object of the game is to try to steal the opposite team's power by removing all their dreams (play balls) without getting tagged; or by imprisoning (sending into a nightmare) all their players. Divide the group into two teams. They stand on their respective beds (the floor mats) at either end of the field (play area).

The basic rule of the game is: whoever runs into the field later than the opponent has the right to tag because she has had more sleep and is therefore more powerful. Players are safe when they are on their own 'beds'. The game begins when the leader calls out '**Wake up!**'. Players leave the bed and try to steal the dreams of the other team or act as bait to the opposing players, who have had more sleep.

However, when leaving the bed, players must watch to see who has more power than themselves – so that they can return to the bed if chased.

If Player A is tagged by Player B with more power, she is sent to Team A's nightmare (on the side of the field, near Team B's bed: see picture). When another player from Team A is tagged, she forms a chain by holding hands with Player A, at the back of the line. This chain is called the 'Nightmare'.

A player may free her 'nightmared' teammates one at a time by tagging the player nearest to the field end of the chain, and then returning to the bed before setting out to free another. When a prisoner has been freed, she must return to her team's bed straight away, and cannot be tagged until she leaves the bed again.

When a dream has been taken, it is carried to the victorious team's bed. The game ends when all three of the opposite team's dreams have been captured.

Variations:

• If four, or a designated number of prisoners are caught and a fifth one tagged, the game is lost, and the other team has won.

> **PLAY AREA:** *35 x 25 paces (a small basketball court)*
> **EQUIPMENT:** Two floor mats (the beds); 6 playing balls (the dreams)

This game has the potential either to be well-formed or to erupt into chaos, which reflects the inner potential of the 12 year old. It also requires a balanced sense of self-sacrifice. Children have to learn to be able to sometimes compromise their own wishes, to accommodate those of others. If they don't, both they and the group will suffer. In this game, the players have to find a balance between going too far out of themselves, and remaining too far in. It is very healthy to achieve this harmony before puberty sets in. At this age there is a last burst of childhood before the weight of adolescence begins in earnest.

Many things happen at once in this game – and the child has to find her own place within a confusing situation. This is a reflection of what's to come: the adolescent, venturing into the world must find her own place. *Waking and Sleeping* also appeals to the children's sense of initiative – they have to move towards an aim (capturing the opposite team's dreams), but must still remain observant, noticing who can be tipped, and who can tip them! As in previous games, neither the overcautious child nor the overconfident child will be very successful. This encourages children either to harness or activate their will themselves, depending on what they most need.

Being able to return to the bed allows the child a chance to 'breathe', and to reorientate herself before rushing forward again.

prison/nightmare

prison/nightmare

203. Strategy Tag

The group line up, shoulder to shoulder, with every other player facing the opposite direction. There are two runners, one is 'it' the other is 'not it'. 'It' runs after 'not it'; both can use the players in the line as 'doors' by gently tapping on a player's back – however the player whose back is tapped is now the new 'it' or 'not it' depending on which runner did the tapping.

Hints to the leader:

- It's a really fun, fast game. The game leader may choose to establish smaller/larger boundaries depending on the needs of the group.
- Include a rule that you may not pick the same 'door' player more than a certain number of times to make sure that everyone is included.

AGE RANGE: 12+

PLAY AREA: Indoor or outdoor, 20 x 20 paces

NUMBER OF PLAYERS: 10+

EQUIPMENT: None

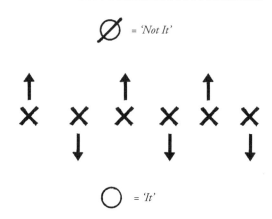

Either player can 'tap out' the line of Xs to take their role.

204. Lord of the Rings (aka Steal the Fire)

Two teams: Orcs and Elves

Players are attempting to steal the frisbees by running into the other team's base and taking the frisbees and running them back to their side of the field. This can also be played by throwing the frisbee back onto your own side of the field. One of your own team members must catch the frisbee. Once a frisbee is caught or brought back to the other side of the field, the frisbees are lined up along the centre line at a designated spot. If you are caught by an opposing team's player (tagged/use flag belts) you must sit down and wait to be rescued by a member of your own team. To be rescued, a player from your own team will come and take you by the hand. Players must hold hands until reaching their side of the field. Once all three frisbees are lined up on one team's side of the field, that team wins the round. Players can then switch sides, reset the field, and start a new round.

Variations:

- Additional rules can be added to increase the action:
  1. Players may only be safe in the frisbee zone on the opposite side for 30 seconds, then they must make a move or run back to their side to reset and try again.
  2. When rescuing a teammate, both players have to run all the way back to their own back line before the rescue is complete, not just back across the centre line.

Hints to the leader:

- Emphasise the rule that when a frisbee hits the ground, it is the offensive team (the stealers) that is responsible for putting it back, not the defensive team.

- Remind players that the signal to not be tagged is placing a hand on your head. When putting a frisbee back into the frisbee zone after a failed rescue, the player from the offensive team places a hand on their head while putting the frisbee back and keeps their hand on their head until they are safely back on their own side.

Age range: 11–13

Play area: Outdoor, large rectangular field area, 20 x 40 paces

Number of players: 10+

Equipment: 6 frisbees (3 of one colour, 3 of another); pinnies for two teams; cones to mark boundaries

For children who may struggle to play this game:

- Players who are afraid to catch the frisbee may benefit from skill-building time playing catch with a partner outside of the pressure of a game. Rather than the standard frisbee, a soft disc may work better. Encourage them to catch with two hands, one palm above and one palm below the disc, in a vertical clapping motion (pancake catch).

Elves   *Orcs*

Chapter Seven
Age 12–13 and upwards

Around the twelfth year children build on an inner sense of form. Their relationship to form grows into a need for 'formation' – a striving to know where their place is in the whole. A balance between the group and the individual is now explored more dynamically. If this is done in a manner that does not give way to chaos, yet encourages individual expression, the children will not only flow into the game but satisfy a deep longing that greatly assists them as they move into puberty.

Many of the games at this age use this sense of 'formation', which is expressed in the way the players position and conduct themselves in the game. It is important that the teacher or leader encourages the children's need for strong team formation, yet without sliding into over-formalised sport, where team form is used merely in order to win. If this happens, a vital developmental step will have been missed out; and while a number of the more physically capable players will, outwardly at least, seem happy, some players in the group will be dissatisfied and resist the game.

Play Versus Sport

It is understandably easy to be misled if you watch children in their free play at around 12 years old: they seem naturally drawn toward sport. But closer observation usually reveals two things – firstly, they are 'playing with sport', not 'playing the sport'. In other words they are not yet playing out of a strong sense of self-consciousness, as adults do. That is, of course, unless they have been put in sporting teams and been over-trained. This is a fundamental misunderstanding of what children need at this age.

Left to their own devices, children will often invent complex rules, imagine great crowds watching, and give a running commentary on the action taking place. The backyard may be Wembley Stadium one day, the Superdome or the Melbourne Cricket Ground the next, in a wonderful blending of the imaginative, creative play of childhood with formalised, stylised, teenage and adult sport. This is a stepping stone into adolescence that must be nurtured, not undermined by over-coaching.

Initiation

Every society has in the past had 'initiation ceremonies'. These 'rites of passage' came at important times of change, giving adolescents recognition and an outer, formalised structure. Can it be a coincidence that the increasing popularity of sport in modern Western culture has come at a time when there is a marked decline in the more formal structures that had influence over our daily lives – such as school, church and family?

Sport can of course be a positive substitute for initiation, providing many values and structures that help a young person define himself. But one vital question must be addressed. If sport is a metamorphosis of initiation, in which certain rites were performed deliberately at certain ages to give

confidence to face approaching challenges, how can it be healthy that seven or eight year olds engage in sporting activities identical to those of teenagers; and that teenagers' activities are identical with those of adults? We see lip-service paid to the needs of different age-groups – in such things as the heights of goals, size of fields and minor rule adjustments – but the basic method of playing a particular game is undeniably uniform, regardless of age.

We complain about the way children are nowadays, and the violence and social breakdown they have to face, so we send them prematurely into battle on the sports field to 'prepare them' – not recognising we may be incubating the very qualities that we fear.

We are in danger of losing any insight into what is appropriate at varying stages of development, of breeding 'adult-ified' children whose childhood has been stolen or at the very least ignored by this generation of adults; we bear a good deal of responsibility, because ours is probably the last generation to have some recollection of what it was like to be allowed the precious freedom to play – simply, unselfconsciously and creatively.

Cultivating negotiation

Each sport has a strict code of conduct, communication and negotiation. These rules and tactics often fill hundreds of pages of detailed and complex manuals. Externalisation of the inner need for convention, which these rules represent, has a very specific formative effect on the individual who is subject to them. At certain stages in life, such regulations and conditions may, though we are unaware of it, be precisely what we need to enrich or help us. Each sport has a different quality, or 'feel' to it, which may appeal to different individuals at certain times in their lives. But prior to puberty, children benefit from a much broader and more flexible set of boundaries in their play, which is, at that stage still, a more inward and creative process. The game is not yet an external event, as it becomes later in adolescence. It is still intrinsically bound up with the child's inner experience of life. The rules that govern the child's play therefore spring from within his own creativity. When he plays with others, he must learn also to take into account their creativity and need for expression. 'Space' is negotiated with the others in the game. In a game of marbles, for instance, delicate and complex negotiations are gone through before play begins. What rules, what size marbles, the value of certain special marbles and what they may be exchanged for, and so on, all have to be agreed. These arrangements often involve passionate argument and problem-solving skills; what is crucially important in this process, though, is that each child meets the other in freedom, and that the outcome is therefore unique to the players involved. In this way children learn both tolerance and the ability to speak up for what they want; they develop the capacities that they already possess as potential.

Contrast this with the external, fixed demands which formalised sport places on young children, and there can be little doubt which kind of activity will help foster healthy, balanced development.

Abdication of authority

Before children reach puberty, adults usually apply creative authority to guide their offsprings' lives. Afterwards, agreements reached through negotiation become progressively more common. The guidelines we give to meet the individual needs of our children spring from ourselves as individuals. When children get involved in formalised sport at this age, parents and teachers often say that they encourage it because it teaches them to obey authority and work as a team. While this may be superficially true, we also need to ask whose authority it is that they are learning to obey. When we involve children in formalised sport too early, we are partially abdicating our own individual creative authority. We are unconsciously communicating to them that the external, outer form of authority is of greater importance than developing an inner moral sense of right and wrong. This could not come at a more sensitive time in the child's biography. At this stage, a great deal of what will later develop into the personality of the teenager and adult is formed. If we want to raise children with an inner knowledge of what is true and just, then we must question whether pre-puberty sport will help or hinder this.

Adult transference

As adults we need to look at why we want our children to be involved so early in sport. The reasons will vary of course, but do we need to explore our own motives? Could it be that the increasing competitiveness of the adult world is leading us to seek an outlet for our frustrations through the success of our children? Are we wanting them to succeed where we have not? Do we find an external authority in sport that we ourselves are not confident to develop within schools and family life? Do we simply place children in sporting teams because that is what is expected of us by our peers? Or is it an attempt to have 'the son follow in the father's footsteps', by encouraging him to take part in the same game that we played and enjoyed at school? If any of these questions have validity then we must surely ponder whether we are projecting our own fears and aspirations onto our children.

Sport as a positive influence

This is not meant to be a rejection of sport's powerful and positive influence in teenagers' lives. Sport does provide an external form that young people at this stage also need. It offers valuable opportunity for self expression, role modelling, safe social situations; it can help form 'work ethics' through training, acceptance of external authority, and engagement in an activity with intensity and concentration.

But parents often feel excluded or powerless about the selection of which sport, and in particular which team, their son or daughter should join. The choice of the team cannot be separated from the coach who will be in charge of it. Here is a list of qualities to look for when making this choice…

A coaching checklist for parents

- Does the coach encourage fair play and a sense of sporting 'honour' and self control?

- Do they place more emphasis on winning or participation? Are they willing to select the players that give their best for the team as opposed to those who are gifted but may be selfish and unreliable?

- Are they aware of the social dynamic in the group and can they relate on a deeper level to some of the issues that they may be confronted with? Are they active in organising social as well as sporting events for the team and their friends and families?

- Are they a good role model? Your child may identify strongly with the way the coach lives. Are you comfortable with this?

- Do they over-train and over-exert the players?

- Do they take winning and losing personally and transfer their frustrations onto the players?

- Do they encourage a positive self-image of all players and affirm their strengths as well as attempting to improve their weaknesses?

- Do they give too much attention to the 'star' of the team, neglecting the others?

- Are they willing to relate to, and not exclude, the parents of the players?

Of course not all coaches are going to score 100 per cent, they are human and have strengths and weaknesses like everyone. However, they are in a powerful and responsible position, and need to be able to cultivate the qualities within themselves that they wish for their players. To 'do as I say, not as I do' is not acceptable to teenagers. This is why it is important to involve yourself in the team that your child chooses. You may then be able to identify any serious problems that arise and be active in solving them.

Children in Martial Arts
The cost

The number of children taking part in martial arts is rapidly growing. All around the world, armies of baggy, white-clad children are being dropped off at local recreation centres, to be picked up an hour or two later. Parents are unwittingly helping to prime emotional time-bombs which will explode in adolescence with shock waves that last for many years.

Martial arts have their origins in ancient times. They were developed out of deep esoteric and religious practices, involving rigorous and repetitive meditation, spiritual instruction, self-denial, and strict diets. All of this was overseen by masters, often monks who had devoted their entire existence to a spiritual path. These mystery centres were often cut off from large population areas, in monastery-type situations. However, there were three crucial aspects to such training. Firstly the students were seeking self-development through esoteric, spiritual disciplines.

Secondly their aim was to understand the subtle energy flowing within the body, and its relationship to the spiritual dimension. Thirdly, they were young adults.

Contrast this with what is happening today. Children are exposed to an increasing level of explicit violence, particularly communicated by music and the media. The nuclear family and community structures continue to break down. Children feel unsafe. Parents not only fear for their children's safety, they often feel unable to supply the necessary security and structure in which to raise their children. The child comes home from school saying that a number of kids in the class are doing martial arts and that it seems 'really cool'. The child seems enthusiastic, whereas so many other things seem to be 'boring'. The parents feel it must be better than hanging around or playing video games, so they agree to the child taking part. They feel, perhaps, that such training will be really helpful.

But let's look more closely at what is going on in modern martial arts. Martial arts, or as it is often called now, self-defence, has largely cut itself off from its cultural and spiritual dimensions, from its source of inspiration and purpose. While lip-service may be paid to this, it is seldom more than an impoverished shadow of what existed in the past. Martial art becomes a hobby, a method to keep fit, or a sport. But at the same time it focuses on the maiming of another human being. No longer does the exponent need to go through all the hardships that would both challenge and prepare him to use this knowledge and power wisely. Martial arts have been adapted to our modern consumer consciousness, our need for instant gratification. And though we buy now, we will certainly, if unknowingly, have to pay later.

There is evidence that in the past, in some martial arts schools, students were taken in at about the age of puberty. In other schools the students would not be admitted until after their teens. What is clear is that in both cases students were not given the overt martial art forms or exercises until they had reached maturity in their late teens or early twenties. There was a very special reason for this. The masters had to wait for the moment when the 'ego' appeared – the time when the adolescent became an adult. It was only then that the young adult had the faculties and the ability to understand and control the special energy and power that they were subsequently taught to develop.

Equipping children with these powers before they have the maturity to deal with them, is perhaps the most dangerous aspect of modern martial arts.

I once broke up a street fight where a young boy of eleven was very seriously assaulting a much older and larger boy. The younger boy was extremely difficult to restrain from further violence as he was badly out of control. The older boy suffered a broken jaw and nose as well as serious knee injuries. Later when I talked to the younger boy he told me he had been studying martial arts for four years. In the last year, which had been quite intense, he had gone in for competitions and done well. I asked him what had happened in this instance. He told me the older boy had been picking on one of his friends and that his friends had asked him to 'sort the guy out'. He agreed; however, in the fight, he said he 'lost it', meaning he had lost all control. He became quite upset, saying that he was really sorry, and that when he had approached the other boy he hadn't meant to hurt him so badly. In subsequent conversations with the boy it became clear that he had become withdrawn and even a little afraid, though he had become a hero of sorts amongst his friends. I was puzzled as to why he should feel reticent. His answer was that he was afraid to get angry now in case it happened again. He told me that at the time of the fight he had meant, and had had the ability, to kill the older boy.

This is an extreme example of what can happen if children are given powers they cannot control. Also, in this case and in other less dramatic ones, children studying martial arts gain a good deal of kudos from their classmates. They are seen as hard or bad figures to be handled with care. Even if the child is actually not very proficient at the skill, he will still develop an aggressive stance toward problems, and the others in the group will pick this up. Gaining status in a group through an undercurrent threat of violence is not a quality that anyone would wish for a child or a group of children. The other effect it may have is to goad other, bigger children into picking on the martial arts student in order to 'put him in his place'; they may even do this in a gang. The exponent often has an over-inflated impression of his own abilities and can be seriously at risk in these situations. The parents who sign their children up for classes in the hope they will learn how to protect themselves, are contributing to a no-win situation. Children may get themselves into trouble by overestimating their ability. It takes years of intense practice to reach the stage of being able to defend oneself properly. But if this stage is reached, then a scenario like the fight I have described may develop.

But there is another aspect. Throughout this book it has been suggested that games, sports and movement play a key role in both the physical and inner growth of the child. Movement in general has a critical task in shaping social and emotional development. Let's look, therefore, at the movements involved in martial arts, and their possible ramifications:

Firstly, consider the body position. The knees are bent, the centre of gravity is dropped. This, like all the movements involved, is continually practised and repeated. Weight and gravity are strongly cultivated. But as I have tried to show throughout this book, it is very important for children to receive a balanced spatial education. Martial arts takes little account of the five other directions in space that need equal cultivation at specific times in the child's life. In martial arts, the aspects of 'levity'* (as opposed to gravity), back-space, front-space, left and right, are either contracted or misused. In more simple terms, the martial art stance is not a natural way for children to stand. It counteracts the healthy experiences they need – of running, jumping, skipping, and all the activities that are involved in levity. An experience of gravity alone, of being 'brought down' without any counterbalance, is not at all helpful for children's development at this age. In many martial art forms, particularly in what are known as 'hard' forms, the hands and feet are used like heavy clubs ready to hit or kick, or like sharp knives prepared to chop or hack. Needless to say this is not what these finely developed parts of our bodies are designed to do, and repetitive use of the feet and hands in this way does little to cultivate sensitivity or 'gentle handling' of a situation. The voice, our most expressive tool, is used in martial arts as a guttural roar.

All these martial movements have a decided emotional as well as physical impact on the student. For example, in some martial arts it is considered highly praiseworthy to be able to punch, kick or even head-butt through an extremely hard tile held vertically by two helpers. The thicker and stronger the tile, the higher the level reached. Any normal, untrained person attempting to emulate this would be badly hurt. It is done by focusing an intense energy far beyond the obstacle – which becomes a mere trifle to be destroyed in the movement aimed beyond it. This consciousness is cultivated through repeated practice. To allow a physical barrier to interfere with your movement towards a goal, is considered a weakness. But this has significant implications in terms of human

---

* a term used to describe an upward-streaming lightness, that can be experienced as the opposite force to gravity.

relationship for the child or adolescent who does not yet have the faculties to control such a power. Take for example a situation where he is told that homework must be done by a certain date, or that he must be home at a certain time at night. If it is his aim not to be in at that time, and he has had it deeply ingrained into his psyche that he should ignore, or punch through obstacles in order to reach his goal, his reaction to parental constraints will be strongly affected. This is not intellectual theory – it has been observed by many educators and parents alike.

A similar outcome is also to be found in the deflective techniques used in many soft-form martial arts. In this case the exponent will deflect and direct the force that he receives back on to and therefore against, the source. This can be devastatingly destructive, depending on the amount of energy directed. But the emotional impact of this technique is also considerable. If, for example, parents ask their son to return home at a certain time, and he disagrees, he may well simply deflect the parents' energy – in this case their instructions – and

be home at whatever time he wishes. If this causes the adults concern or anger, which is directed at the child, he may deflect this also. The more intense and concerned his parents become, the more he will direct their frustration back at them.

Finally, in each kick, hit, or throw the student practises, he is imagining a vulnerable or sensitive part of his opponent's body. It may be a kick designed to dislocate the knee, or rupture an internal organ; it may be a hold or a throw designed to break an arm or dislocate a shoulder, it may be a punch aimed at the nose, designed to force the cartilage back into the brain. One should be in no doubt that inherent in each movement is the intent to cause harm. It is this picture that the child has before him when he practises for hour after hour. To suggest that these things have no adverse affect on children would be naive. If they feel vulnerable in a world they perceive as violent, then we their guardians must seek to reassure them and give them the warmth that will lead them back into the safety and innocence of childhood.

Children in Ballet
Strung up, strung out

Along with opera, ballet is one of our classic artistic forms. Why is this? And why is it that so many children undergo a classical ballet training?

Ballet is a highly stylised, perhaps the most stylised, of all movement forms. While an ordinary human being can kick, strike or bounce a ball, punch or wrestle, perhaps even do a roll or turn a cartwheel, there are very, very few who can move like a classical dancer. This is not surprising since it is exactly the point, the aim of ballet. The movements are designed to appear not only graceful but 'other-worldly', to lift the audience up and away from earthly existence; another, connected feature of ballet is that it is almost totally audience-centred. Of course the dancers experience feelings – particularly pain! – but they must not communicate this to the onlooker. They must appear as if the earth with all its cares and limitations does not exist. Gravity is overcome and denied. The dancer seems to draw us away into another dimension.

This denial of gravity shows itself in many ways. The most obvious is the tutu, and the costuming in general. The tutu extends out from the waist and forms a frilly band around the dancer. It draws a clear distinction between the body that shows above the waist, which is often gaudily and attractively dressed, and the lower body which is as far as possible plainly adorned in tights. The tutu emphasises the dancer's upper body, and also prevents her from seeing her own legs and feet.

The whole posture of the dancer is developed and sustained by training the muscles, particularly of the abdomen and the legs. The dancers spend painful, feet-distorting hours, learning the *en pointe* technique, in which the knuckles of the toes are forced to carry the entire body weight. This increases the illusion of weightlessness, as only a tiny surface area is in touch with the floor, reinforcing the impression of a negative attitude towards the earth – the least possible physical contact with it the better. The feet move in tiny steps that seem to float the upper body across the floor; or the dancers are thrown and leap high into the air, seeming to hover there like a bird. The gaze is directed up and away. The arm movements generally begin at the waist and move upwards, seldom dropping below the tutu. A stylistic copy of the way a child moves with ease and levity is sought and parodied.

So ballet audiences, particularly since the industrial revolution, were encouraged to leave the world behind, with all its increasing materialism and mechanisation, and be transported to higher, more graceful realms. Not to appreciate this art form was considered to be the mark of a Philistine, someone who was cut off from the more noble aspects of cultural life.

In fact, a child's movement and inner intent, particularly at play, could not be more different from the ballet dancer. Whereas the dancer undergoes hours of training to achieve a technique-based levity, the child moves with an effervescence and buoyancy that is as beautiful as it is unconscious. The classical dancer's movements are highly stylised, the child's are totally natural. The dancer draws a sharp divide between inner experience and what can be externally observed, while the child knows no such divide; the way the child moves is strongly motivated by the way he feels. Whereas the dancer deals in abstraction, the child is immersed in reality. The dancer's moves are carefully directed, the child's are spontaneous. The dancer moves for the appreciation of an audience, the child plays because it is a natural expression of life. The dancer's aim is to rise above an earthly existence, the child's energies are completely opposite – he wants to learn about the world and become a part of it.

To encourage children to take up ballet is to impose an adultified concept of beauty on those that have no need of it. If the child is repeatedly exposed to this form of training, he will eventually begin to adopt the adult values of the dancer; this is to invite emotional disturbance and to restrict the child's full experience of childhood.

The school of ballet of today, vainly striving against the natural laws of gravitation or the natural will of the individual, and working in discord in its form and movement with the form and movement of nature, produces a sterile movement which gives no birth to future movements, but dies as it is made.

The expression of the modern school of ballet, wherein each action is an end, and no movement, pose or rhythm is successive or can be made to evolve succeeding action, is an expression of degeneration, of living death. All the movements of our modern ballet school are sterile movements because they are unnatural: their purpose is to create the delusion that the law of gravitation does not exist for them.

The primary or fundamental movements of the new school of the dance must have within them the seeds from which will evolve all other movements, each in turn to give birth to others in unending sequence of still higher and greater expression, thoughts and ideas.

To those who nevertheless still enjoy the movements, for historical or choreographic or whatever other reasons, to those I answer: They see no farther than the skirts and tricots. But look – under the skirts, under the tricots are dancing deformed muscles. Look still farther – underneath the muscles are deformed bones. A deformed skeleton is dancing before you. This deformation through incorrect dress and incorrect movement is the result of the training necessary to the ballet.

The ballet condemns itself by enforcing the deformation of the beautiful woman's body! No historical, no choreographic reasons can prevail against that!

It is the mission of all art to express the highest and most beautiful ideals of man. What ideal does the ballet express?

from *The Art of Dance*, by Isadora Duncan

The Twelfth-Year Threshold

To recap then: roughly three years have passed since the child experienced the last major threshold – when he stepped out of early into middle childhood. The experiences have been rich: the ten year old discovered his individual place in the order he grew to recognise around him. The eleven year old began to harmonise with his new-found individuality, developing a sense of beauty and grace, truth, and the budding ability to express it. The twelve year old stands at the doorway of late childhood and puberty. Dramatic changes lie ahead as he gathers the strength needed to face them. He prepares to take leave of those direct influences of the home and family that have nurtured him, and is dimly aware that he will have to become progressively more self-reliant. This is both exciting and unsettling.

He therefore begins to demand a sense of form and order – from himself and from those around him even more so. He sets off on a forced march to the boundaries of what he can achieve, and to discover what the adults around him will accept. When he reaches these boundaries, he will begin to test his strength – at first tentatively but, as the years pass, in an increasingly probing, personal way.

If he finds these boundaries weak, or lacking consistency, he may push beyond them and wander into a land he is not yet equipped to navigate. He may become fearful, resentful and lost.

Break outs and boundaries

He may then begin to look for subcultures to lean on – like drugs and gangs; or may turn inward and cut himself off from what he experiences as a formless world. These actions may be distress flares which he sends up in the hope that they will attract the attention of potential rescuers. If they are not noticed, though, he will wander further into these strange lands.

Gradually the memory of the warmth of the past will fade. What he has seen with eyes that were too young will come to seem normal. He will defend it aggressively against anyone who seems to threaten the only way of life he knows. Very careful overtures will be needed to approach this feral soul. He will need the food of unconditional love and acceptance, and will not return without a good deal of reassurance to the place which he originally deserted because of its threatening chaos.

At this age, then, the child needs secure boundary-walls; but they also need to be adaptable, changing as the young person develops. At twelve they need to be strong and straight: easily identifiable, with only a little flexibility, and no ornamentation. The discoverer of these walls has not yet acquired the subtlety to search for the cracks that will appear in them in the coming years. The builders of these walls do not place them there in an attempt to imprison – the opposite is actually the case. They give security and reassurance at a time when this is what is being asked for. There may be 'break-outs', but the escapee knows where the boundaries stand, knows therefore that he has gone beyond them, and where to return to find them again. In the coming years he may discover on returning from one of these breakouts, that the caring walls have shifted and expanded somewhat; but at twelve there is little movement. They are straight, strong and predictable.

Around the age of 12, circus skills are of particular benefit. These include tightrope walking, flying trapeze, unicycling, acrobatics, devil-sticks, diabolos, and of course, juggling. Just at a time when the 12 year old wants to test her new found strength and consciousness, these skills can be introduced with great success. They demand all-round skill, spatial awareness and at times great courage.

205. Juggling

Step 1:
Start alone by simply throwing and catching one beanbag. Any kind of throwing will do – and one can be quite creative!

Choose one juggler at a time for the others to copy: a kind of throwing and catching follow-my-leader. Then change to another leader, etc.

Step 2:
In partners: while maintaining eye contact with your partner, throw the beanbag from your hand to your partner's.

Step 3:
Throw the beanbag from hand to hand, following a lemniscate pattern (or figure-of-eight – see below: both the hands and the beanbag move in this pattern).

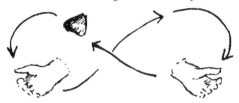

Step 4:
Facing your partner, mirror each other's movements, throwing the beanbag as in Step 3: so one partner will start with the beanbag in their left hand, the other in their right.

Step 5:
With your partner: one partner holds his beanbag in his left hand, the other holds his in his right hand. Begin as in Step 4, but after three throws, the next (fourth) throw will be to your partner. (The beanbags therefore swap over.) Throw from your right hand so that your partner catches in his left, and vice versa.

Equipment: For each juggler, 3 soft, triangular beanbags (each side is about 4 inches, or 10cm, long) – these can be made in the craft lessons, or on a rainy afternoon at home

I tell the children at this point that they should imagine that their hands are soft golden spoons, and that the beanbag is a heavy but precious object. (This helps to prevent 'snatching' catches.)

Step 6:
Kneel on the ground and work alone. Holding a beanbag in each hand, throw the one in your left hand so that it lands on the floor in front of your right knee; and then the right-hand beanbag so that it lands in front of your left knee. Pick up the beanbags and repeat. Make sure the beanbags land at the same distance in front of each knee.

Step 7:

Take a beanbag in each hand. Throw them in an arc towards each other so that they 'kiss' (meet, collide) in the air.

After doing this for a while, tell the jugglers that this is what you don't do when juggling.

Step 8:

Kneeling on the ground again, take a beanbag in each hand. First, the right hand throws the beanbag so that it lands in front of the left knee. Then the left hand throws the beanbag so that the right hand can easily catch it. Swap around, so the left hand throws first, the right hand second.

Step 9:

Repeat Step 8, but this time the first hand that throws, throws to the other hand, and the second hand throws its beanbag so that it lands on the ground.

Step 10:

Repeat Step 8, but catch both. Make sure that there is a definite rhythm set up by the steady 'one, two' throwing of the right and left hand.

- If a juggler has difficulty in throwing from right to left or left to right (i.e. throws up vertically and catches with the same hand), suggest that, holding a beanbag in each hand, she rhythmically touches the right beanbag to the left shoulder, the left to the right shoulder.

- If a juggler throws from one hand so that the beanbag consistently lands much further from the knee than the other beanbag, stand behind the juggler and ask her to throw the beanbag with her 'faulty' hand over the opposite shoulder. Catch the beanbag and return it to her, so she can repeat this action over and over again.

Step 11:

Both partners lie on the floor, on their fronts, facing each other with their arms forward. One is the catcher, the other the juggler.

Tell the students that the catcher is 'gravity', and imagine he is above the juggler, suspended above him by a rope. The juggler has one beanbag in each hand, the catcher has one in his right hand. They will

throw/slide the beanbags along the floor.

The juggler throws the beanbag in his right hand to the catcher's left hand. The catcher throws his beanbag to replace the one that has left the juggler's right hand. Then the juggler throws the beanbag in his left hand to the catcher's right hand. The catcher replaces this one.

This is repeated. Then the partners swap over, so that the catcher has a turn as juggler. Tell the jugglers that now their brain is successfully juggling!

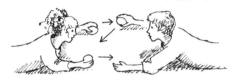

Step 12:

The juggler kneels on the floor, with one beanbag in each hand. The catcher stands above him, with his palms outstretched.

The juggler throws the right beanbag to the catcher's left hand. He catches it at its zenith. Then the same is repeated on the other side. The catcher then lets the left beanbag drop into the juggler's left hand, and the right into his right hand.

- If a juggler has a tendency to be too retentive: the catcher can put one hand, palm down, just above where the beanbags will reach their zeniths. The juggler then throws the beanbags, aiming to make them reach their zeniths at this point.

- If a juggler tends to try to 'fill up' an empty hand with a beanbag, you can do two things. First, the catcher puts his hand between the juggler's two hands, and asks the juggler to juggle.

Or, teach the juggler 'The Dancing Lady'. The left hand throws the beanbag in an arc while the right hand throws (more of a pass, really) its beanbag to the left hand. Then the right hand throws the arc, the left hand passes. (So the same beanbag is always being thrown in an arc.)

Step 13:

Hold two beanbags (one and three) in the left hand, and one (two) in the right. Beanbag three will remain in the left hand at all times. The left hand throws beanbag one to the right hand, and the right hand then throws beanbag two to the left hand.

Then throw beanbag two back to the right hand, beanbag one to the left. Repeat. Then practise holding beanbag three in the right hand while doing the same.

Step 14:
Kneeling on the ground: Repeat Step 13, but when beanbag two is at its zenith, just drop beanbag three.

Step 15:
Repeat Step 14, but instead of dropping beanbag three, throw it away somewhere, anyhow…

Step 16:
… drum roll (this is the moment we've been waiting for!)… Repeat Step 15, but now throw beanbag three in an arc and catch it.

Step 17:
Mark beanbag one in some way. Practise a flowing rhythm of juggling with all three beanbags, particularly emphasising beanbag one.

206. Pillar and Protector

Build a 'pillar' in the centre of the inner circle with the tin cans. One person is chosen to be the 'Protector'. They must guard the 'pillar' from being hit by the ball. They stand just outside the small circle, facing the direction the ball is coming from. They are not allowed into the small circle.

The rest of the players are 'Killers'. They stand outside the larger circle and throw the ball at the pillar, trying to knock it down, from any point on the outside circle.

The protector shields the pillar with their arms, legs and body – if they can get round the small circle fast enough to face the oncoming ball!

Passing amongst 'Killers' is permitted. The Killers are not allowed inside the large circle. If the pillar is hit, then a new pillar is built and a new protector chosen.

Variations:

> **Equipment:** A soft practice volleyball; a lit candle in a candle holder, or a rose or another flower

- Instead of a pillar made of tin cans, in this variation there are two players in the circle: one player is a 'pillar of stone', and stands in the centre of the small circle holding the lit candle (or rose). This person is not allowed to move, except to pivot on the spot, so as to face the oncoming ball. (This is a hard task – one's reflexes to duck or dodge the ball are very strong: but that is the challenge!) In the same way as before, the other person in the circle, the protector, tries to keep the ball away from the pillar. (I often let the 'pillar' choose their own 'protector'.)

> **Play area:** Draw a large circle 10–15 paces across, around a small circle 2–3 paces across – the size of the inner circle can be adjusted according to the skill of the protector: a smaller circle makes their job easier, and a larger circle increases the work!
>
> **Equipment:** A soft practice volleyball; a set of seven tin cans that can stack on top of one another

I first played this game when I was working with behaviourally-disturbed children; it met with great success. *Pillar and Protector* is a game that deals with issues of cruelty, protection and vulnerability. I give the 'pillar' a lit candle (or a flower in a vase) in order to make him feel as vulnerable as possible. Not being allowed to protect oneself from the ball, but sometimes having to rely on the protection of another, is something we all need to come to terms with: it does not always come easily. This game can also raise the consciousness of those who bully and taunt others. It can be helpful to make the bully protect his victim, as well as putting the bully himself into the vulnerable position of the pillar.

207. Matilda

The players stand in a circle, approximately 15 paces in diameter. The leader begins by standing in the centre of the circle. She throws the ball straight up into the air, and calls out the name of one of the players, e.g. 'Ben!'.

All the players, except Ben, run as far as possible away from the ball. Ben then tries to catch the ball on the full. As soon as he catches it, all the other players freeze. However, if he doesn't manage to catch the ball, the other players secretly decide on a new name for him, e.g. 'Harry'. The leader then throws the ball and names a player again.

When 'Harry' is called, Ben, who knows he has a new name, must be awake enough to go into the centre and try to catch the ball. You may end up having a large number of fictitious names for players who dropped the ball.

> **EQUIPMENT:** One play ball

If Ben does catch the ball on the full, he tries to brand one of the players from wherever he caught it. If he misses, then the circle reforms, but this time, Ben throws the ball up and calls a name.

But if Ben manages to brand a player, say Jo, then Jo has to throw the ball from the centre of the circle. Or, the player branded has to sit out. In which case the game ends when there are only three players left.

This is a very exciting extension to dodge-ball games played at the age of ten. In *Dead and Alive* (page 189), however, almost all the players are both dodgers as well as throwers.

208. Down Basketball

Three or four players are 'It'. They try to brand all the players with the ball. All branding must be below the waist. Any 'It' can pass it to another 'It', but is not allowed to run with the ball.

If a player is branded, he sits down with crossed legs, wherever the ball hit him. (He is now a 'down' player.) However, a player (an 'up' player) can catch the ball on the full (without it having bounced), or deliberately pick up the ball off the ground – without fumbling it so that it falls to the ground – and try to shoot a basket. If he is successful, all the branded players are freed and can stand up again.

When a player is holding the ball, he can be tagged by any 'It'. He then loses the chance to free everyone, and has to sit down.

Any down player may pick up the ball if it comes close enough to him. However, a down player cannot shoot a basket, but must pass the ball to an up player. Down players may protect up players by shielding them from being hit by an 'It'.

> **PLAY AREA:** A basketball court
> **EQUIPMENT:** One soft play ball; 2 basketball goals; 3–4 coloured vests

Variations:

- As in *Hounds, Hares and Hunters*, a variation may be played where a down player, who has his legs crossed, can tag a running 'up' player. Then the up player must swap places with the down player who tagged him.

- Another way for a down player to get up is if he can get the ball and throw it at one of the 'Its', and hit them without them catching the ball. The 'It' does not go down, though, but continues to play.

Down Basketball is a terrific way to introduce basketball. It can also be used as a training aid; and has always proved to be popular. The players must be able to keep calm and carefully judge the risks they take. Any player who panics or does not keep alert in this game, will not succeed.

209. Dead and Alive

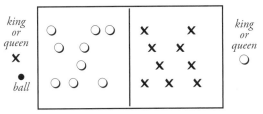

beginning position

> **PLAY AREA: Space** 30 x 20 paces for 30 players, marked with wall lines
>
> **EQUIPMENT:** One play ball

Divide the players into two teams. Each team stands in one court, facing the ball. From each team choose a player to be the thrower (King or Queen). These stand at the end of the opposing team's court.

To begin the game, give the ball to King or Queen A, who throws the ball at the players of Team B, and tries to brand them from the waist down. The dodgers on the court have two options:

- To dodge the ball. But if a player is branded, then he is 'dead', and becomes a thrower for his team. He does this by going to the same end as his King or Queen and helps to brand the opposition players.

- Or to intercept the ball. If a player intercepts the ball he must catch it on the full (without it having bounced); he has then earned one 'life'. (This means that he can either forfeit this life and invite one of his team's throwers back onto court, or when he is next branded himself, he stays on court and the life is used up.) He can then turn to face the opposite team, and pass the ball to a throwing teammate, or take a shot at one of the opposing team's dodgers.

If a player tries to intercept the ball, but fails to catch it on the full, he becomes a thrower, and joins his teammate behind the opposite team.

The game continues until all the dodgers on one team have been branded and gone off court to become throwers.

Variations:

- When all the dodgers on one team are dead (have become throwers), the original King or Queen from the team takes the court and makes an exciting finale, trying to survive attack from the opposition by accumulating lives, and by trying to brand the opponents. The King or Queen is given three lives to start with.

This is a dynamic, fast-moving game – one of the best and most popular I have come across for the 12–13 year old.

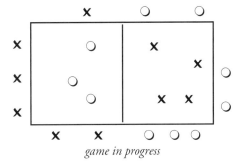

game in progress

210. Bottles

Another variation of *Dead and Alive* (above). Instead of having to protect oneself from being branded, the dodgers have to protect a skittle – each player has one skittle to protect. However the skittles can be also knocked down by mistake by one of the dodgers. Whoever does this is out.

211. Buzz
Devised by Craig Taylor

This is a simplification of a traditional Indian game. Divide the players into two teams. Each team is numbered one to ten (or up to as many players as you have on each team). One team will run first (Team A) while the other team will catch and avoid being caught (Team B).

- Team A waits, ready to start, on one side.

- The first player (player A) moves towards the centre line, and as he does so, takes a deep breath.

- As he steps over the centre line, he starts saying 'buzzzzz' in a loud voice without pausing.

- He may not take another breath until he is back on his own side.

- He may stay in the opponents' half for as little or as long a time as he likes providing his 'buzzzzz' does not run out.

- While in the opponents' half, he can tag the members of Team B, who will be running away and avoiding him as he enters their field. When they are tagged, they do not immediately sit out but they must do so if the player who tagged them manages to make it back over the half-way line into his own safe territory.

- When Player A has run out of breath, and cannot say 'buzzzzz' anymore, he can no longer tag any of the B players.

- However, when he runs out of breath, Team B can try to catch and hold him without fear of being tagged. If this is done then he is out. The two teams alternate in sending a 'buzzzzz' player in.

- They may do so as soon as the opposing number returns. (If player number two from team A has just returned over the line, then player number two from team B can immediately cross the line and begin to 'buzzzzz'.)

PLAY AREA: 25 x 15 paces

There are two ways that Player A can be caught:

- Taken unawares by player from team B, Player A is held in a bear hug round the waist, until his 'buzzzzz' (breath) runs out.

- When his 'buzzzzz' runs out while he is running, Team B can catch Player A in any way they can, and hold him on their side of the centre line.

- Once he is caught, Player A tries to drag his restrainers over the centre line, to Team A's side. If he is successful, the person (or persons) who were holding him are out.

- When a player is caught he may call 'Stop!' which means he has submitted and agrees that he must now go out. The holding players must release him straight away.

- The first phase ends when there are no players remaining on one of the teams. Alternatively, the leader can give each team two minutes of running, and then two minutes of catching; when this is up, each team counts the number of captures they have made. The team with the most captures wins.

Variations:

- Build up the number of raiders crossing the line at any one time, until you have two or three saying 'buzzzzz' together.

- If a player is tagged by the raider, instead of sitting out, he can join the raiding team.

Hints to the leader:

- To increase the chances of catching a raider, the running team can run away from the centre line when being chased by the raider, so that when his breath runs out, he has less chance of escaping to safety across the centre line.

This is one of the few games that I have never liked much, but that the children love! This may be because it involves a marked sense of combat, and players have to be courageous. In order to play successfully, players must not panic – they must 'keep their heads'. This game also introduces a structured and fun-filled environment for physical contact between players – which is healthy for children at this age.

212. Comets

As developed by Jaimen McMillan

Level 1:

The players stand in a circle. (The circle can be described as the universe, and the beanbags are comets which fly through space.). They stand and throw the beanbags to one another at random, trying not to let them fall to the ground. The number of successful catches can be counted. When a beanbag is dropped, the counting begins again at one.

Level 2:

The players turn to their left (or right) and start slowly walking around in a circle, continuing to throw and catch the beanbags, and counting. Every time someone drops a beanbag, the direction of the circle changes and the counting begins again.

Level 3:

To make this game even more challenging, ask the players to jog very slowly (more of a light run than a jog, really) round the circle.

Variations:

• Make two circles of players one inside the other. The inside circle should have fewer players than the outside circle. The circles run in opposite directions, passing the comets between them.

> **Equipment:** 5 bean bags

This is a game that relies on all the members of the group: to reach a good number of successful throws, the players have to both throw and catch consciously. They also have to make contact with one another – they cannot just throw and presume their job is done. Each person has to be involved in the catch of the player they threw to. Another challenge of this game is to learn to throw the bag or ball into the space in front of the oncoming catcher, recognising the space the catcher will occupy rather than the space they did occupy at the time the ball was thrown.

This game is also good for teenagers because players at this age are very unforgiving of others. You may well find, as I did, that one child struggles to catch the beanbags thrown at him, and is jeered at and frowned upon every time he 'lets us down'. But to play *Comets* successfully, the failure of individuals has to be forgiven. The bean bag or ball must also be thrown very sensitively to the player who cannot catch as well as the others. This helps encourage sensitivity for the needs of the other, rather than simply becoming frustrated at his weakness.

213. Coupe

One player is 'It'. He chases the other players and tries to tag them. The game begins by It naming the first person that he is going to chase, e.g. 'Keisha'.

However, if 'It' is chasing one player (say, Keisha), another player (say, Jessie) can run between It and Keisha, shouting 'Coupe!' at the very moment he intersects the 'It's path, and raising his hand to identify himself. 'It' then has to chase Jessie. Jessie in turn may be rescued by another player (say Jack) who cuts in between 'It' and him. It must now pursue Jack, who runs away hoping for rescue. This is repeated until 'It' has caught one of the players.

When a player is tagged, he becomes 'It', and calls out the name of the first person he is going to chase. Those players running between 'It' and the runner must run across their path clearly (see diagram). Hint: it helps if the leader names the player who has shouted 'Coupe!' e.g. he can call out: 'Sarah is coupe... Ming-na is coupe' etc. as the coupe changes.

This is a game that has both form and chaos. Initially the player who is 'It' can only tag the player who is named; but anyone can call the chaser onto themselves by shouting 'Coupe!' To intersect the line of intention between 'It' and the child being chased, requires timing, courage and quick thinking. These are similar to the skills needed for *Running the Gauntlet* (game 184).

coupe

214. Medusa's Raft
As related by Jeremy Dunleavy

All the players stand on the mat. This is the raft around which swim hungry sharks. The raft is sinking so the players try to push each other off. If you are pushed off you are out. The last few players on the raft win.

This is a very simple game, which I play with children from the age of fourteen. It helps them experience using their balance and, in particular, their weight – learning to 'earth' themselves.

EQUIPMENT: 2–3 gym floor-mats pushed together, or a chalk rectangle marked on the floor, measuring a total of about 6 x 10 feet (1.8 x 3 metres), for 15–20 players

215. All Against All

There are no teams in this game. Two balls are used at the same time. The aim is to throw the ball at any other player on the field, trying to hit them below the waist.

If you get hit you are out. You immediately go to the side of the playing area, remembering which player threw the ball that hit you. You may re-enter the game if the player who got you out is later hit themselves and leaves the field. This player may have got only you out or they may have got many people out. You are all free to enter the game if this player is hit and leaves the field. If you are unsure who hit you then you go to the side and pick any player on the field. When that player is out you may re-enter the game.

No one may run with the ball. You may run freely if you do not have a ball. If you have one of the balls in your hands when you are hit, you may not throw it.

> **Play area:** 25 x 20 paces for 25 players – it is helpful if this playing area has either a fence or walls around it, otherwise the balls will be difficult to retrieve.
>
> **Equipment:** Two soft practice volleyballs

You must place it on the floor and leave the field. If you catch a ball on the full (without it having bounced) then the person who threw it is out. If you try to catch it and you drop it, you are out. You may not protect your legs with your hands and arms. If they are struck while in front of your legs, you are still out. The game ends when either all the players are out except one (this rarely happens), or when a set number of player remain (for a group of 25 you may say five players), or when a set period of time has elapsed.

216. Team Against Team

The rules are the same as in *All Against All*, except that there are now three teams on the field at once (you may introduce a fourth later on).

The aim of the game is to get as many of the other team out as you can. All other rules relating to being hit, going out and coming back in are the same as in *All Against All*.

> **Play area:** 25 x 20 paces for 25 players – it is helpful if this playing area has either a fence or walls around it, otherwise the balls will be difficult to retrieve.
>
> **Equipment:** Two soft practice volleyballs; 3 or 4 sets of coloured vests or sashes

Chapter Eight
Age 13 and beyond
Symbolism and History of Sport

Like all great athletes, he was the lord of time and space. In other words, he played in an environment of his own choosing at a rhythm dictated by his own mood and inclination. He was beautiful to watch no matter what he was doing on the field of play. He was blessed with a natural, unhurried ease of movement that, along with the absence of frill or flourish, is the hallmark of a true stylist. He was everything an athlete should be; graceful and gracious, outrageously talented and naturally modest. Perhaps his most attractive and endearing attribute was that he didn't understand what all the fuss was about. Still doesn't.

This article describing the cricketer Sir Garfield Sobers, written by Michael Parkinson in a national British newspaper, *The Daily Telegraph*, could also apply to a very select number of athletes who have taken little interest in the hype and vastly inflated financial incentives that surround and pollute much of modern sport, preferring to draw their inspiration from the fundamental spatial dynamics of the game itself. In doing so they not only become outstanding players, but also unwitting beacons of moral light in a world in need of it. Surely this is what we wish for our young athletes of today.

Much of this book has been concerned with younger children. Let us now turn to the subject of sport for teenagers. A case has been made for not beginning sport too early in the child's life (see Chapter Seven) and some mention has also been made of the positive influences that sport can have on teenagers. This is a fascinating and huge area of study and may form the basis of another book at a later date. Nevertheless, a brief overview of an ideal programme is worth exploring here.

The Origins

In order to do this we must take a glance back at the origins of sport. It is commonly agreed that the ancient Greeks were among the first and most successful in developing what we now call sport; they elevated bodily movement from the mundane and the combative. The Greek striving to build an earthly connection between the gods and mankind reflected the overall evolution of human consciousness. With the coming of the Greek era, the gods gradually became less intimately and directly influential upon life and culture than had previously been the case.

This was a momentous change – and one whose effects continue even to the present day. The new emphasis was brought about by an increasing sense of independence and individuality, of ego. What better way to foster and enhance this than by competing, by matching yourself against your fellows? Not just in order to see who was the fastest or the strongest; but to use the body as a vessel, an instrument for striving toward a reconnection with the divine. This is why so much of a child's education in Ancient Greece was given over to athletic prowess. There were few divides between sporting, cultural and spiritual life.

Evidence of this is best seen in the Olympiad and the original Stadium. The word Stadium is defined as 'a stage in a process'. The Sanctuary of Olympia, which includes the Palaistra and the Gymnasion (practice areas) as well as the Stadium, was built around the temple of Zeus. The athletes and spectators involved in the Games preserved a deep connection with both funerary customs and religious practice and festivals.

In the transition from the Classic to the Hellenic and then to the Roman era we see a further grounding of this need to be more fully on the earth, to develop individuality. The religious nature of the Games began to fade. A very telling step was taken, when, in the 5th century BCE, professionalism began: athletes were given large sums of money, special rights, and lavish gifts by their cities. After the Roman conquest of Greece, Sulla transferred the games to Rome where the so-called 'heavy events' of wrestling and boxing became more and more popular, and fighting to the death between gladiators or man and beast was introduced. Whereas previously, in Greek times, these events had been seen as a dedication to the gods in which both onlooker and athlete were involved, they now became bloody arena spectacles. And seldom before in history had anything so precise and incisive been experienced as the armies which now amassed rank on rank in perfect formation. Physical prowess was still, at this point, vaguely connected with the divine; but the signs of a separation became apparent, which continued and grew ever more marked through the succeeding ages.

By the time of the European Middle Ages this divergence had become clearly defined. The spiritual world could now only be approached through the intermediary of the priesthood. A guarded doorway was put firmly in place between the individual and his God. The body was viewed as a tainted, fallen image of God, to be reviled and overcome. Knights became, at this time, an elevated caste – often pictured on horseback – whose gaze was turned up and away from earthly reality.

It took the mechanism and materialism of the industrial revolution to accelerate and form modern sport. The structures that had for so long been held in place by community and extended family, began for the first time to fall apart. The priesthood, the church, and mankind's relationship to God were brought into question. Into this void stepped sport. Sport not only attempted to free people from the grinding hardships of the factory and reconnect them with each other, it also sought a new view of human

beings and their physical and spiritual place within the world.

Since then there has been an increasing dislocation of the family and community; a rapid increase in industrialisation, which has led to an isolating technological environment; a decline of the church's central role; and an increasing awareness that people must now walk alone and forge their own path in relationship to spirituality. The corresponding massive growth of sport can therefore hardly come as a surprise. Hundreds of millions of people are involved in sport. Very few children in school in any country in the world are not exposed to its formative influence. It is therefore high time that the seed which the Greeks planted long ago begins to be nurtured, if it is to bear fruit and aid our evolution. This is why it is of such significance that we begin to educate our children in a way that recognises the differing dimensions that sport and movement offer. We must develop comprehensive movement programmes that give our young people opportunities to play games and sports which mirror their developmental stage; which allow them to unfold at their own speed, in activities that nurture the whole individual not just the physical body. If we remain chained to our bodies alone – indulging in beauty contests, aerobics and body building, treating the body with allopathic medicine that denies the soul's and spirit's role in healing, taking performance-enhancing drugs; if we continue to be dominated by a rampantly demanding fashion industry and a two-dimensional media culture, and, most widespread of all, a hard, competitive, aggressive, body-centred form of sport – then we will have missed a unique historical and evolutionary opportunity.

Sport can be a vehicle for dynamic human growth; or it can lead us into a wasteland subculture of vain self-seeking, of aggression and soullessness.

The symbols of the modern mystery

Let's look at some of the parallels that exist between religious and devotional life, sociological and emotional needs, and modern sport. Symbolism exists all around us. It attempts to build a representational bridge between the visible and the invisible, between physical and spiritual worlds. It is celebrated in art, poetry, music, prose, dance – indeed wherever the human being strives toward higher ideals. Pushing beyond the normal expectations and limits of life is also a hallmark of sport. So sport too must have its symbolism.

The goal

The goal is perhaps the clearest to define. We all have our ideal picture of what we want to achieve in our life. We call this our 'goal'. It may be as mundane as replacing your car with a new one every two years and keeping up with the mortgage repayments so as to provide a secure home for your family. You may set yourself a target to do with your work; or place great value on your social and personal relationships. You may feel drawn to prayer and meditation. Whatever goal you have, it will always contain a striving to move forwards, to improve your life, whether on a physical, social or spiritual level. A true goal is not something you only occasionally recall and wistfully regard; it is a quality you integrate with everyday life through diligence and daily practice, and by overcoming obstacles.

A goal in sport contains a very strong reflection of this striving quality. Difficulties have to be overcome to score a goal. Skill is built up through regular practice. Tactics are discussed in order to optimise a team's chances. The way each individual relates to the others is of vital importance. All these aspects are then put into place on the day of the game to make goal-scoring possible. Outdoor pursuits such as canoeing and rock climbing also have these features, only in this instance the tactical side of things is a much more individualised process, and the goal is not so clearly or visibly defined and restricted. Some sportsmen and sportswomen are paid huge sums of money because of their prowess at goal-scoring; and there is jubilation when one is scored. We, the viewing public, unconsciously recognise the symbolism and the parallels this has in our own life. Fully realising our abilities can come only after hardship and regular practice. The achievement arising from this practice is a clear proof that the athlete or sportsperson has

raised herself to a higher plane.

For a modern civilisation that has left behind many of the old rites of passage – considering them no longer appropriate to the way in which we now live – goals remain a powerful representation and metamorphosis of such nodal, threshold moments. Goals are all about challenges: thresholds we strive to pass through. This is why it is so important that the right sports be given emphasis at the right age. Initiation ceremonies, once common to all cultures and faiths, all recognised that certain values and spiritual realities needed to be made available to children and young people at very precise moments in their lives. It was not a random, hit-or-miss activity. Yet nowadays we see very young children engaged in the same sport as their fathers. If we should suggest to a mother that she should go through the same initiation ceremony as her daughter – let's say confirmation which happens around twelve in the Christian faiths – she might well be somewhat upset at being placed on the same developmental level as her offspring. Or, perhaps more to the point, it would be clearly inappropriate to ask a twelve year old to take part in an adult-only ceremony. Though she might be very willing to be seen as one of the adults and feel flattered, she would be unlikely to have developed the capacity to understand what was happening. Worse still, she might be exposed to something she was not yet ready for, and be negatively affected by it. We do not present a Cubist painting or a stream-of-consciousness poem to an eleven year old and repeatedly, insistently expect her to understand. We might feel it was more appropriate for a sixteen year old. Sport, too, has its developmental stages and benefits, which it is up to us to discover.

The ball

It is so often said that modern culture is speeding up. Life today calls for quick responses. The media flash a whole succession of images at irregular intervals to keep our attention. In most primary schools we change teachers every year; in secondary schools we change teachers every lesson; food from any country can be bought regardless of the season; travel abroad, which gives many an experience of short-term climatic and cultural change, has becomes common-place. It is getting much harder to find continuity, to develop a theme, thought or enduring relationship over a long period.

Sport, particular practice with the ball, allows us the situation, space and time to shut out these fast, flickering images and focus on one activity to the exclusion of all else. It allows us to focus our thinking and bring our will into a more repetitive, even meditative quality. Whilst this has many beneficial aspects there is also an inherent danger: this kind of activity can, depending on the individual, become compulsive; it can be used to shut out the real world and develop a fantasy world based around practice and sport.

Boundaries, rules and referees

We only have to look back into the recent past, perhaps the pre-1950s, to see a society that exhibited a great deal more respect for authority than we do today. The boundaries between what was acceptable and unacceptable were much more sharply defined and adhered to. It is no coincidence that as these boundaries have broken down, there has been a corresponding increase in the numbers of people taking part in sport. While there may, in many ways, be chaos all around us, in sport we find commonly agreed conformity, and rigidly enforced consequences for overstepping the boundaries of what is acceptable. This provides a secure basis from which we can more readily explore our relationships to others and our individuality. So much now rests on the individual's shoulders; people nowadays must make decisions and decide on their own criteria without the guidance of an accepted code. It is therefore of great importance that sport depends upon clear-cut rules. But this is, again, a double-edged sword: the individual runs the risk of losing her individuality within the structure of a club and a game, becoming weakened and reliant on external forces. A chosen sport should hopefully be a means of developing individual potential, rather than an activity which only enforces group consciousness.

In general we can see that sport provides a valuable structure within which we may define ourselves and make space to discover and strengthen our individuality. It is clear that modern sport has filled some of the vacuum left by the decline in orthodox religious practices and commonly respected community values. But a great deal of sports activity is conducted in a very unconscious way – by both the players and the coaches. This must change if we are to realise our potential for freedom. Only increased self-awareness can aid us in setting goals – both for ourselves and for human development in general. We must face the fact that the unconscious structures which previously sustained society have fallen away; and that we are in the process of creating new ones. If the nature of this change becomes arbitrary or random – and let's not forget the huge social influence sport has – we will have missed an enormous opportunity to take a giant step forward.

The 'In-coming'

In Chapter One we said that child development in the first fourteen years may be seen as an 'in-coming' or 'in-carnating' movement. The child journeys from the periphery to the point. We have many sayings that unconsciously express this, such as: 'She has come into her own.' We only need to compare the light skipping of the seven year old to the heavier yet more conscious movements of the fourteen year old, and the gradual transition between the two, to recognise this basic 'in-coming' principle. But 'what is it that is incarnating?' On a physical level it is clear to everyone that children grow bigger and heavier. But as soon as we move away from the visibly physical aspects of development and into the invisible, subtle levels, there is much more room for debate and disagreement.

Most would now recognise and have few problems with the concept that life has a psychological dimension. Sport does not, of course, exist in isolation from life, and there are now many practising sports psychologists. But these professionals are mainly concerned with performance enhancement, rather than any wider issues. Yes, there are commendable campaigns to encourage general participation – such as 'Sport For Fun', 'Sport For All', 'Life Be In It' etc. In fact, much money is spent by government agencies on these media drives. But this really only proves that the main focus of sport is on winning and improving performance; why, otherwise, does so much effort need to be put into promoting 'Sport for All'? The simple answer is that it has not developed along participatory, inclusive lines. Governments recognise this and spend vast sums to try to redress the balance. This is admirable – even if the motivation is somewhat limited to physical health and a vague notion of feeling better.

But let's return to the challenging idea of 'the invisible' dimension of life, sport and movement in general. Psychology used to be recognised as the study of the soul – and still is today in many circles. Philosophy examines aspects of life which are in many ways connected with the spirit. Psychology and philosophy have partly sought to 'materialise' and bring into practical, quantifiable existence what is invisible.

So we have sports psychologists. But the term 'counsellor for the spiritual aspect of sports' would at the very least raise eyebrows in the rugby changing-rooms. It is clear, of course, that sport does not exist in a vacuum, that it is interwoven with our culture.

Religion and spiritual life still play a large, if somewhat diminished part in most societies. Why then should the notion that sport has connections with spiritual dimensions of existence, cause concern, scepticism or laughter? Is our spirit something we hang on the peg along with our ordinary clothes when we change into our sports kit? When designing a sports programme for teenagers we must look at the whole developing individual, not just at the physical and vague, narrowly-defined emotional benefits such as standing up for oneself, and toughening oneself up. Even the rationale of developing self-esteem, though a positive goal in itself, is really only the first step in the path of development which a wholistic movement-programme can achieve. Self-esteem can be roughly defined as how one stands in relationship to the world and how one consciously feels about this perceived position. But it is crucially important to see that the way a young person views herself changes year by year through the turbulent time of adolescence. If the self-esteem and the overall spatial development of the teenager is to be strengthened, any educational sporting programme must give sharp definition to the appropriateness and helpfulness of particular activities at each particular age.

The Phases

Throughout this book the nodal points and the step-by-step developmental stages of childhood have been identified. Of course each child will grow up at her own pace in her own unique way. What has been explored here are archetypal phases and the kind of activities and dynamics that give a spatial expression to inner experience at any particular age. It may be that a stage identified here may come later or earlier than described, or be lightly passed over so that it may seem it was hardly gone through at all. What follows is not a prescription but a guide.

Thirteen

In the first teenage years young people begin to turn inward. They long for independence and solitude. Yet at times they can show amazing energy for things that capture their imagination and arouse interest. A fine interplay begins between external and internal worlds. It is also a time when a more conscious interest in the outer world takes the form of wanting to sample all sorts of aspects of life. The family norms and guidelines begin to give way to those dictated by the young person's friends, the peer group. It is a time of discovery.

The thirteen year old still maintains some of her child-like qualities. Her body has not yet become as heavy as it will in later years. She will still be able to play and move with some lightness and innocence. However she is 'falling into weight' and as the year goes on she will experience this more and more.

So there are three main principles at work at this age. Firstly the interplay between inner and outer worlds. Secondly, connected to the need to experience the external world, is the theme of exploration. Thirdly, the impending fall into weight together with the remnant of light, agile, child-like 'springiness'. We should try to respond to all three in any games and movement programme.

The need to 'taste' many different things can easily be facilitated by allowing the teenager to experience a smorgasbord of activities: **basketball**, **softball**, **cricket**, **tennis**, many different athletic events – particularly **running** and **jumping** – **netball**, **korfball**, **volleyball**, **swimming** – with an emphasis on diving. In a school setting, each of these sports may be experienced, preferably for no more than six to eight weeks, before the next activity is introduced.

In gymnastics*, much can be expanded from the previous year's work, which had as its theme the supporting of one's own body weight, expressed in handstands and various support positions on the bars. **Vaulting** can recap on the basic moves such as astride (leap frog) and squat or through-vaults; however the springboard is placed further and further back from the box so that the students have to really leap to clear it. The big moment comes when the students are asked to test what they have learned in their handstands, and perform a long-arm. This is a vault in which they launch off the springboard, achieve a handstand on top of the box and then flip over on to their feet, landing on the other side of the box. In parallel and asymmetric bar-work, simple dismounting moves from swinging support are built on; however, for the more capable student, activities like swing-to-handstand on the parallel, and beat-to-handstand on the low bar of the asymmetric can be attempted. A tension drop is a very good example of falling into weight. The student stands on the low bar of the asymmetric bars, with her sacrum touching the high bar. She grips the high bar with both hands. The leader, of course, stands below. Keeping her body straight, she leans back away from the low bar, raises her feet and comes into a full

---

* Some of the terms used in descriptions of the gymnastics exercises in this chapter may be unfamiliar to many. I have not explained each one, since only a trained instructor should attempt them.

inversion position. She now pikes (bends at the waist) and drives her feet towards the ground. She then quickly releases the bar from her hand-grip and lands on the safety mats below. A more advanced method is to repeat what has been described, but this time the hands are raised into a backward arc beyond the vertical position, arms straight. This arcing thrust with the arms creates the momentum to fall backwards and dismount from the high bar. High twisting, tuck, and straddle jumps for the **trampoline**. **Tumbling** and **acrobatics** centre around handsprings, flick-flacks and fast gymnastic display routines of basic moves involving a team of acrobats performing in tightly synchronised choreography. This can all be put together with the further development of circus skills such as unicycling, flying and static trapeze, juggling, diabolos, devil sticks, and tight- and slack- rope walking, that can be introduced in the twelfth year. Here, once more, we see a balance being struck between childlike play and formalised activity. Circus skills are an excellent way to achieve this. They are both individually challenging, spatially demanding, and playful.

Orienteering should be given particular emphasis. Basic courses can be set out with markers placed in a range of about two miles from the base, with their positions marked on a map. The students divide into groups of three and are given their own maps, upon which they must carefully draw the markers in the right position. Once they have found a marker on the course, they record the colour or a distinguishing feature of it, to prove they have found it. They should try to complete the course in a given time, 45 or 50 minutes is usually enough. For every marker they find they are given ten points. You may give more points for finding the markers that are further away and a bonus of 50 points for finding all the markers. For every minute they are back after the designated time they have ten points deducted from their score, but for every minute they are back earlier than the designated time they receive an extra ten points. In this way, speed, accuracy and initiative are encouraged and rewarded. Orienteering is a wonderful way to give expression to the qualities of exploration, independence, and the play between the inner (the map reading) and the outer (the hunt).

The leader of these activities should remember that it is not yet necessary to make too great a leap by over-formalising or hardening the movements. In the school setting the student should experience at least one, and possibly two gymnastic lessons and two games/sports lessons (a double lesson is best) of 45 minutes each per week.

These should have an introductory and enjoyable quality. For example, in a basketball lesson the teacher could devote the first third or more to playing *Space Ball* (game 150) or any of its variations. In volleyball, *Prisoner* variations (games 193, 196, and 197) can be played. Basic rules are introduced, leaving aside the more complex for later on. The thirteen year old will benefit if these rules, although only a framework, are strictly enforced. They provide the boundary, the safety, within which the young person can feel secure.

The thirteenth year is a *springboard* into puberty and all that lies beyond.

Fourteen

Inwardness may now reach its most intense contraction, from which point the journey back out into the periphery, into the world, begins; but now the young person sees what is around her with a new, more critical and conscious faculty. She will feel much more ready to face the world and challenge what she feels is unjust. She will feel more earthed. Discussion, debate, and laughter will bubble up in the expressing of new-found ideals. The ability to make judgments, especially about rules and aesthetics, begins to emerge.

So in a movement programme the main aim will be to give expression to this strong dynamic between gravity and contraction; and between awareness of the periphery and movement towards it.

In sport a continuation of the areas covered in the previous year goes on, but with an exploration of weight and how to use it. Sports such as **Rugby** and **Hockey**, **American** and **Australian football** can be introduced. These games emphasise weight and its use, punctuated with delicate and accurate speed and levity. Perfect for the fourteen year old. It is important that the rules are modified so all players can take part without fear. For example, in the football games a flag or touch rule can be used: instead of tackling an opponent the player may be stopped by a double-handed tag or by removing a piece of material about 12–18 inches (30–45cm) long that has been tucked into her waist-band leaving 8–10 inches (20–25cm) showing. The player may prevent her flag being taken, by weaving and dodging, but may not hold onto it in any way. A situation may be reached in which some players nominate themselves as 'full tacklers'; these may now tackle and be tackled. Others may wish to stay as 'touch'. These players may not be tackled but can stop anyone on the pitch with a touch, and in turn be stopped with a touch. This is of particular benefit in playing with mixed physique and sex groups.

Shot putting is very much enjoyed at this age.

The athlete takes hold of weight and hurls it forward, pressing dynamically into the earth in order to throw.

Wrestling can be used, with modified rules and many variations. For example, line wrestling. In this form the two wrestlers stand on a line, (a court line-marking on a gymnasium floor is ideal, a crack in a floorboard, or a chalk line on the floor will do); they place both feet on the line. It is important that their toes point along the line so that they do not gain an advantage by turning their back foot sideways. The two wrestlers put their front feet forward so that their toes touch each other – this prevents their feet slipping. They then join one hand each with their opponent. Now they must try to pull or push their opponent off the line, using just the one hand. The first wrestler to move a foot off the line loses.

Penguin wrestling: Two people stand about one foot (30cm) away from each other. They should be facing each other. They place their own feet tightly together. Their hands are raised to chest level, palms facing each other, but not touching. Now they must attempt to slap their opponent's hands so that she is forced backwards and has to move one foot in order to avoid falling over (this movement looks very much like a penguin, hence the name). But if an opponent tries to make a hit on the other's hands and the other quickly withdraws them, the aggressor may lose because she topples forward (this often ends up in a laughter-filled hug). The match is lost when, as a result of either hitting or missing, one of the wrestlers moves her foot – even a tiny bit.

Greek wrestling: This type of wrestling can be experienced in a quite new way at this age. For a full description see the wrestling section in Chapter Five. **Roman wrestling**: This is much more the type of wrestling used in modern times. Opponents must be matched according to weight. Great stress needs to be placed on safety when playing this with young people. This wrestling should only be done on gymnastic mats (although a lot of fun can be had doing it in knee-deep water). A circle is drawn on the mats about four to five paces across. The two opponents face each other, placing their hands on each other's shoulders. At a given command they try either to lift their opponent up so that both her feet leave the ground (some clever wrestlers may wait until their opponent is down on the ground and then lift her feet up, thus almost avoiding the need to lift any weight. This would still count as a win) or wrestle her to the ground and pin her shoulders to the mat. This pinning rule can be adapted so that the leader may choose a one-, three- or even five-second count before declaring a winner. The bout can also be won by pushing the opponent so that a part of her body goes outside the circle on three occasions in one game. *No throws, holding of clothes, locks that either hurt or go against the normal directional movement of the limb, are allowed. If there is any risk of injury the referee must immediately step in and stop the bout. Any wrestler deliberately attempting to hurt another is immediately declared the loser.*

Group wrestling: a good example of this is *Medusa's Raft* (game 214), described in Chapter Seven.

In **gymnastics**, the exploration of the principle of weight, contraction and expansion is also undertaken. One of the principle exercises to master is the somersault in all its many forms. It is a perfect expression of the principle of gathering one's forces (the run and/or the preparation to jump), coming into oneself (the tuck position), and emerging into the periphery (the opening stance at the end of the exercise). This can take up the work done in previous years in tumbling, especially the forward roll and back roll. This can then move on to the dive roll onto safety mats, both from standing and running take-off. The dive-roll then progresses to dive-rolling over objects. The next step is the somersault itself. This somersaulting action can be taught using a variety of apparatus including a trampoline, a double mini trampoline, a mini trampoline, a spring-board; but best of all it should be taught using no apparatus, just the floor to push off and perhaps a mat to land on

---

* In acrobatics the many variations on human balancing exercises are a great test of strength and allow the young person to experience gravity.

and some helpers standing either side who may assist in the standing in*.

In outdoor activities, **caving** and **potholing** form the ideal focus at a time of weight, earth and gravity, and also call on courage and perseverance. The basics of rock climbing and abseiling can be introduced, but these will be picked up much more strongly the following year.

In general, young people at this age feel a need to measure themselves against challenges. As a teacher, leader, or parent you may well experience your own values being challenged and questioned by the adolescent. The type of clothes you wear, your social media profile, the values you hold, and in sport, the way you play – and more importantly the way in which you interpret and enforce the rules – will be put to the test. The adult response is of particular importance. For the teenager it is a vulnerable time of rapid change; she will seek security in challenging the *status quo* and observing and experiencing the adult response. Whereas in the past the adult may have relied on a creative authority, this now gives way to an increasing degree of negotiation. No longer will the teenager accept rules at face value – and she is right not to. She has the awakening capacity to look 'behind the scene' and question why a certain adult stance has been adopted. She may do this with varying degrees of tact and social sensitivity, and sometimes cause flare-ups. She may need guidance to challenge in an appropriate way; but of greater importance is the response of the adult. It may be, as is very often the case, that the teenager spots an area in the adult that is somewhat unresolved and therefore sensitive. She has never really noticed it before or if she has, has not had the courage to stand up and challenge it. An adult on the receiving end of this may initially react by protecting herself, telling the teenager that it is none of her business, and not to be so rude. This usually has two results. Firstly the teenager will know she has hit the mark and secondly that the adult may be unwilling to face up to weakness. When this happens it is an unsettling experience for the adolescent; she wants to see a world that is willing to work on weaknesses, not hide from them. She wants a role model who can show her how she can face her own self-doubts and go forward into the future. If the adult response is to encourage her to speak about what she sees as unjust or unresolved and engage her in what causes her concern, the aggression often falls away and can be replaced with genuine compassion. If the criticism is aimed at the adult directly it may be possible to admit that this is an area that is sensitive, even giving a background to why this came about, and how you are working on it. Teenagers know the adult world is not perfect. It is fairly unrewarding to pretend it is. But it empowers the teenager to see adults around her who are willing to admit both their weaknesses and strengths.

At this age one may also begin to negotiate boundaries in such things as bed and home times, and acceptable and unacceptable behaviour in group or family activity. It may be, for example, that the group leader, teacher or parent offers a framework of possible choices. The teenagers are then asked to prioritise what they would like to take part in. The discussion then moves on to how this can be achieved. What are the ground rules? The next crucial and often overlooked step is also to agree the consequences for these ground rules being broken. If this last step is not taken, it can easily happen that everything goes well until a rule is broken or deadline not met, and then the adult is placed back in the role of authoritarian sanction-giver. The group has relinquished a vital part of its ownership of the whole process. And the adult gets cast in the 'bad guy' role. All this is not to suggest that the adult should abdicate authority; rather, that this authority gradually transforms itself into guidance. In this way the young person feels that the changes she is experiencing are being recognised. It is what Julian Sleigh** refers to in terms of a development from the authority of the king to the care of the shepherd.

---

* Standing in: A specific holding technique to ensure child safety.

** Julian Sleigh, *Thirteen to Nineteen: Discovering the Light*, Floris, 1989.

Fifteen

A cycle has been completed and a new one begins. The 'growing in and growing down' of the previous two seven-year phases has now been completed. A true growing 'up' and 'out' into the world now begins. A theme that will run throughout the next four years will be a growing interest in the world. This may be expressed, for example, in fashion, dance, drama and music, hobbies, environmental issues, political systems and rights, youth organisations, and most of all peer groups and friends in general. It is a time of dualism: on one hand we see great activity and enthusiasm in groups; and on the other, inwardness and a need for solitude, compassion for the plight of the disadvantaged people of the world. It can be a time, also, of very personally hurtful attacks and extremely self-centred behaviour; exaggerated self-belief alongside acute self-doubt and criticism; aggression yet vulnerability; retreat into the security of home and school punctuated by 'breakouts' such as truanting and not coming home; demands to be treated as an adult – yet excuses for immature behaviour, such as: 'What can you expect, I'm just a kid?' While this pendulum movement between two poles can be exasperating for the adult, it is an essential way for the teenager to find the middle ground.

Another important feature of this time is the intensification of subjectivity, expressed in extreme views. This is a refined form of dualism: the fifteen year old will approach the world in terms of black and white, wrong and right. Once, when negotiating with a fifteen year old a coming-home time from a party, and being faced with an elaborate explanation for all the reasons why a later time was okay, I threw up my hands and said: 'For goodness sake, do you have to be so subjective?' The memorable response was: 'What do you expect? That's my job.'

The unborn baby calling on its will to struggle through the birth canal into the world outside the womb, is echoed in the life of the fifteen year old. What is being born in the teenager is consciousness. In particular, consciousness of her actions and their implications, her feelings with all their complexity and mobility, and her thoughts now better able to look incisively and clearly at the world. Each of these three qualities must be harmonised with one another if a morally guided, balanced life is to be led. In the education of the adolescent the cultivation of action, feeling and thought – in this order – is vital. It should be remembered that these qualities are, in their own subtle way, just as vulnerable as the physical body of the baby. They are both new-born.

We begin this cultivation by focusing on the development of the will. This forms the foundation around which other qualities may grow. A normal fifteen year old displays abundant will. Anyone who has spent much time with young people at this age will have little doubt about this. Inner development at this age will also have its expression in space, in the way a young person moves. She may still display a residue of heaviness but a new quality of will has been added.

She carries the weight, the gravity, but now seeks to shift it in a self-guided way.

Given that a dualism runs through the life of the teenager, it also follows that there are 'spatial polarities' as well. In the fifteen year old this expresses itself in the polarity between the space that stands before or in front of us, and the space that is behind us. The front space: representing the future, 'stepping forward' – and the back space: the past, 'taking a step back'. This has a strong link with the fifteen year old emerging from the previous phase of life, standing on the threshold looking toward the future and all that awaits her there. The 'frontal' plane of space calls upon the will of the fifteen year old embarking on the journey into adulthood.

In sport this can be fostered not so much by changing the activities of the previous year, but by changing the emphasis, the way they are presented. While this may seem subtle, such a shift is absorbed by the teenager on a very deep level, and builds naturally to the development not only of good all-round skills and spatial understanding, but to a well-rounded, balanced individual. For example in **basketball**, the players are asked to focus on one-to-one skills in both defence and taking the offensive – taking on an opponent and trying to get by her successfully, while the defender responds quickly by adjusting position. The same principles can be applied in **rugby** and **hockey**. **Handball** can be introduced, as these qualities are easy to develop in this game.

Archery is also a good sport to be introduced at this age. The action of standing one's ground, pulling the bowstring backward in order to release the arrow's forward movement, is a perfect metaphor for the fifteen year old.

In athletics, **hurdling** and **high-** and **long-jumping** develop the qualities that are sought. The athlete has to bring her will into the foreground by sprinting, approaching the obstacle, using her weight to press down into the earth and then up and over. In long jump the principle is the same, but you strive to propel yourself as far forward as possible. The length of the jump, of course, is totally dependent on the amount of energy you are willing to exert. **Shot-put** is another activity that can be taught. As with long jump, the athlete has to press down into gravity and explode with will to propel the shot forward. However, like archery, she stays where she is and the object is hurled forward. She must not get too caught up in the throw – otherwise she will fall beyond the ring and the throw cannot be counted. So the will must be called upon, but must not overcome the athlete: she must harness and master this power. Simple tug-of-war is also enjoyed at this age particularly. This involves a long length of thick strong rope, two teams holding the rope and attempting to pull the other over a designated line.

Although **swimming** will have gone on for many years, it has particular importance at this age. Unlike walking or even running, it takes the young person out of her everyday movement environment. The swimmer's only means of moving, and indeed – in some cases – of not sinking, is to call on her will and motivate herself to swim through the water. While in running or land-based activities you may choose to stop if you lose your motivation, in swimming this cannot be done. The swimmer must go on until she has reached the end. Then she may rest. This sounds rather obvious, but in a world of instant gratification, where you may have something now and pay for it later, swimming is rather a good antidote.

In gymnastics, **vaulting** manifests much of what is needed. Again we see a barrier being placed in the gymnast's path, one that requires her willpower combined with skill to overcome. This activity can be slowly built up over the months to a stage where quite difficult and challenging vaults are attempted. There is little need to stay within the narrow boundaries that competitive vaulting sets, in which only a box and springboard are used. Mini, double, and full trampolines can be adapted. Both uneven and parallel bars can be vaulted, and the setting gradually raised. The distance between the obstacle and the springboard/mini-trampoline can be widened so that the flight needed to make contact with the box is longer and more challenging. The boys can attempt simple moves on the **parallel bars**, **rings**, and **pommel** (or vaulting horse). This should involve strength and determination to push oneself to the limit of one's endurance before relaxing and recuperating for the next attempt. For the girls, simple moves on the **uneven bars** and **balance-beam** should give emphasis to courage and strength. Basic moves such as forward and backward rolls, or even hand- and headstands, can now be attempted on the balance beam; on the uneven bars, release and catch moves and dismounts can be tried, involving bravery and skill. On the floor, both the boys and girls can continue **handsprings**; but a new challenge can be introduced in the form of a **flick-flack** (sometimes known as a backflip). This has been prepared for by the previous year's somersaults. This can be further developed with thrown-back somersaults, in which a gymnast runs towards another stationary gymnast or thrower, places her foot in the cupped hands of the thrower and her hands on his shoulders.

She is then thrown up into the air, back in the direction she came from; and while in the air she executes a back somersault, landing on her feet facing the thrower. Of course careful attention needs to be paid to the technique: as with all these movements, this should only be attempted with the aid of an experienced leader.

There are many steps in preparing for a flick-flack, involving take-off from inclined springboards and/ or raised platforms such as vaulting boxes, when the hands make contact with the end of the box and the dismount to the floor is to a lower level. One must stress the fact that the gymnast's arms need to be straight, the back-bend being full and dynamic, the head and eyes looking back towards the heels; and most of all, the explosion of energy off the floor.

Rock climbing and **abseiling** are also wonderful activities to be focused on now. Real quality time needs to be devoted to this activity, that so meets the needs of the fifteen year old. Here we see the dynamic frontal planes of the climber encounter the static frontal plane of the rock wall. Courage and willpower need to combine with endurance and a cool head. Once at the top, the climber has earned the pleasure of abseiling back down the face. In order to do this she must stand at the edge of the rock, facing away from the fall, pluck up her courage and launch herself backwards, over the edge, into space. Here again we see the dynamic interplay between front and back space, gravity and will. **Canoeing** and **kayaking** can also begin. Here the will is strongly involved: the paddler is required to exert a thrusting downward force into the water in order to propel herself forward. If this motion ceases her movement simply stops. **Hiking** and **cross-country skiing** also fit perfectly with this stage. **Snorkelling** and especially **scuba diving** are very popular and beneficial activities. These help the student to explore weight and its effects, as well as engaging their will to influence it.

Sixteen

The foundations have now been laid, the life of the will continues to play its part in offering solidity and motivation; but now a new dimension emerges, the life of feelings. The sixteen year old is no longer a child. Instead one now encounters a true 'young adult'. Some of the defensiveness of the past begins to change. She is likely to be more ready to accept the consequences of her own behaviour. The individual begins to emerge and the role of the peer group shows the first signs of becoming less important. In its place can come a more intense one-to-one relationship with another, quite often with a romantic attraction element. The young adult seeks to define her place more in terms of her individual relationships with her friends and also, perhaps, her romantic partner. How she feels about people and issues, and certainly how others feel about her, become somewhat central in her life. Whereas her relationships were previously governed by reasonably cohesive peer group and family structures, she will now attempt to redefine these in a much more individualised way. She will look around herself with an appraising eye – like a captain on board a ship surveying the horizon – ensuring she is on the right course, enjoying the sunshine but checking for potential storms and hazards.

In spatial development at this age we can see a strong relationship to the horizon and the horizontal plane. What lies above and below the horizontal plane becomes more sharply defined. While the will activity of the previous year was mainly experienced through the limbs, the horizontal plane is more closely related to the trunk – the place in the body that has the strongest relationship to its own rhythmical movements. We can see this in the movement of the heart and lung, and even in the peristalsis of the intestines. Here also is the focal point of the feeling life.

In **sport** many activities of the previous year can be continued, but again a shift of spatial emphasis is required. Rugby, wrestling, hockey and football may become less valuable. Now the accent moves more strongly to the player's relationship with her fellow teammates or her position on the court. She will have a greater capacity to understand that she need not chase the ball, but can move into the right position and make herself available for a pass; or even distract other opponents, thus giving the ball-carrier more space to move. She may sacrifice her own 'glory' for that of the team. This needs to be encouraged and praised. Sports which may have been previously introduced, such as **tennis**, **badminton**, **softball**, **baseball**, can now be focused on more strongly; for in the batting and stroking of the ball and shuttle, the horizontal plane comes to the fore in a wonderful way. **Ice-skating** is another activity that lends itself splendidly to the dynamics required at this time. **Volleyball** can be further developed with particular emphasis on passing, both in digging and volleying. Ball games such as **netball**, **korfball** and in particular **basketball**, are very appropriate at this age; they emphasise the patient build-up of passing, and the total awareness of all players on court. Tight refereeing is important, to allow the player to be more proactive and not encroach on the opponent's space, thus committing a foul. Creating screens for your teammate to shoot over; 'picks' for her to run off; give and go moves; creating a momentary distraction or moving clear of an area, to create space for your team-mate; or alternatively being aware of when space is being created for you: these are all skills that transform basketball from what can at times be

an aggressive to a flowing, total-awareness, spatially sensitive game.

In **athletics** the **discus** should receive pride of place, with its clear experience of the horizontal plane. An interesting adjunct to the programme can be **learning first aid**. In this area the young person can both develop valuable skills and be given a safe context in which to express her feeling for the well-being of another person.

In **gymnastics** an artistic approach is needed. Much will have been learned over the past years; now the separate moves are arranged together to form routines and choreographies. At first these may be simple and the instructor will prompt often. But in time the sixteen year olds will enjoy working out their own routines in an attempt to express themselves in an aesthetically attractive and spatially dynamic way. The routines may take the form of gymnastic display work, in which a team of gymnasts will perform a series of split-second manoeuvres arranged in an artistic and energetic way. These can often be performed for parents and peers at assemblies and festivals, or simply be done for their own sake.

Water sports form the core of the outdoor education programme at this time, particularly **sailing** and **windsurfing**. Here one literally has a clear horizon and a need to be extremely sensitive to the environment and the changes in both the currents and the wind. If you are lucky enough to have access to surf beaches, then this also has a fine role to play around this age. Basic **downhill skiing** can also be developed. In such an activity there is a need to be very aware of one's surroundings, making quick adjustments when needed.

Seventeen

At seventeen begins a phase of looking forward. Decisions are made around this age that will have implications for many years to come. Many possibilities will present themselves; the essential and the non-essential will need to be carefully sorted out and a direction found. While parents and teachers may be called on for advice, the process is largely in the hands of the young person herself. This process may well go on for several years. If we cast our minds back only two years – to the stage of the fifteen year old – we can see evidence of the rapid changes that occur during adolescence. A basis was laid around fifteen, then followed a phase in which the feelings of the individual became more conscious; but what now begins to emerge are incisive, clear qualities of thought. This will be of great assistance as the seventeen year old begins to assess where she is now and where she wants to go. She will be reasonably realistic about her skills and limitations. The harsh subjective criticisms of the past begin to give way to a new objectivity. The 'no' phase is largely over, the 'maybe' phase, though still present, begins to give way to a 'yes' phase. However the 'yes' will only be affirmed if it stands up to the teenager's own intense, analytical, penetrating focus of thought.

The seat of this thinking is our head, which is the part of the body least involved in movement. A possible analogy for the threefold relationship between head, heart and limbs, is the following: the limbs are like horses, full of power and responsive to any command, that make it possible for the carriage to move; the carriage represents the trunk, able to respond to the bumps along the way, mediating between the road, the horses and the passenger; the passenger is like a king or queen, carried by the carriage, able to sit quietly with a certain interested detachment, sure of its role and control of the situation. In terms of spatial development, the dissection of left and right, and the symmetry that exists between the two in the vertical plane, is similar to the process the seventeen year old goes through when determining the essential from the non-essential and finding a path forward. It is necessary to become conscious; by balancing what is to the left and to the right, we find the plane that exists between two extremes. We come into harmony and symmetry and can truly relate to what is vertical, what is upright.

As in previous years, this new psychological and spatial development needs to find its place in the movement experience. We are attempting to give expression to the qualities of verticality and conscious thought.

Many of the sports of the previous year can be continued, further developing the will/frontal, and the feeling/horizontal planes; but now emphasis shifts to the thinking/vertical. In games such as **basketball**, for example, the focus moves to shooting; in **racket sports**, to accuracy – particularly in the overhead smash and serve; in athletics to **sprinting** and **javelin**, which provide a clear experience of symmetry and total focus on the finishing line; in **softball** and **baseball** absolute accuracy in throwing in the field and in pitching. There are some other activities which are perfect at this age: in **cricket** we see one of the most gracious and clear examples of symmetry and verticality. This is most obvious in the predominantly straight or vertical bat-strokes that can be played with force or with wonderful finesse. Symmetry is beautifully expressed in the bowling action, and in the position of the wicket at the centre of the field of play – the ball may be stroked either to the left, right, forward or behind, over the fielders' heads or along the ground. In short it is one of the few games that encompasses all six spatial directions.

While **volleyball** will have been built up in the previous years, it is at this age that it comes into its own.

Digging, volleying and setting demand symmetry: both hands or arms must make perfectly equal contact when playing the ball; if this happens then the pass will be accurate, but if it is only a fraction out there will either be a foul or the ball will fly out of control. In serving, and particularly in spiking, there is a need for fine control yet power, and a strong relationship with verticality. This is especially obvious in the vertical jump that proceeds the spike.

Another major theme at this time is cultivating the ability to move with accuracy, precision and speed. This requires lightning reflexes, an ability to perceive an opening, and most of all, keeping a 'cool head'.

These moments can be found in many sports but they are most 'distilled' in **table tennis** and in particular **fencing**. If at all possible, these qualities should be strongly encouraged at this age.

It is also beneficial for the seventeen year old to acquire a very good **knowledge of the rules** of each game. Talks and projects may be set in this area. Short courses can be given, followed by a rotation of players taking it in turns to referee part of a game. This facilitates a further development of the ability to see beyond the surface and calls for real clarity of perception and reaction.

In **gymnastics**, the previous year's efforts in display work can be developed further; but now this can move into more individually-based routines. **Trampoline** work is of particular benefit, as many of the moves require a solid understanding of verticality. However these dynamics can of course be found and accentuated in all areas of gymnastics. In **orienteering**, map reading and compass settings are further developed, with the courses becoming progressively more difficult. **Kayaking** and **downhill skiing** require all the faculties previously mentioned in connection with fencing, but to a still greater degree. **Rowing** is of special importance as the boat's linear direction through space – in this case through the medium of water – is totally dependent on the individual or the team exerting equal pressure on the right and the left of the boat. This is an excellent example of the threefold qualities of the head, trunk and limbs. The legs press away and back, the arms strain at the oars, the trunk tenses and relaxes rhythmically with each stroke, and the head remains still and focused on the task.

In general the seventeen year old should be encouraged not only to play the game but also to understand what lies behind it. She will, for example, benefit from being offered frequent opportunities to plan and execute tactics – such as increasingly complex motion offensives, or set-play isolation moves in basketball. The same goes for volleyball, with crossover shoot, and quick or short-set spiking attacks; in table tennis, the role of top and backspin in setting up for a smash; in orienteering, the careful planning of the route to optimise efficiency.

Eighteen to Twenty-One

The time between eighteen and twenty-one is of great significance; this has been recognised throughout the ages, and is especially expressed in initiation rites following puberty. The young person now stands at the doorway leading from adolescence into adulthood, looking back to the past and forward to the future. The strength of the threefold qualities of soul expressed in willing, feeling, and thinking that have been developed since puberty, are now brought together and play a vital role in how the young person makes this step. It is a time of testing, exploration and risk-taking, in an effort to find one's limits and potentials and then attempt to push out beyond them. This often takes a physical form but can also be an inner, spiritual quest. It is a time where ideals and hope flourish – which can sometimes end in great disappointment. The young person will look about herself and see the weaknesses and contradictions of the world, and how they need changing. If she has developed inner soul strength in the time since puberty, she may just see a way that she can make a difference. This is also a very special time in terms of spatial development. The three planes and the six directions of space have, we hope, been thoroughly experienced. What can follow is the conscious realising of these in every activity.

We can encourage such an exploration by looking back and briefly experiencing the many stages of spatial development that have been passed through. One may even look as far back as the baby's journey through postural stages in the striving towards uprightness. This begins at a 'plant' stage (lying on the back), then passes through the following: 'bird' (lying on front with arms and feet outstretched so that only the pelvis touches the ground); 'fish' (lying on the front, feet raised, with legs bent at the knee, arms bent with hands palm down near the shoulders); 'reptile' (same as the fish, but push upwards so that the arms are straight); 'quadruped' (classic crawling position); and finally the 'human being' standing on two feet. Then one can progress through the singing, finger games and hand games, skipping, and all the other stages that have been comprehensively described in this book. It is often heartwarming to see these young adults now secure enough within themselves to be willing to go back and play the games of their childhood. Although this is often riotous fun, the aim of the teacher is to bring the young adult into a conscious understanding both of the stages of spatial development, and of why certain games – and later sports – were played at quite specific times. In other words, the teacher now draws back the veil on all that has gone before. This will often leave the eighteen year olds with a new-found respect for the process they have passed through, and, even more importantly, the space in which they move now.

It is at this age that teenagers will often feel the need to become very proficient at just one or perhaps two sports. As far as possible this should be facilitated, both within school time and after school, in clubs. They should be encouraged to pass their newly developed expertise on to younger children who are just beginning their sporting journey. This can be done in after-school clubs or on class or group outings. By encouraging this, the adult is recognising the maturity of the young adult, is challenging her to further develop and deepen these skills by doing what also needs to be cultivated at this age – helping others.

In each sport, great emphasis should now be placed on being aware of the threefold planes of space and how they interact. For example in **athletics**, especially running, it can be pointed out that to run with both speed and grace the legs and arms must move powerfully; and yet the trunk must not over-tense and in a subtle way try to do the job of the limbs; likewise the head must remain still and focused, not moving from side to side or contracting back into the trunk so that the shoulders become hunched. Each of these three aspects has its own job to do and needs to be given the freedom and awareness to do so. This example is true for every sport; indeed, it is actually true for every movement, even brushing teeth and washing dishes. At this time, then, in every sport and activity, the young adult should strive to stay conscious not only of what she achieves but how she moves to achieve it. This theme of pure, free movement is also taken into **gymnastics**. Every exercise, no matter how simple, should be executed with strength, grace, and clarity. This is also an ideal time to teach the gymnast standing-in or spotting techniques, so that she can deepen her understanding of even very basic exercises.

In outdoor pursuits, as far as possible, a freedom of choice should be given. The kind of activities that are often popular are those that are the physically most thrilling and dangerous. More advanced **downhill skiing**, and **rock climbing** are popular. **Hang-gliding** and even **parachuting** have at times been pursued and very much enjoyed. At this age there is, again, a need to push the limits of what can be achieved.

217. Zip-Zap-Zop

This game keeps you on your toes!

In this game, the order is always 'Zip-Zap-Zop'. A circle is formed with everyone facing in and someone begins with 'Zip', sending a spatial gesture clap in a very clear direction to another person in the circle with eye contact – that person then sends along 'Zap' to the next person, 'Zop'... and it keeps on going until someone breaks the rhythm. If you break the rhythm, you are out – each round is played by fewer and fewer survivors until there is a face-off with just two people and then one eventual victor.

Variations:

- New words may be created by the group – single syllable words allow a steady beat.
- When players are 'out', the game leader can choose to put them on a task (i.e. start classroom chores, fitness challenges, etc.)

AGE RANGE: 12+
PLAY AREA: Indoor or outdoor, any
NUMBER OF PLAYERS: 8+
EQUIPMENT: None

- Players that are 'out' can try to **silently** distract the players that are trying to concentrate.
- As skills improve, the tempo may be increased.
- An additional rule can be added that a player can be 'out' if their signal is not clear. The game leader must have a keen eye for this. This encourages players to be good senders as well as receivers.

Hints to the leader:

- This game can be stressful for some students, and is only really fun when all people playing are game for some serious competition.

218. Equidistant

The game leader asks each player in the group to choose two people (in secret) from whom to stay equally distant. The goal of the game is to eventually come to stillness. Once everyone has chosen their secret two people, the game leader calls 'Ready, Set, Go'. All players then move/adjust their own position according to the (now ever-changing) positions of their two secret people.

Variations:

- Hero/Villain: Same concept but players secretly choose one player as their Villain and a different player as their Hero. When the game begins, each player is attempting to position themselves so that the person that is their Hero is standing between them and their Villain, 'protecting them' if you will. When using this variation, encourage players not to only choose their best buddies.

Hints to the leader:

- When setting up, don't start in a circle. Encourage

AGE RANGE: 12+
PLAY AREA: Indoor or outdoor, large room or open space, 20 x 40 paces
NUMBER OF PLAYERS: 10+
EQUIPMENT: None

the group to be in an unorganised clump. This gives the game more action/movement.

- The game leader can ask the group to bring their awareness to those who may have chosen them and can eventually have each person show their connections by pointing all together. What would this look like if you connected all of these connections with string? Birds-eye view?
- This is a fun game to do with adults (parents, teachers, etc.). A non-running/non-standing player can play this game in a chair that has wheels on it (i.e. an office chair).

219. Eye of the Tiger

The group holds hands in a circle around a large (soft) central object (a big bean bag chair works great.) This is the 'Eye' of the Tiger, and if you touch it, you're out. If you break hands, you're out. The group tries to push/pull/move any which way so as to get others to touch the 'Eye' without doing so themselves.

Variations:

- Those that are 'out' can be the first to start on chores, work on their fitness challenges, etc.

Hints to the leader:

- This can be a satisfyingly rough game – not everyone's cup of tea. For more sensitive players, they may choose where to place themselves on the circle (specifically, whose hands they feel safe holding!).

AGE RANGE: 12+

PLAY AREA: Indoor or outdoor, 20 x 20 paces or a large room

NUMBER OF PLAYERS: 8+

EQUIPMENT: One large beanbag (tiger)

For children who may struggle to play this game:

- An additional role may be added for those who wish to not get pulled around: Referee – calls the outs when a players touches the beanbag or when players break their hand-holds.

children in circle holding hands

large bean bag or cushion in centre

220. All Play! an adaptation of *Capture the Flag* for all of the temperaments (aka Storm the Castle)
by Cory Waletzko and Kevin Quigley

The players are Knights who have been sent on a perilous mission – to steal the Royal Orb from the opposing team's castle without being captured and sent to the dungeon.

This is a version of *Capture the Flag* that was created as the culminating event for the sixth-grade rite of passage Knighthood Ceremony and Medieval Games Tournament at the Upper Valley Waldorf School in Vermont. This is a community-wide game, played by about 100 adults and middle school students on a large open field, that addresses the different temperaments of the players: the Cholerics (the fiery go-getters heading straight into action), the Melancholics (the stalwart protectors taking up guard positions), the Phlegmatics (the passive observers, on the side-lines or day-dreaming away), and the Sanguines (the flighty dabblers, chatting and bouncing around trying a little bit of everything.) Play: Two teams, marked with different colour pinnies or ribbons, try to run to the opposing team's side, take the Orb, and return it to their side without being tagged. The round ends, either when one team captures the opposing team's Orb by running it through the Lake of Mist back to their own side **or** when all the players on a particular team are captured (which is highly unlikely). Then players switch sides and start another round.

Field Set-up:
The field is divided into three sections: each team's home territory and a no man's land in between. In each team's home territory is a Castle hoop that holds the Royal Orb (a small throwable ball) and a Dungeon hoop that designates the jail. There are also at least four Sanctuary hoops on each side. At any given time, one player may guard a particular hoop. Guards must be five steps away from any hoop that they are guarding; a Sanctuary hoop, the Dungeon hoop, or the Castle hoop that holds the Royal Orb.

Sanctuaries:
Sanctuary hoops are 'safe zones'. A player cannot be tagged if they make it into any hoop (Sanctuary)

AGE RANGE: 12+

PLAY AREA: Outdoor, 20 x 40 paces, large rectangular flat field

NUMBER OF PLAYERS: 12+

EQUIPMENT: 12 hula hoops; 2 balls (Orbs); 4 corner cones; low cones to mark periphery of the field; 1 chair; 2 long streamers (life-lines); low cones to mark centre area (Lake of Mist); 2 different coloured pinnies or ribbons (enough for all players)

with at least one foot. Only one player may occupy a hoop at any given time. When a teammate steps into an occupied hoop, the player who was previously standing within it must exit.

Lake of Mist: Spirit of the Lake, Lifelines
Between the two opposing sides is the Lake of Mist. In the Lake of Mist, the two sides can mingle, neutral territory. A player cannot be tagged in the Lake of Mist – unless they carry the Orb. If the Orb is to be captured, it must be run through the Lake of Mist safely to the other side without the knight being tagged.

Option:
For an injured student, or anyone who does not wish to stand or run: in the centre of the Lake of Mist, sits the Spirit of the Lake (a player sitting in a chair with two streamers tied to each side.) The Spirit of the Lake has the power to grant a Lifeline to one knight at a time on each side. The Lifeline is a long streamer or ribbon. The Spirit of the Lake, if asked in a knightly fashion, may grant a Lifeline by handing one end of the streamer to the knight of choice who may then venture into the opposing side. As long as they hold the Lifeline, they cannot be tagged.

A knight may not hold the Orb and the Lifeline at the same time. When the Lifeline is released, the Spirit of the Lake reels it in to offer it to a new knight. If they are not the recipient of the Lifeline, players may not touch it, even accidentally, or they automatically go to the opposing side's Dungeon. The Lifelines should not quite reach into any of the Sanctuary hoops.

Action:

If a player is tagged while in the other team's territory, they place both hands on their head (the signal that they are not currently in play) and go to the other side's Dungeon to await rescue. Players may form a chain in the Dungeon, linking hands so that one end of the chain has a foot in the hoop and the other end is closer to the home territory.

All prisoners are rescued when any one of them is tagged by a free player from their own team. When rescued, players place both hands on their head and hightail it back to their home territory. Once 'home' they may re-enter play.

Orbs:

The Orbs can be thrown from person to person as long as they are not dropped. If dropped, an Orb must be returned to it's hoop by the team that dropped it. Orbs may not be thrown into or out of a Sanctuary – but they can be run into a Sanctuary. They may not be thrown over the Lake of Mist – but they must be run through it to win the round.

The round ends either when one team captures the opposing team's Orb by running it through the Lake of Mist back to their own side **or**, when all players on a particular team are captured. Then, switch sides and start another round.

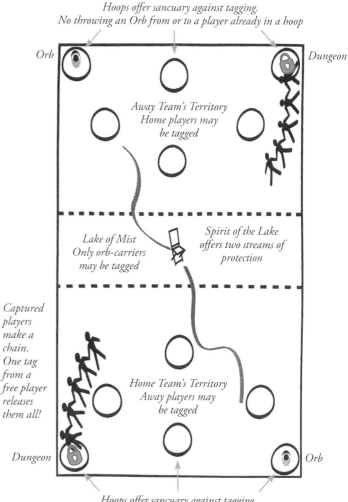

Hoops offer sancuary against tagging.
No throwing an Orb from or to a player already in a hoop

Orb   Dungeon

Away Team's Territory
Home players may
be tagged

Lake of Mist
Only orb-carriers
may be tagged

Spirit of the Lake
offers two streams of
protection

Captured
players
make a
chain.
One tag
from a
free player
releases
them all!

Home Team's Territory
Away players may
be tagged

Dungeon   Orb

Hoops offer sancuary against tagging.
No throwing an Orb from or to a player already in a hoop

221. Disc Golf

Similar to traditional golf, disc golf is a series of 'holes' in which participants traverse, trying to hit their targets in as few throws as possible. Players start at an agreed area called the 'tee box', throw their disc towards the target (or to a strategic location that gets them closer to the target), then walk to their disc to throw from the location where the disc lands. This process is repeated until a player throws their disc and hits the agreed target (usually a tree, marker, or other physical feature in your area).

To set up a disc golf course, all that is needed is an open area and a few hours to establish the following:

- The course layout.
- Establishing the targets, or 'holes' – a nine-hole course is good for beginners, and it means that the players will be able to complete the course within a 40- to 45-minute period of time. 18 holes is the traditional length of a course.
- Establishing the 'tee boxes' (starting throwing areas for each hole) that correspond to each identified target.
- Placing targets near the next tee box creates a nice flow to the course, and can keep multiple players from accidentally throwing into each other's areas of play.
- The 'par' for the course – 'par' is a term used to describe the number of throws it should take a very good player to eventually hit the target with their disc.
- If using standard *Ultimate* frisbee discs, some children can throw a maximum of 60 yards, with most children throwing an average of 40 yards.
- A formula to calculate the par for each hole is to take the total number of yards between the tee box and the target, divide by 40, round to the nearest whole number, and add two. For example, a 90-yard hole would be calculated like this:

  90 yards / 40 yards = 2.25
  Round 2.25 down to 2
  2 + 2 = 4
  A straight, 90-yard hole would have a par of four.

AGE RANGE: 12+

PLAY AREA: Outdoor, open area with options for targets, or 'holes' – school campuses or public parks work well

NUMBER OF PLAYERS: The number of holes on the course x 6 (a 9-hole course can accommodate up to 36 people comfortably and 54 with some waiting for others)

EQUIPMENT: One disc / frisbee per player, pencil and paper to keep score (optional: ties or markers to identify each target)

Variations:

- Team play is possible on a disc golf course. Establish teams of two to four for most disc golf games.
- 'Best Disc' – In Best Disc format (commonly called 'Scramble' in traditional golf), each player throws from the tee box, then the team chooses one disc that is most advantageous to **all** throw their next turn from. In this format, the team is taking their very best throw from the group each turn and the team gets one score that can be compared to other teams playing the same format.
- 'Best Score' – In 'Best Score', each individual on the team plays their disc all the way to the target keeping track of their score. The team then takes the best score from the whole team and only records that score for the team.
- Soccer-Golf – A similar course can be set up using a soccer ball instead of a disc.
- For more advanced play, different types of discs can be used for different length throws. There are 'driver' discs that are smaller and go farther, and 'putting' discs that are easier to control and go shorter distances.

Hints to the leader:

- Determine a plan for 'lost discs' – if a player throws a disc that gets stuck up in a tree, for example, have extra discs on hand but also determine a fair consequence (i.e. that person adds two strokes to their score or must make a plan to retrieve the disc at a later time, etc.)

- If possible, have players practise different kinds of throws for target practice. It is not necessary, nor always advantageous, to throw the disc in the same way one would when playing *Ultimate* (game 227) or a game of catch with a disc.

- A good course has a mix of challenging and relaxing holes. Players should have triumphs and pitfalls in every round. A course that is too easy gets boring quickly. A course that is too challenging will not be fun for anyone but the most skilled players.

For children who may struggle to play this game:

- Some players will never be able to make 'par' on any of the holes. This can be an unnecessary frustration that leads to low self-esteem. Helping players develop their own sense of par can be a liberating educational process. The player can be asked how long they can throw the disc if thrown with accuracy and strength.

This number is then put into the par formula to create an individualised par for that player. For example, if a student can throw the disc 20 yards with accuracy, the same 90-yard hole would be calculated like this:

90 yards / 20 yards = 4.5
Round 2.25 up to 5
5 + 2 = 7
A straight, 90-yard hole would have a par of seven for this student.

222. The Gauntlet

Two teams of equal numbers. One group is stationed in the field, each player in a stationary position. One group is 'up'. One at a time, the players who are 'up' toss the ball out into the field and run to a designated area across the field and back. The team in the field tries to peg the player as they run. The player attempts to dodge all throws and return unscathed. The number of 'hits' are counted cumulatively. Every player on the side runs the gauntlet. Count the score then switch sides.

Variations:

- Add more balls and increase the distance for a larger group.

AGE RANGE: 12–14
PLAY AREA: Indoor or outdoor, 30 by 30 paces or a large room
NUMBER OF PLAYERS: 12+
EQUIPMENT: One soft-skinned ball

Hints to the leader:

- Wait until players are at least 12 years old to introduce this game. At that age they are ready for it, and it's a good time for them to begin to think about defence.

- This is also a good game to develop proper arm mechanics needed for throwing.

- Use a softer surface, spongy type of ball, seven-inch diameter so they can get a good grip.

- No head shots!

223. Speedball

Soccer meets football meets handball – this game levels the playing field!

Speedball is a fast-paced team game that combines the most exciting elements of many sports all together. Two teams, one ball.

Each team is trying to score by getting the ball either:

- kicked into the goal (two points).
- run across the end zone (one point).

The game begins with a jump ball in the centre. The game leader throws the ball straight up and players then try to get the ball to their goal/end zone. The catch is that, if the ball is on the ground, the ball may only be kicked (soccer rules). If the ball is kicked or thrown into the air, the ball may be caught/passed/run with (football rules). However, the ball may not be picked up from the ground.

Switching possession: If the ball is kicked or thrown out of bounds, that team loses possession and the other team may then throw the ball in from the place that it went out.

If a player is holding the ball/running with the ball, that player may be tagged (two-hand touch) by a player on the opposing team. If tagged, they must put the ball on the ground at the place they were tagged and the opposing team is the first to kick the ball back into play from that spot.

> **AGE RANGE:** 13+
>
> **PLAY AREA:** Outdoor, soccer-sized field
>
> **NUMBER OF PLAYERS:** 10+
>
> **EQUIPMENT:** One ball (soft-skinned or soccer ball works well); cones to mark outside boundaries and soccer goals or cones to mark goals; pinnies to identify two teams

Variations:

- 'Air dribbles' may be added – any player may throw the ball up and away from them and catch it again.
- 'Kick-ups' may be added – using both feet to hoist the ball off the ground so that it can be a legal 'catch'.

Hints to the leader:

- Rather than a jump-ball to begin the game, the game leader may wish to use a kick-off. This avoids possible head bumps/collisions and does not give advantage to taller players that are generally the ones who are able to take possession from a jump ball.
- This game helps to 'level the playing field' – players that have a lot of practice playing soccer, for example, are given the chance to use their hands in this game, and players that have a lot of practice playing football get a chance to use their feet.

224. Parkour Course

Parkour (or Free-Running) is basically a timed obstacle course that encourages participants to use strength, flexibility, momentum, and creativity in order to traverse from point A to point B as efficiently (or interestingly) as possible. The simplest approach is to visit a playground site and envision/try out creative movement challenges that take you through the various playground structures in ways that are not necessarily conventional to the actual structures that exist. For example, if there is a playground slide, one of the stations may require participants to run up from the bottom to the top (rather than sliding down.) If there are swings, the challenge may be to run through them while they are swinging in alternating directions/speeds, etc. The game leader must make sure that each of the stations is doable, safe, and (hopefully) fun. Once the whole course is mapped out, and thoroughly tested by the game leader for possible glitches/unsafe areas, each player may run the course while being timed. They then have the option to try to beat their time.

Variations:

- When working with a group with a wide range of physical ability, the game leader may create options at each station (an easier version/a more challenging version.) This way, players can self-select the level that is appropriate for them.

AGE RANGE: 13–14

PLAY AREA: Outdoor, playground with various play structures

NUMBER OF PLAYERS: Any

EQUIPMENT: A stop-watch or other device to time the participants

Hints to the leader:

- It can be helpful to have participants work together in pairs or trios so that every runner has a spotter (or cheerleader!) as well as a timer. This fosters a sense of camaraderie as well as covers basic safety precautions. Having a partner time a runner also relieves the runner of worrying about the time/stopwatch so that they can fully focus on the challenge at hand.

- This activity is especially great for teenagers as it gives them a good balance of risk and creativity. They can also create their own courses, or help to establish different levels of challenge at each station.

Activities to Develop Spatial Awareness

Age 16+

The activities that follow are a blending of games and spatial exercises. They are aimed primarily at the teenager and the adult. They will be of little benefit to the pre-puberty child, who will not yet have developed the faculties for understanding them.

225. Equilibrium

Each player has a partner. Facing a partner, the players hold their hands at chest height. The two staves are held between the partners' hands with a firm pressure. Tell the pairs to increase the pressure, ensuring that it is very firm.

One partner is the leader, the other the follower. They move in silence. The follower tries to maintain the pressure of both staves, mirroring the leader's actions. For instance, when the leader walks backwards, the follower must maintain the pressure on her hand made by the staff, as she moves forwards. The second stage is for the follower to close her eyes while doing this. The leader must not move too quickly, and is responsible for preventing any collisions!

She must guide her partner safely through the room full of other pairs.

Variations:

- The number of followers per leader can increase. Build the number up slowly; start with two then three followers. Three followers and one leader is a good number as they will then form a square when they hold their staves between each others' hands.

  They will try to keep this shape as they are led. But with more than one follower, the leader also has the option of calling out 'Stop!' Then the followers stand still, open their eyes and correct themselves. (For instance, two of them may be about to collide with each other.)

  Whatever happens, the equilibrium must be kept at all times.

> **Equipment:** One wooden staff for each player

It is possible for 20 people to play this in a circle. If I am the leader in such a group, I ask the players to keep their eyes closed. I then stand as still as I possibly can, not varying the pressure on the staves either side of me in any way. Almost invariably, the same interesting and very funny thing always occurs: although I haven't moved, the circle moves, perhaps because that is what everyone is expecting. Since the leader must not respond in any way, but only initiate movement, a staff will eventually fall to the ground and the communication between staves breaks down. I then suggest that the group try again, trying to listen more carefully to one another. This is an exercise that asks the participants for acute spatial sensitivity, as well as for clear communication between them. I have played this game with such diverse groups as drug-addicted teenagers, drama students and in-service trainees in firms and corporations. It never fails to be a revealing experience for the participants – both in terms of how they affect others and how they respond to events.

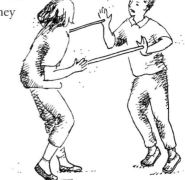

226. Help!

One person is chosen to be 'It' and chases the others, trying to tag them. The other players are safe from 'It' when they are holding a beanbag.

If someone is in danger of being caught, she can shout 'Help!' to the others – and, hopefully, a beanbag will be thrown to her before she is tagged. When caught by It, the player leaves the game.

Begin by throwing the beanbags into the air, so that all players have a chance to catch one. As the game progresses, slowly collect the beanbags, so that there are always too few to go around. About 60 per cent of the players will at any one time have one in their hand.

This game tries to encourage players to become a little more aware of one another's needs or plight. In one school I taught in, I had continually observed that when the bell rang and everyone had to pass through the front doors of the building, none of the teenagers ever held the door for the others behind them – even if they had just been knocked in the face themselves by it! This was an example of how self-absorbed young people are at this age – each one the only sun in the universe. *Help!* is a game that tries to help people move beyond an 'each one for herself' attitude.

I have also played this game successfully with adults on various training courses, as well as in work settings and in-service training days.

It is interesting to observe who is prepared to sacrifice the safety of having her own beanbag, for the

> **EQUIPMENT:** Beanbags (enough for 60 per cent of the group)

sake of another student who is in trouble. There are also those who tend to selfishly hold on to their own beanbag – but they lose out on the thrill of a narrow escape. The experience of being chased without a beanbag and not getting help, is a bit like a bad dream – everyone could save you but no-one will!

At other times you are being chased and will have bean bags thrown to you, but because you are panicking you do not have the presence of mind to catch them.

At this age, I feel it is appropriate to discuss the social dynamic of such a game – it fits the adolescent's growing interest in self-awareness and self-development.

227. Elf and Goblin Boots

The aim of the game is for the Elf to avoid being touched by the Goblin. However in this game there is no need for the leader to call out, because every time either the Elf or the Goblin moves, the bells around her ankles will make a noise.

> **EQUIPMENT:** Two blindfolds; four elastic garters or bands with a small bell sewn or threaded on top of each of them – they should be big enough to slip over, or tie around the ankle – follow the same guidelines as in *Night Watchman* (game 233).

228. Ultimate

This is a variation on the well-known game of the same name developed in the United States.

The frisbee is placed on the ground where it was dropped. A player who will initiate the next play stands near it.

The opposition team then make a line facing the other team, about five paces away. No-one can break out of these lines until one of the players with possession of the frisbee picks it up off the ground and attempts to make a pass.

If a throw is intercepted by a clean catch, by Player B, for instance, then Team B is awarded possession of the frisbee (a 'turnover'). If a turnover occurs, then all downs no longer count, and the team in possession of the frisbee is allowed three downs.

However, if the interceptor drops the frisbee in her attempt, possession is given to the team that was attempting the pass.

After three drops or 'downs' the frisbee is given to the other team from the place where the last down took place. However if Team A, for instance, throws the frisbee beyond the field of play, then Team B is awarded possession from the place where the frisbee crossed the line.

Divide the players into two teams of about 11–15 players each. Each team starts off with three 'downs' or lives. During one of their 'downs' they have uninterrupted possession of the frisbee. To score a point, a player must throw the frisbee to another player on her team who is in the end zone. Any player is allowed in an end zone for only five seconds at a time.

No player may run with the frisbee in her possession. She may pivot. Any player may only hold the frisbee for five seconds. Any longer than this and it is counted as a 'down' (or a lost life). No defending player is allowed within two arm-lengths of the player with the frisbee. If this occurs and the defending player does not retreat, then the attacking player may call for a five-yard penalty; she may then advance five yards towards her end zone and the offending player must then stand one yard behind her until she has taken her free throw.

When a point is scored, for instance by Team

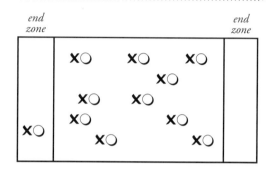

PLAY AREA: A large empty space: e.g. a hockey pitch – mark off the two 'end zones' field, facing their end zone, at about the place where the frisbee was dropped

EQUIPMENT: Bibs or vests to mark the two teams; one frisbee or an aerobie

A, then Team A gets possession of the frisbee and starts by throwing it as far as they can away from their own end zone (where they just scored). Team B will be waiting where they calculate the frisbee will land, to begin a new attack. If a catcher doesn't catch the frisbee, she declares it a 'down' by raising her arm. She then waits while the two teams form a line. This is done by the team in possession of the frisbee forming a line across the field, facing their end zone, at about the place where the frisbee was dropped. The frisbee is placed on the ground where it was dropped. A player who will initiate the next play stands near it.

The opposition team then make a line facing the other team, about five paces away. No-one can break out of these lines until one of the players with possession of the frisbee picks it up off the ground and attempts to make a pass.

If a throw is intercepted by a clean catch, by Player B, for instance, then Team B is awarded possession of the frisbee (a 'turnover'). If a turnover occurs, then all downs no longer count, and the team in possession of the frisbee is allowed three downs.

However, if the interceptor drops the frisbee in her attempt, possession is given to the team that was attempting the pass.

After three drops or 'downs' the frisbee is given to the other team from the place where the last down took place. However if Team A, for instance, throws the frisbee beyond the field of play, then Team B is awarded possession from the place where the frisbee crossed the line.

Variations:

• You can agree not to play the line-out rule. Players may take up any position on the field and not have to run back and form two lines after each down. This makes the game more flowing and usually necessitates man on man marking (one player exclusively guards only one player from the opposition team).

• If a player has the frisbee, she can decide to run with it: but then she can be chased and touched by a player from the opposite team. This touch must be made with both hands simultaneously. This would then count as a down.

Ultimate is based loosely on American and Australian football, but instead of bone-crunching tackles, there is laughter, long flying throws and running free of worries about physical contact. In the official *Ultimate* game there is no referee.

Players must follow a sporting code and own up to any fouls or drops that may have occurred. If there is a dispute then the players involved have to negotiate and sort it out before play can continue.

229. Space Disc aka Cone Ultimate
Created by Pepper Williams

Do you love Ultimate, but find yourself in the middle of a global pandemic – supposed to stay six feet away from others? No problem! In this game, you get to 'Space Out'!

Here's how the game is played in a nutshell:
The field is covered with cones placed in a honeycomb pattern, where every cone is separated by about eight yards from every other cone. As in normal ultimate, offensive players throw the disc to each other and try to catch it in the end zone. But the big twist is that you must always catch (as well as throw) the disc from within three feet of a cone. You're free to move without the disc at any time, but you can only move from the cone you're on to an adjacent cone (so unless you're on a sideline, you always have exactly six options to choose from). Furthermore, once you start moving toward another cone, you must continue to that cone.

Defensive players also have to move from cone to cone, though they're given a little more leeway, as described below. If two people start moving toward the same cone, the first person to yell 'mine' gets the cone, and the other person must immediately turn around and go back to the cone they came from (you cannot immediately switch directions and

> **AGE RANGE:** 12+
>
> **PLAY AREA:** Same as for *Ultimate*
>
> **NUMBER OF PLAYERS:** 8+
>
> **EQUIPMENT:** One disc; pinnies in 2 colours, 10 normal cones, 57 (for full size field) 'shorty cones'

switch to to another cone). So the end result is that players are forced to keep themselves separated; the rules specifically prohibit people from entering each others' spaces.

Field setup

• The field can use standard *Ultimate* field dimensions or smaller, depending on the number of players.

• Distribute cones throughout the field, in a honeycomb-like pattern with 'rows', every cone separated by a distance of approximately eight yards from the six cones surrounding it.

• The two rows on either end of the field are the end zones. Ideally, 'shorty' cones should be used for the 'field cones' and the back row of end zone cones, and the first row of each end zone should be marked with slightly taller cones.

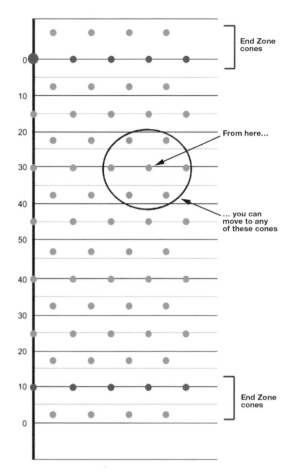

End Zone cones

From here...

... you can move to any of these cones

End Zone cones

Basic game flow

As in standard *Ultimate*...

- You can play with teams of up to seven players on a side.
- One team is always playing offence and the other defence.
- The offensive team scores by catching the disc in their end zone.
- A turnover occurs any time the disc touches the ground.
- When a turnover occurs, teams switch roles so that the team that was playing defence is now trying to score.
- *Here's the twist:* offensive players are only allowed to touch the disc if at least one of their feet is within a yard of a cone, and any cone can only be 'occupied' by a single player.

To start the game

- As in ultimate, the game begins with a pull.
- Each defensive player must start at one of the cones in the end zone they're defending, and each offensive player must start at one of the cones in the opposite end zone.
- The player pulling the disc must be within three feet of a cone when they release the pull.
- As soon as the pull is released, all players are free to move from cone to cone.

Stall count

- At the start of a point, or after an offensive player catches the disc, any defensive player can start a stall count. The offence has five seconds to throw. If the count reaches five, it's a turnover.

Hints to the leader:

- This is so important that it's worth emphasising again: everyone must always be moving directly from one cone to another adjacent cone. It's very tempting, especially when playing defence, to just move where you need to be to make the block (because that's what you do in regular *Ultimate*), but unless you've planned things out so you're moving from one cone to another adjacent, unoccupied cone, you can't do it.
- This game serves as a good lead-up game to the original *Ultimate* in that it slows the game down and levels the playing field so that even the more timid players can find their way – *Ultimate* meets chess! Even if social distancing is not required in your community, this version is interesting and fun.

Note that the game is still evolving.
See the up-to-date 'official' PDX Masters' rules here:
https://docs.google.com/document/d/1GzeSEXg-jZ
DSOgSqR4ZkGD9ZG9ynwyLy7qQ8BGklluM/
edit?usp=sharing

230. Candles

The next game is one I developed on the spur of the moment, although since then I have seen it played in other parts of the world too! When I think of this game, the comic picture of (often) clumsy teenagers daintily trying to save their flames from being extinguished, comes to my mind!

Each player has to try to blow out the others' candles, without letting theirs be blown out. Also, players must be careful not to extinguish their own flames through sudden movements or by tipping the candles too far over.

Variations:

- One person is designated to be the one from whom the other players can relight their candles.

- Or, players can relight their candles from any lit flame.

- Give each player two candles, one for each hand.

> **EQUIPMENT:** Lit candles in simple candle-holders so that each player has one

231. Night Watchman

The players form a circle about 10–12 paces across. One player is chosen as the Night Watchman. She is taken into the centre of the circle, blindfolded and given the foam 'stick' and the bunch of keys. A Burglar is chosen. She is placed inside the circle near the edge of it. She is blindfolded and given the bag with tools in it.

The aim of the game is for the Night Watchman to find the Burglar and hit her gently with his stick. The Burglar tries to avoid being caught. Both players are free to move about the circle. If the two blindfolded players are about to leave the circle, one of the players standing nearby will gently and silently guide her back in.

If the game leader senses the Burglar has no idea where the Night Watchman is, she calls out 'Night Watchman'. The Night Watchman must then rattle

> **EQUIPMENT:** Two blindfolds; one set of keys on a key ring; a bag with a few tools in it; a 2-foot (60cm) length of cylindrical foam pipe insulation – if this can't be found a thinly rolled-up piece of newspaper about the same length will do

her keys. The Burglar now knows where her pursuer is and quietly tries to move away from her. The Night Watchman listens for any noise in order to locate the Burglar.

If the game leader senses the Night Watchman has no idea where the Burglar is, she calls out '**Burglar**', who must then shake her bag of tools, giving the Night Watchman a clue to where she is. The game ends when either the Burglar has escaped for enough time, say two minutes, without being caught or the Night Watchman succeeds in hitting her gently with her stick.

232. Stick Through Water
Developed by Jaimen McMillan

Divide the group into pairs. The pairs stand holding hands, one pair behind another, in the centre of the room, but facing towards the far wall. These pairs are the 'clear water' through which the 'stick', a single player, will move.

The stick stands on the opposite side of the room, facing the clear water. The stick moves towards the line of players forming the water. The water also moves at walking pace towards the stick. The stick goes through the centre of the partners who release their hands in the same direction the stick is walking, just at the moment the stick is in front of them, spinning off as they do so.

The player who was the stick waits quietly while the turbulence of the others dies down. Another player can now be the stick.

The pairs reform, now at the other side of the room (where the previous stick began), and the second stick approaches them. Continue until each player has had a turn to move through the others. When teaching such an exercise for the first time, ask the players to follow your movements like an echo – so they learn through doing, and not always through verbal descriptions.

Once a 'child' is 16–18 or older, the games generally appropriate for them are games that are suitable for adults as well. With 16–8 year olds, you can spend time reviewing the games curriculum – playing games from previous years, and explaining to the participants why such games are important. This is because they are now secure enough in themselves not to be embarrassed about stepping out of their 'age' and entering into a game for younger children. Although they play such games now with a different consciousness, they also have a lot of fun. As well as entering into such a game with warmth of heart, they can also use their emerging thinking to understand the psychology behind it.

They begin to reflect on their own behaviour and ways of being in the context of the game. How did I relate to the others on my team? Why was I always caught when I was the mouse? By discussing such questions, the adolescent can come to insights about their own character; and by bringing this to consciousness, take a first step towards changing.

233. Peg Tag

The object of this game is to collect as many pegs as you can. Each player puts a peg on the back of their shirt. At an agreed signal the game begins. All the players are free to move about, trying to steal the peg from another person's back, without having their own taken.

When you are successful in stealing a peg you put it on the back of your own shirt. While putting on a peg, a player cannot be 'attacked'. You may not protect your peg/s using your hands.

Give the group three minutes to take as many pegs as possible off the others' shirts, and to put them on their own shirts.

Around puberty, one's space contracts. Games at

EQUIPMENT: Clothes pegs (one per player)

this age should help the individual awaken to a broader awareness of the space and world around them. It is particularly valuable to work on developing children's awareness of the space behind them – 'back space'.

This game helps players develop a sense of back space and a general spatial awareness. It is also an image of how to develop individuality in a healthy way: taking from the world (taking others' pegs) but at the same time guarding what one has already achieved (protecting one's own pegs).

234. Hand Tower
Developed by Jaimen McMillan

The players make a tower of hands: they hold one of their hands about two or three inches (5–8cm) above the hand below theirs, palm over palm and trying not to touch anyone else's hands.

It is helpful to imagine the following: if a thin golden beam of light that could penetrate matter, was shone through the palm of the player's hand at either the top or bottom of the tower, it would pass directly through the centre of the palm of every other player.

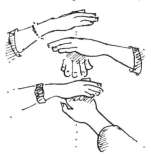

Everyone should put one hand in the tower – which will probably mean that the players will have to huddle closely together, turning sideways on. They should all put the same hand in. Arms should be fully extended and roughly horizontal.

The player whose hand is at the top of the tower, lifts her hand up and away; the other hands move up and out of the tower, following or being 'drawn' by the hand above. This movement continues until each outstretched arm and hand is raised vertically above the head. This is done quite slowly and consciously.

At the moment the last person raises her hand and arm to the vertical position, the first person begins to lower her arm and hand again, back down to its original position.

Then the tower can reform into its horizontal position. When this is achieved and the whole group have brought their hands back down into the tower, continue the movement of the arms and hands down until they are resting at your side.

A powerful image that can accompany this activity is to picture your hand above hot coals when it is by your side. In raising your arm and hands to the horizontal and forming the tower, you share this heat. As your hand is lifted higher you begin to experience a greater coolness.

This activity allows life forces to stream into the hands, warming them. Often the players realise this with surprise and wonder. It also helps them differentiate between the qualities of space above and below us.

235. Follow the Humming Bird

Each person should have a partner. One partner closes her eyes. She is the follower. The other partner is the humming bird. He has his eyes open. He stands about three feet (one metre) behind the follower, facing her. He begins to hum in a constant pitch. He slowly begins to walk backwards, humming. It is the follower's task to respond to the moving humming bird by following where she thinks the humming bird is moving to.

The follower and the humming bird both walk slowly backwards. After about 30 seconds the humming bird will stop. The follower must try to respond to this by also stopping and not bumping into the humming bird.

If there is a group playing this, each pair must wait quietly when finished, so as to let the others also finish without being distracted.

236. Swap the Humming Bird

Follow the directions given for *Follow the Humming Bird*. But this time, when the humming birds are moving about the room, they catch the eye of another humming bird and at a given signal leave their follower and swap over with the humming bird they signalled to. Both humming birds now have a new follower.

The followers must quickly reorientate and set off in pursuit of the new humming bird.

This manoeuvre may be repeated several times in the two to three minutes the game lasts. At the end of the game the players gather in a circle and the followers try to guess who, at various stages, were their humming birds.

237. Dragons and Angels

This game has many differing roles that can be taken up by children aged seven to 18. It is a game that requires courage; the only way of protecting oneself against the evil dragon is to join forces with others, and stand firm in the face of danger – for this reason this game is particularly suited to Michaelmas or Harvest Festival in autumn.

A large number of children can play, but it is important to play in a wild area – it heightens the adventure and sense of danger! This game can be quite frightening for younger children, but they can take refuge in designated safe places. For the older children who are the dragons, it is important that they agree to play in the spirit of the game: they shouldn't scare the little ones too much, but can let rip a bit more with older children. I have played this game for a whole morning – but it is hard to keep track of so many children over such a large area, so it is good to have a few more adults to assist you.

Divide the children into three groups: a quarter of the children dress up as dragons, usually the 13 or 14 year olds. Another quarter of the children dress up as angels and are given a gong each (usually the 15–16 year olds). The rest of the players are the children playing in the forest.

The dragons try to catch the children. If they catch one, the child goes to the dragon's lair, where she can be freed by a passing angel who takes her by the hand and leads her back to the fairy place. The children's

PLAY AREA: This game works best played in a large area which is quite wild, with trees and bushes; one area – a rock, little hill, a clearing – should be designated as the 'fairy' place; another area is the dragons' lair

EQUIPMENT: Enough gongs (or musical instruments, e.g. French horn, triangle, flute) for each angel; costumes and make-up for the dragons

only protection against a dragon is to form a circle near an angel, and sing or hum in harmony to the note of the gong which she is striking.

To capture a dragon, she must be encircled by a ring of singing children. When a dragon is captured, she is taken to the fairy rock, and takes off the dragon's make-up and costume, becoming an angel.

The angels move through the woods, and when they see a dragon they hit their gong, so that the children are warned. The children listen out for the noise of the gong. When they hear it they can choose to run away from the dragon, or run towards the angel and make a circle (with more than two children) and begin singing. The dragon is powerless against the singing.

The game ends when either all the dragons have been caught or, after a suitable length of time, a note is sounded from a whistle or flute. All the children are then safe to gather in the fairy place and see how many dragons have been captured.

PART THREE
Considerations for Creating Inclusive Culture

Chapter Nine

The Five Cs
Inspired by master movement teacher Julianna Lichatz

To inspire a lifelong love of movement, one can consider the development of skills and abilities as a continuum, whereby certain capacities build upon one another. When choosing movement activities for your child, consider this developmental sequence: 'The Five Cs'.

1. **Creativity** – Imagination rules! Free play outdoors allows the child full freedom of motion and expression. The world is their oyster, anything is possible. A ball is not just a ball; it is a comet, or a bird, or a giant blueberry! Their universe is far more vast than win/lose, in/out, black/white. If we allow children to create, we give them the capacity to 'think outside the box' which leads to flexible thinking in later years.

2. **Coordination** – It's helpful if the child has basic coordination before they are put under pressure of a game with repetitive movements, strict rules, and scores. Knowing right/left, having a sense of balance and spatial awareness helps a child feel confident. Free play outdoors (woods, playgrounds, playing catch with a friend, made up games) helps the child build up their 'coordinates' – 'I am here', 'The world is out there', 'I know where I am in the world'.

3. **Cooperation** – We encourage the children to learn to play with each other before they play against each other. Activities where children can learn to problem solve together are healthy and satisfying for all. This is not to say that they should avoid conflict; conflict is a vital element in learning. Building a fort together, for example, is a way to work through differing styles and temperaments in a group environment that helps build a sense of purpose and belonging. This cultivates adaptability, a key ingredient to work successfully in a group or on a team.

4. **Communication** – Giving children the opportunity to practise articulating what they want and listening to others do the same is an essential life skill. Before putting children into a competitive situation, it's helpful to make sure that they have the capacity to communicate their wants and needs. Without communication skills, children can feel quite powerless. We want them to be able to navigate challenging situations by being able to speak up for themselves and others.

5. **Competition** – When all of these capacities have been put into place, we set children up for success in the competitive arena. They are well-equipped and eager to test their mettle. Without having practised these skills, a child is likely to place their sense of worth on the extrinsic game or score rather than the intrinsic joy of the activity itself. Many children become risk averse when competition is introduced too early, which defeats the purpose altogether. When choosing a team or sport, it's helpful to observe the style of the coach. Do they practise inclusion? Do they value the 'win' over the experience of the players? Do they inspire a love of the game?

Game Conduct/Sportsmanship

1. **Tagger's Rule** – I have had success in using 'tagger's rule' – this says that, even if you don't feel it, if the tagger is 100% sure of the tag, then there is no arguing, you just accept the tag. This helps the taggers toward honest reflection and the taggees toward accepting that life is not always fair.

2. **Ro-Sham-Bo** – If there is any question, or any disagreement, it is settled with, 'Ro-Sham-Bo, Ready, Steady, Show!' (Rock, Paper, Scissors) Conflict resolution 101. This has permeated the culture of our school so that on the playground, many infractions or arguments are settled with Ro-Sham-Bo. Worth its weight in gold!

3. **Play(s) of the Day**, inspired by master movement teacher Katie Moran – After a game, the group gathers down on a knee and is asked to think about the game quietly for a moment and then raise hands to name a 'play of the day'. This is something that someone did, or some play that was extraordinary – something we would want to see in an instant replay. This way we all celebrate the outstanding moments and end the game with positivity and a reflective, meta-perspective on the game (a great way to transition into the next activity rather than the heat of the game interfering with whatever is next.) When I forget to do this, the students request it!

4. **Making Teams** – The process of creating teams can make or break a given game and create unnecessary exclusion and stress. For younger players, the game leader can simply determine the teams, avoiding the 'team captain' approach where the more skilful players are chosen immediately and the less skilful players are left as stragglers at the end of the gruelling ordeal. In adolescence, the desire to 'test one's mettle' emerges, and the time is ripe to give young people opportunities to seek out the level of competition that is right for them. The game leader can give the instruction, 'Stand opposite a partner that is a good match for you today'. Both partners have to agree, and eventually two lines are formed, creating the teams for the game. For the next level of 'fairness', the game leader can say, 'If you can't live with these teams, and you have a suggestion for a switch, speak now'. The group then, together with guidance from the game leader, assesses the change, and the group must all agree to the switch. It's not enough to simply complain that the teams are not fair; that same person must then propose a solution to their perceived imbalance. Since most players just want to play and have fun, the micromanaging of the teams does not go on forever, but it gives the players a sense of ownership over the 'fairness', which could be argued to be just as important as the activity itself.

5. **Playing Catch** – The ultimate social experience: two human beings imbuing a seemingly empty space between them, and filling that space with an agreement or a pact – we're in this together. I need you and you need me. When one of the players makes an errant throw, it is common to hear, 'I'm sorry' or 'My bad', or some other form of apology. Game leaders can encourage players to change this dynamic. Rather than apologising for a bad throw, what if the player thanked their partner for going out of their way to retrieve the 'bad throw'. Rather than a field full of players yelling, 'Sorry!' we have a field full of players saying 'Thank you!'. This minimises the fear of making mistakes and encourages an overall sense of gratitude.

Recess Duty
Some tips to consider

- **Self Care:**

  Have you taken care of your own basic needs?

  Bathroom, nourishment, clothing/footwear for comfort outdoors, what helps you?

  To provide quality care for others, we are at our best when we've taken good care of ourselves. Are there ways your school can support you so that you can be present, grounded, and comfortable while on recess duty? Can a fellow colleague offer you brief coverage support before recess? What might you be able to offer to another along these lines?

- **Collegial Check-ins:**

  Sometimes it is necessary to check in with a colleague during recess duty, though it's not the purpose of recess duty. The primary focus should always be on the children, so if we must have adult conversations, it's good to keep them brief. It may be helpful to walk with a colleague while checking in so that both can keep an eye on the recess activities.

- **On the Move:**

  If possible, keep moving through the various recess activities so that you have an idea of the whole picture. Try not to get stuck in one place, though if you must stay in one place due to a 'hot-spot' situation, other colleagues on duty should see this happening and cover the unsupervised spaces accordingly.

  Like a good sports team, we should know where our supervising colleagues are positioning them-selves throughout the recess so that we can adjust our own positions to support the whole. Go Team!

- **From the Heart:**

  At least once each recess, try to connect with one of the activities with a spirit of positive curiosity; Help build a fort, ask what's for sale at the store, join in on one of the games, share your interest

with the students in who they are and what they are doing. To build a relationship of trust that balances all the times we have to say 'no' to a given activity or behaviour, it is important for the children to experience that the adults around them have a true interest in their world.

- **DADD – Disapprove, Affirm, Discover, Do-over**
  A social inclusion approach by Kim Payne
  (*fuller description on page 224*):

  Adults hear about one in ten put-downs; research has shown that bullying incidents begin with put-downs, so we must intervene each time we see/hear it happen.

  Disapprove: 'That's not okay.' If we do not interrupt and disapprove of the behaviour, children see this as tacit permission to continue or worsen the behaviour.

  Affirm: 'That's not your best.' Find some authentic language where you can affirm the inherent goodness of the student, even though you are disapproving of their behaviour. It is important to distinguish the child as separate from the behaviour. If we do not make this distinction, the child can develop a negative self-image; 'I can't do anything right – I'm just bad.' Research shows that 'shaming' may work short term to stop negative behaviours, but the long-term effects can include depression, disengagement, low self-esteem, self harm, and bullying behaviour.

  Discover: 'What's going on?' Letting them share their story/feelings/frustrations regarding the incident. Try to embody as much compassion as possible in this space (even if you are frustrated) so that the children will want to share with you.

  Do-over: 'Let's find a way to make this right.' Ask them what they think will be helpful in order to make amends and move on. Saying 'I'm sorry' is not as effective as some kind of action. You can guide role plays so that they have a chance to do it differently during the 'replay'. Using humour or sharing your own story from when you were young is sometimes helpful as you guide this last step.

As we work with this, it is important that we look at our own social habits in terms of blame, shame, and put-downs as we strive to be authentic adults, worthy of imitation.

- **Preview / Review:**

Consider if it might actually save time in the long run to make time before and/or after recess for the class to go over with you, 'What are the plans for recess?' and then 'How did that recess go?' Nervous/anxious children often benefit from knowing ahead of time what the games will be and who will be doing what so that they don't have to navigate these things on the spot. Children with attention challenges often benefit from the review; How did that game go? How did my actions/words affect another? You may want to work with a peer collaborator on these topics. Visiting each other's classes and observing each other's transitions may provide helpful insight.

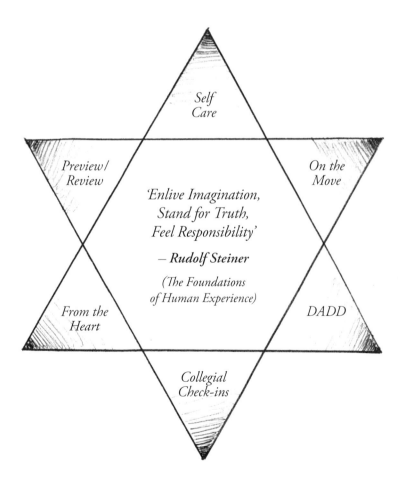

Self Care

Preview / Review

On the Move

'Enlive Imagination, Stand for Truth, Feel Responsibility'

— *Rudolf Steiner*

(*The Foundations of Human Experience*)

From the Heart

DADD

Collegial Check-ins

We-Directions
For the younger child

Redirecting kids when they are finding something difficult and becoming defiant or stuck often is a struggle for the parent or educator. The key reason this happens is that the adult can unintentionally still give the child the feeling they are being 'sent away' to another place. If a re-direction is changed into a we-direction a subtle but important message is sent to the child:

A 'we-direction' is when the child/teen is helped to move rather than get stuck, but the movement happens with an adult close by. Terms like, 'Let's both...' or 'We need to...' or 'Come with me and...' 'I wonder how our...' often pop up during a we-direction.

If a child is struggling with their behaviour during play time or a game:

- **Distraction for Cooperation.**

  I wonder if we can visit with the big children as we walk back to our room. They should be coming out around about now. Let's tidy up quickly now so we can find out.'

- **Change the Environment.**

  'Looks like we are going to need to sort this out when everyone has calmed down a bit more. Come and help me pack away the jump ropes and we can sort things out later so that it feels better.'

- **Acceptable Alternative.**

  'Oh Molly, those soft play balls are not for kicking. I'll show you how to throw them over the net.'

Avoiding the down sides of we-directions

1. **Facing Social Discomfort:**

   While we-direction and distraction can be especially helpful for toddlers and young preschoolers, it may discourage older children from using their problem-solving skills and avoid social discomfort.

2. **Problem Solving:**

   Use a we-direction to help the child/student out of a stuck or escalating situation, but when the time seems right, quietly talk to the child/student about what was happening and develop some ideas of how things could be done better.

3. **It Becomes Your Problem:**

   We-directing a child away from difficulties can risk placing responsibility for resolving the issue on you instead of the child/teen. This is a problem because your child/teen may get the message that they can act recklessly and that you will swoop in and make everything all right.

4. **Making the Task Doable:**

   Even though you are we-directing, still be careful not to set yourselves a task too big and complicated as the point is to help a kid come back into themselves and connect with you, and completing what you set out to do gives a child a good sense of accomplishment.

Crossing the Line
Blame-free accountability in action

So often our children 'go too far' without intending to be disruptive, mean or excluding. Doing this simple exercise done with the students can help clarify boundaries. However it's main use can come when a line does get crossed. Then the teacher can draw the student's attention back to the *Crossing the Line* agreements.

This avoids blame, opens a healthy conversation about the situation and increases the chance of coming up with ideas about how to put things right.

'Joking around crosses the line and becomes teasing when…'

• *[example]* 'everyone doesn't think it funny.'

• . . . .

• . . . .

• . . . .

'Playing a game crosses the line and becomes excluding when…'

• . . . .

• . . . .

• . . . .

• . . . .

'Standing up for yourself crosses the line and become hurtful when…'

• . . . .

• . . . .

• . . . .

'Talking to someone in the class after a game crosses the line and becomes hurtful when…'

• . . . .

• . . . .

• . . . .

• . . . .

Disapprove – Affirm – Discover – Do-Over (DADD)

An everyday tool for working with children's arguments, put downs and misbehaviour.

This tool can be used to explore and reframe a social or behavioural problem, or it can be used over the space of days when the issue is more complex. The aim of learning this strategy is that when the children need help, you will be better able to intervene with quiet confidence without seeming to be on anybody's side.

First… Disapprove

Begin by expressing clear disapproval for the action, 'It is hurtful to behave as you did.' 'We don't speak that way in our family/class.' Speak with quiet directness. Mean it.

And… Affirm

We know that we are supposed to separate a child's actions from their whole being but it's not always easy. To achieve this disapproval needs to be followed up right away by an affirmation… 'You hardly ever speak like that.' 'So often you say helpful and kind things.'

You may feel the situation calls for you to reverse the order and 'Affirm' first and 'Disapprove' afterwards. Agree **Truce** and then, when the time is right…

Discover

Then the adult discovers what the subtle issues are. 'What's up?' 'Something must be bothering you.' This question must come at the right time to get an honest response.

Finally… Do-over

When the issue is a bit clearer the adult can help the child to do over. 'Let's work out a way to say what you need to say without being hurtful', or for a young child 'Let's go and help your brother fix his broken fort.'

In this way we honour everyone's needs while acknowledging our responsibilities toward others.

Considering the Temperaments

Considering the temperaments is the last and very important component to this new regime if it is to be right for each child. Timing is all-important in DADD practice and there are few better ways to get this right than to know the temperament of the child. If it is tricky to determine the child's temperament try asking… 'Which temperament is my child least?'

- **The Choleric** needs to be spoken to away from friends and usually after they have calmed down. Key words: Defer, Deflect until you can be Direct

- **The Melancholic** needs to be spoken to with an understanding of the vulnerability they often experience. Key word: Safety, Empathy with Quiet Accountability.

- **The Phlegmatic** can become very stubborn if they feel their side has not been heard. Don't take them by surprise. Let them know for example, that after class you will want to understand why they are speaking in that way. Key words: Fairness and Timing.

- **The Sanguine** needs to be tackled right there and then. If you don't they will wonder what you are bothering about ten minutes later. Key words: Implications of Actions.

Responsibility – Request – Redo
A quick and effective playground dispute tool

When a disagreement flares up on the playground between children who normally get on most of the time, first ask them, 'Are you all working this out, or do you need a little help to get back to playing?' This offers the children a chance to pause and consider. Of course, if they say they are 'fine' it's still a good idea to stay nearby to make sure their assessment is right. If they need help a simple intervention from the teacher is often all that is needed to make the shift for the game or activity to continue. The key features of this tool are:

- It asks each child to reflect on what their role may have been in the dispute and have a safe space to speak about it.

- Having done that it makes good sense that each person now has earned the right to make a request of the other child they are in dispute with.

- It avoids long and escalation-prone 'talks,' as well as strained or false apologies and offers all the children a chance to do-over the situation and get on with the game or activity.

Here is how it works…

Step One: Responsibility.

Bring both/all children together. Assure them that there were probably things that everybody did that led up to the dispute. Tell them that in a moment you will ask them to say one thing they take responsibility for, and after that they can make one request. Also let them know that this is a very quick way of sorting things out so that they can get back to the game. One person is going to speak at a time. If there is play object such as a ball or rope, the person holding the object is the only person to speak. When their turn is done they hand the object back to the teacher, who then hands it to the next person who has something to say.

Now ask each one of them in turn to say one thing they may have done or said that, '…might have been a part of the problem.' It is okay if they can't think of anything right away. They can 'pass' and can speak in a moment when others have given their perspectives on what they might have done.

Step Two: Request.

Now that each child has taken some responsibility for what happened they may make a request of the other/s. They should begin the request with, 'I ask that…'

It is often surprising how doable and straightforward their request tend to be. However if it seems like a big request the teacher can step in and ask something like, 'what would be a good first step to having it be that way for you?'

Step Three: Re-do:

Finally each child is asked if they can agree with the request that was made. This is usually not too problematic because the teacher has worked to make the requests small and doable. The children are free to get back to playing. It is important for the teacher to stay close to the activity for a while to make sure the requests are honoured.

The key to this on-the-spot problem-solving strategy is to not 'get into it' too much. The aim is to get small agreements that shift the trajectory just enough to get back to the game and trust in the healing powers that play can often bring. Even if the 'real' problem is not really sorted out, just the fact that each child took a little responsibility for what happened can be very helpful if the situation needs more attention later on.

A big thanks to Nikki Tausch Lloyd and the team from Novato Public Waldorf School for this wonderful strategy.

The Outside In Playground
Playground Support

This plan is based on giving the right amount of space and autonomy to a student so that they can be supported and coached to navigate recess and feel successful rather than 'always getting into trouble.' While it limits the area a child has to play it increases the support.

Why is Playground Support Needed?

Fringe Dwellers.

Traditionally students who tend to need to most support during recess are just the ones that move around the periphery of the playground or recess spaces and receive the least support and interaction with the playground supervisors.

Getting Out Their Energy

Letting children run freely at recess is a great thing… if they can cope with it. Sometimes in the name of 'getting their energy out' what happens to the student who has problems with self monitoring in the first place, gets more and more out of control and wild.

The Bad Lands

Many children who might be less assertive or concerned about their safety during recess tend to avoid going out into the 'bad lands, where there be dragons.' They tend to cluster around the areas most frequented by the supervisors or close to the school building and doorways. The problem with feeling the playground is a place to survive rather than enjoy is that their understandable concerns can become escalated into daily anxieties. Also, the whole idea of the playground being a place to 'run around', may only be true for a minority of the fringe-dwelling, socially-less-able kids.

The Control–Rejection Cycle.

Most experienced teachers would tell us that children who struggle with social issues on the playground are drawn to games that they feel they can control. These are often situations involving children who play in more of a low-key or cooperative way that does not seem to have one dominant player. The child can see this as a leaderless game and moves in to a role that the other players do not like or want. Controversy ensues and the game either dissolves or the child is rejected. This pattern repeats itself over and over as the child drifts from one game or play situation to another and can result in the child feeling intense and broad-based rejection.

The Outside In Playground

The solution to this dynamic is simple; bring the kids on the edges of the playground into the centre where they can get informal coaching and support to play in a healthy way. This opens up the playground for the majority of children to now repopulate the playground because now it is safe to do so. By doing this, a subtle but huge shift takes place in the playground culture.

Here is a well tried and tested way to support children who need help to play in a helpful and safe way:

Check in and Plan

This is a simple system where a child reports to the duty or class teacher at the beginning of every recess and lets the teacher know where they will be playing. It needs to be one specific game or area and the child may not leave that area without checking back in. The teacher may see that what the child is suggesting is fine or, that it needs some adapting. Now the teacher does not have to follow the child all over the playground mediating in each social controversy that arises, as they may only play in the designated area agreed. It also means that the child can get the support and coaching he or she needs to have a happier recess.

1. Meet with the child in need of support and let them know or remind them about the check-in process.

2. Listen to the child's plan about where they will be playing.

3. Very briefly speak to the child about any potential problems they might encounter and what their plan will be to work it out.

4. Tell the child that this is the only place they may play and that if they wish to change games or places they must check back in.

5. Make a point of visiting that area often and supporting the child if it is needed.

Added support can be given by assigning a couple of older students who act as 'Game Helpers'. This kind of student citizenship is a wonderful thing to cultivate and further creates a healthy and safe playground.

It is important that the child knows that they will be doing this before every recess until the play is going well. It should be at least for a week and can last as long as three to four weeks. One or two days on this plan are not usually enough to shift old ingrained habits.

Problems involving shared times and spaces need a shared response.

This simple plan can be one of the single most effective ways to support a healthy playground culture. Countless numbers of teachers have been very surprised at the positive changes at recess. However, the level of success of this plan will be in direct relationship to the involvement of all adults in the school particularly playground supervisors. It does require broad 'buy in' and coordination from the playground supervisors/teachers. Of course, our schools are for academic achievement but they are also stand for social learning and the playground is just as much a learning environment as a classroom.

Afterword
The Deeper Significance of Games

How playing healthy games helps children develop in the *senses* of movement and balance in the electronic age

Cheryl L. Sanders

From playing to watching

Until a few decades ago children's play was their work. Playing was created by children when they were not otherwise engaged in helping or learning. During the latter half of this century a startling phenomenon has occurred, mostly precipitated by the advent of television. Beginning in the early to mid 1960s children gradually began to play less and less – and watch (TV) more. *This gesture of watching will prove most revealing.*

Not just in the West, but areas of the planet that began to be called 'developed' became subject to the loss of children being able to play spontaneously. What has been lost? And why have we not noticed this transformation with alarm? We do not seem to notice the loss until children become adolescents, then our attention is riveted because of the problems that seem to appear 'out of nowhere'. Suddenly our precocious 'little adults' become unreasonable 'big children'.

Perhaps our lack of attention to what happens with and around children today, and for the last three to four decades, is because we, too, have just been watching. The problem when we watch television, even 'good' television (as in program content) is that we only watch. We do not do. There is little to no movement, not even of the eyes that are watching. We seemed to have missed the early indications, even as we were becoming enamoured of and/or dismayed by the culture that resulted. At the outset TV influenced culture and moved it from evolving through the arts and humanities, to mimicking what was advertised. As our attention becomes more and more diverted toward what to buy and how to look, we no longer see where it is that we are paying most dearly for what we have received so cheaply.

So where do we 'pay'? In the realm of education,

we have discovered something called 'learning disabilities'. To be more appropriate, this should be called teaching dis-ability, for no child cannot or will not learn. Only our lack of consciousness as to who is before us and what is asked limits any child's ability to learn, or to learn what we wish to impart. The label 'dyslexia' became a diagnosis in the 1960s, and we can follow an increase in its occurrence through the 70s and 80s. In the 80s hyperactivity, and now ADD (attention deficit disorder) and ADHD (attention deficit/hyperactive disorder) are epidemic in the schools. Proportionally there has been an increase in drug abuse, perhaps in direct relation to the increase of what we euphemistically call 'medicating' any child who does not sit still at school enough to be properly 'taught', with such drugs as Ritalin. (This medicine can be extremely helpful for one to two per cent of cases, but enormously destructive to the 80 to 90% who receive it for behaviour modification.) Also crime and violence among adolescents and young people have increased. In addition, the numbers of people who are depressed, anxious, fearful, even suicidal are startling, and these are not just adult symptoms. Children are also characterised by these diagnoses, in a time when childhood is revered and supposedly sacred. Why? It is also worth noting again that the same phenomenon can be documented with each third world country introduced to the marvels of technology, most especially television. (e.g. Jerry Mander's *In the Absence of the Sacred*, Sierra Club Books, 1991)

The question certainly arises, 'What do we do?' We cannot go back to the time before television. What has been lost cannot be found by pretending, or acting like TV does not exist. This is not a game. The transformation of this powerful presence is only possible by facing it consciously, neither allowing ourselves to remain in the communal trance into which we have plunged, nor reacting out of a fundamentalist position. We need to be fully present to the world as it is the nature of the child to be fully present. But what is the contemporary world the child enters now, and why does so much that once we learned spontaneously have to be developed consciously, even taught? Carefully and consciously knowing what needs to be taught can only manifest in the school curriculum by learning from each generation of children what they have not brought with them. Children can teach us what they need to be taught if we can truly observe in them those places that are waiting for guidance.

In this time, those places can be met most fully through books like *Games Children Play*. For what we see now is that children need to be taught the relation of their bodies to the world, and most especially, to others. For example, in a world where 'watching' is not necessarily seeing, vision must be taught, or at the very least nurtured to the true capacity of seeing what is perceived as a creative activity between the seer and the seen. This is not given by the simulated world of television or computer screen images.

What has this fundamental gesture of 'watching' given us? If it is transformed into a spiritual capacity, then we begin to actually see what we are watching. What does one see when we watch that which we love most deeply, namely our children?

In 1906 Rudolf Steiner introduced the nature of the human being's sensory organisation in a whole new light. He outlined twelve senses, and briefly described and referred to these twelve senses in only a few lectures.* To see the needs of children today, we must be able to watch them with living vision, and learn from them what they need to be taught first, in this most basic realm of the body. What we see if we look closely is not only what they are most in need of, but also where we ourselves are in need of healing. In the first four senses Steiner spoke of, the most fundamental rudiments of being a human being are given at birth to every healthy infant. These are born with us in all the senses, but we will focus on the most primary, lower, or corporeal senses. Normal

development demonstrates the unfolding of these senses of touch, movement, balance and what Steiner referred to as the life sense. (The senses of vision, taste, warmth and smell are the middle, or world senses, and hearing, thought, speech and individuality are called the higher, or communal senses.)**

It is assumed when we see an infant move that it knows how to move, and that movement is healthy. Then, in a year or so, the baby stands on wobbly little legs, and eventually takes off into the world walking. It appears he or she has found the sense of balance. But we have come to a time when these two elements of our being in the world can no longer be assumed to be mere normal functions of the body. We must now begin to understand movement and balance as actual sense activities. As such they are subject to disruption and distortion, and can only be taught to function in healthy ways if we realise the need to do so. It follows that *Games Children Play*, and other books like it, are not just nice compendiums of games and 'age appropriate' things to do with children. They now contain some of the most crucial elements in education.

We are being called to wake up and become conscious of who we are, what we are doing and how we are relating to each other. The disruption of the senses, especially the lower senses, is so primary that we cannot see it in others, even children, because we do not see it in ourselves. To teach something, one must first know it personally.

What do we know about movement and balance as senses?

The Sense of Movement

The sense of movement senses whether we are still or in movement. We feel the movements of our body primarily by means of the muscle system. This system senses not only the larger movements of our body, such

---

* Rudolf Steiner, *Anthroposophy, A Fragment*, Anthroposophic Press, Hudson, NY, 1996; and Rudolf Steiner, Study of Man, Rudolf Steiner Press, London, 1966.

** A grasp of the senses of movement and balance is vital for understanding the importance of *Games Children Play*.
For a full exploration of the senses, see A. Soesman, *The Twelve Senses*, Hawthorn Press, Stroud, U.K., 1985.

as that of our arms and legs, of the feeling in our neck when we move our head, but also much more subtle movements, such as the movement of the eyes, the movement of the fingers and toes, the movement of our chest and belly when we breathe in and out. When the sense of movement functions in a healthy way, we experience a bodily sense of having a reason for being here; we have a sense of purpose. In the present world, the sense of movement is either too cramped or it becomes too muscle-bound. Sitting all day at work or school, or even in day care, and then being carried everywhere by car, bus, or subway, the inner sense of movement dims and we feel more like we are lugging our body around. On the other hand, the ways in which we try to balance the feeling of being cramped – through going to the gym to work out on exercise machines, or playing games such as organised sports or jogging, (or for children the release of running around frantically or banging, breaking or smashing things); these activities do not result in a healthy sense of movement either. We may feel the tingling of muscles, and get a temporary high from the increase in blood circulation, but it is more like a momentary breaking through the barrier of confinement than moving in purposeful and meaningful freedom. Observe your own body after watching TV for even just 30 minutes. It feels a little sluggish, heavy. Then look at children who are watching TV, and follow the manner in which they move for the first few minutes after. They either move manically, as if out of control, or they will appear to be 'warming up' to being in a body at all, and seem to take a while to 'get going'.

For the newborn baby, movement has been happening since before birth. An infant moves in direct relation to the sounds in its environment, most especially the sound of the mother's voice. Each of those movements that seem so erratic and non-directed by the infant is the body responding to, answering, dancing with the sounds (and to a lesser degree sights) by which it is surrounded. The choreography of the first movements of the body are evidence of the deepest learning that takes place from the moment of birth.

As we once were steeped in a world of the voices of the family and the natural sounds of wind and storm, the world's voices of animals and water, we are now adrift in an increasingly simulated world of sounds of all kinds coming from the pervasive electronic media. This is not to say that any of these sounds is intrinsically bad, just that they are different. What does the difference mean? For the infant, movement is directed from a different realm, and becomes a different kind of activity. Well, babies still move the way they always have, in that adorable, chaotic way that charms the soul of adults. But children are having more and more difficulty with movement at younger ages than ever before. If we see movement as learned at a deep level through the environment, we can begin to understand it as the subtle language of the soul, and distinctly different in different cultures. Movement teaches us to speak through imitation of the movement of the larynx, as well as the imitation of heard sounds. It guides the nature of our thinking, it illustrates our temperament and what we think of the world. We are more and more disconnected from the sense of movement as a sense because we move less naturally or spontaneously than we once did. For example, movement is given back to us in the things we manufacture and surround ourselves with in the world. When we were surrounded only by simple, handmade tools, our movement was natural and flowed freely from within us as we created the world around us and dwelt in its heart. However, with the industrial revolution and the overwhelmingly rapid invention of untold numbers of machines, things changed. As we began to work with and around machines in factories, on farms and wherever we live, work or play, at every level of society, our movements began to change. We take on the movement of the mechanical, and the model of what we work with and around; machines are in factories, on farms and in our homes, schools and businesses, so at every level of society, our movements have changed. Having taken on the movements of the mechanical, the model of what we work with or are surrounded by, becomes our model for the body, instead of vice versa. For example, watch people in large cities walk down the street. They walk as if they were cars manoeuvring through traffic. There is a distinct characteristic to the movements we take on as a result of inventing and then emulating the machine.

Now, in childhood there is the simple yet profound reverence for the adult that is manifested by the deepest imitation. This imitation is not the simple mimicking of outer activity, but imitation on the most profound level, one could even say on a cellular level. The imitation reaches to the spiritual gesture behind movement. If the adult moves in quick, jerky, rapid or disconcerting ways – the child will take this into the deepest realm of their own being, and move in the same way. The child does not have to personally meet the specific machinery or electronic device the adult has absorbed into their soul, and manifested in their actions. In education we never consider the question, 'How has this child learned to move in the world?'

Movement is not just the movement of my voluntary muscles in response to my wishes. It is also a response to the world. If I wish to open the door, the door is as involved in my movement toward it, and it draws me to fulfil the goal of opening the door, as my wish to open the door is in me. Thus my opening the door, just as any other grand or simple movement we make, is imbued with purpose, and the origin of our sense of purpose.

As we have seen, movement is the origin of our sense of purpose. The disruption of the sense of movement wholly disrupts our capacity to live in the world with a sense of purpose. This is perhaps the single most destructive outcome of the disruption of this sense, for living without a sense of purpose sets us up for depression, despair, and a loss of the inner relation to our own activity as essential to the world.

Hyperactivity was invented as a diagnosis at about the same time we technologically 'broke the sound barrier'. It has become a distinct presence in schools as a diagnosed learning disability. It will probably become more prevalent as we take up computer technology and attempt to emulate the movement of the computer, whizzing along in cyberspace. Movement gives us a sense of freedom, and a sense of direction. If our movement is dictated by an unconscious imitation, and no consciousness

is brought to this sense, that sense of freedom becomes a prison of frenzied activity out of control and bouncing off of and into everything outside of the self. This makes a mockery of freedom, and it becomes impossible to conceive of what true freedom is for the individual, as well as precluding ever coming to that inner sense of knowing my purpose, my destiny. This is of significance in our time because of the increasing numbers of people who seek a sense of this for themselves, and fall into despair because they cannot find such a sense.

In a child the extremes of disruption of the sense of movement may be hyperactivity, but it can also manifest as a sort of inertia. Inertia is often labelled low self esteem, when in fact the self is debilitated by the sense of movement being assaulted by either over stimulation or relentless alteration.

We can only approach the healing of movement for children through interaction in and with the natural world. Although movement as a sense must be approached for adults through community and interaction with others, for children, the games and activities in this book will help bring healing to the imitation of movement as mechanical, or electrical. Through teaching children to play, one strengthens the capacity of the body to bear the demands of a world in which our own learned movement is as simulated, or artificial, as the movement we see.

It is also interesting to note the work of Dr. Harold Levinson, in New York City, who treats hyperactivity and certain forms of dyslexia with over-the-counter motion-sickness medication, with remarkable results.*** His work is mostly scorned by the LD (learning disabilities) and medical communities. Is it too simple and straightforward? Or just too threatening to find the true source of the problems that fuel large markets? If one is always overwhelmed by movement, or a little off-balance, would one not feel the dizziness of 'motion sickness'?

*** For further study on the now approaches to the treatment of dyslexia and ADHD, vastly more complex than the reference made here, see H.N. Levinson, M.D., *A Scientific Watergate, Dyslexia*, Stonebridge Publishing Ltd, Lake Success, NY, 1994.

The Sense of Balance

The sense of balance, centred in the inner ear, senses the relationship between the earth's gravity and our own body. When the sense of balance functions in a healthy way we are not only able to stand upright and move around in the world without it swaying because we have lost our point of reference, there is also a more subtle feeling; we feel inner calm and security. With the sense of balance we are able to take our place in the world as human beings between the sky above and the earth below. We will remain uniquely our self in the midst of all the other selves. The inner calm and security is a corporeal feeling of ourselves as spiritual beings of the earth.

In the present world there is much that throws us off balance. The extreme instance, when, for example, there is an inner ear infection, is vertigo. But much more subtle states of imbalance occur. Then a kind of vertigo occurs, but it feels more like a vague sense of being swallowed up by the surrounding world. If one does not have the sense of being a spiritual being, which is a very corporeal feeling, not some kind of out-of-body experience, it is like feeling the ground is at any moment going to give way. In the modern world, we often feel that we move from one thing to another throughout the day – answering phones, going to meetings, solving one crisis after the other, trying to meet all the demands that come toward us in a kind of frenzy. After a few hours of this we can feel dizzy or even disoriented. If you are in this kind of situation, and take a short break by walking outside, there is an unmistakable feeling of a return of calm and inner security. The sense of balance, of equilibrium, has a little chance to recover. But imagine what it is like when there is not this respite. Life is lived out of balance.

The interesting thing about balance is that it is directly related to the sense of our Self in relation to the world. The world is what makes it possible to maintain balance. It does not give us balance; it makes it possible for us to stay in balance. We each at some point quite early in our career as human beings, stand upright. Unless there is some physical infirmity, we each balance ourselves on our own two feet. No child ever has been known to say, 'Oh, I'll wait awhile for standing, maybe when I'm five or six, I'll be stronger then.' Every child stands before he speaks. Every child learns balance as the first major accomplishment only he can bring about for himself. This milestone in life gives the body the means by which one can eventually speak the word 'I'. 'I' learn of my self only when standing. What do we do to infants who, when raised to their feet only weeks after birth and, because their muscles automatically flex when placed in this precarious position, we smile in our ignorance and say, 'Look, he's trying to stand all ready!' Or, 'Oh, he loves it when I stand him up', without realising he is not 'trying to stand', but that his immature muscles are being put under enormous strain and imposition, and possibly damaging what only later should be strengthened out of the child's own forces? Those forces are debilitated by our game of holding babies in this premature position. When a baby is allowed to pull himself up when he is ready, and, in spite of all the falls and bumps, brings himself to the moment of standing upright, then the body is strengthened for the moment of speaking of one's self as a free, independent individual. This simple misunderstanding makes it possible to disrupt the sense of balance even before the age of three. Any early disruption in the sense of balance profoundly affects the will forces that are developing and informing the child of his own tasks and responsibilities in and to the world. The accomplishment of free, individual balance is the foundation for communion with the world, others and the divine.

But what if one were always a tiny bit disoriented in the sense of balance? And how would this disruption manifest in the behaviour of a young child? Being slightly off balance may not cause too much of a problem in the earliest years. We have an enormous capacity to compensate to the extent that no one, not even our mother, can detect that any compensating is occurring. And we, of course, do not know that is what we are doing. It does, however manifest its repercussions a bit later, when one is attempting to coordinate the body in space to finer gestures, such as the eyes moving across a white page filled with obscure black shapes and forms called letters. Or the even more dramatically complex activity of the hand on a piece of paper with a pencil, trying to make those same strange shapes. The physiological activity requires enormous balance to hold these things together and not become literally seasick. Even more confusing is that this activity creating imbalance does not necessarily indicate a lack of gross motor coordination. Coordination can vary from being disturbed at all levels, to being disturbed only on the most subtle (true dyslexia). In mainstream education we do not recognise the twelve senses as in need of nurturing or training toward harmonious interrelationship. Were this the case, balance would receive a great deal of attention, for here we have the 'I' attempting to orient itself in the world in a harmonious flow.

So as we see, balance as a sense is not simply my standing up and not falling over, but it is activity in relation to the world; activity that gives me my self back and allows me to maintain my equilibrium in the face of whatever the world brings. If we look out over the Grand Canyon we are to varying degrees, momentarily dizzy. If one stands for a moment, the dizzy feeling may pass. We have filled the Grand Canyon with our presence, and it has given us our selves back. It participates in our sense of equilibrium. If we are never able to experience the world giving us our selves back, the sense of balance becomes disturbed, disrupted, out of balance. The disruption of balance causes a certain sinking feeling in the stomach, a dizziness that might be similar to spinning about 10 or 12 times then trying to walk straight. Imagine if this feeling were present every time you wanted to read, or write. What if the experience were much more subtle, so that you could not quite figure out what it was, but you knew you were feeling awful when at school, especially in some classes, but not in others, like art or music. Even recess can be disastrous if the disruption of balance extends to the whole body, as it often does, not just to fine motor skills. And what if lack of coordination is extended to any attempt to participate in games, or even just trying to run across the playground without being laughed at?

As we move into an increasingly technical imagination of education, we become even more fascinated with the tools of education, and decreasingly interested in the whole point of it all, the child himself. Our enchantment with our own cleverness, not only with the gadgets, but also of pedagogical forms that are in theory wonderful for children, is the most dangerous element in the disruption of the senses. This enchantment keeps us inattentive to who is being educated, and attending mostly to how we display our own facility (whether with the tools or the pedagogical ideals). Also, the lack of attention to the actual child is a mirror of our lack of attention to our own presence; the activity of our presence and what it conveys merely indicates the disruption of our own senses.

In not attending to these things, lack of balance is an ongoing element in education. If no 'stand' is ever made in relationship to the other, the 'I' of the child is not only not recognised, nurtured and encouraged, but no worthy model of a healthy individual is present in the teacher. This is the ground from which our current dilemma of 'poor self esteem' stems. Being a teacher filled with self esteem is not the fundamental gesture the young child needs to imitate to learn self esteem and thus become imbued with his own self esteem. When the child says 'I', self esteem is present. The teacher who is attempting to convey 'high self esteem' through his or her own self confidence or great facility with every problem or question might just as well be teaching egoism or self righteousness. Being a person able to maintain inner balance – to be one's self and simultaneously present to the other and all the other others – lends an integrity to the soul of the teacher that is worthy of and joyously imitated by the child who is thus being 'taught' to 'fine tune' the fundamental sense of balance. Children were once the inventors of a myriad of games joyously created in a moment and as readily forgotten in the next, for a new one would appear in a flash to delight the senses. We now enter an age when the senses no longer give us the world, but the simulation of the world we have created. If we teach children to play games that are by their very nature allowing the child to move and interact freely with one another, we return the child to the body and bring about healing in the senses. Children are asked to learn a great deal at increasingly younger ages and we forget that learning to read at three will not quicken in the child a love of learning, but only present the world with a three year old who can read. But a three year old who can run and jump and climb and twirl and sweep and turn a somersault is much better prepared to enter the world, and meet that world with equanimity and purpose in later life, because this child lives in balance and with capacities for moving through the world in freedom.

There is much one can do in the realm of activities for children. It is essential that we know why we teach certain skills at specific ages. We must become awake to those things in the world that are calling us to awaken, such as television, computers, electronic and mechanical simulations of the world itself. With each new development of technology, we must renew and strengthen our capacity to observe and be present to the body as the highest expression of the spiritual nature of humanity. Here we must be grateful to technology as the avenue by which we are forced to bring consciousness to that which was once given, but through which we only gazed at as if through a mirror darkly, but are now able to see clearly, face to face. Clear vision requires greater responsibility, so we must teach the body that which it senses is its own, and not the imitation of the lesser gods, such as modern technology. That is why this book is a blessing disguised as play, a therapy for the soul of the world.

Cheryl L. Sanders, ms
School of Spiritual Psychology
Great Barrington, MA, USA, Autumn 1996

Dr Cheryl L. Sanders-Sardello (1951–2015), was Co-Founder and Co-Director of the School of Spiritual Psychology with Dr. Robert Sardello.

About the Authors

Kim John Payne has been quietly and passionately working to help tens of thousands of people give voice to the feeling that something is not okay about the new normal of overwhelm that so many people are now experiencing. He offers do-able ways to realise the hopes and values we all have for ourselves, and build deep connections with our children that gives families resiliency and simple joy.

A consultant and trainer to over 230 US independent and public schools, Kim John Payne, M.ED, has been a school counsellor, adult educator, consultant, researcher, educator and a private family counsellor for thirty years. He regularly gives keynote addresses at international conferences, and runs workshops and trainings around the world. In each role, he has been helping children, adolescents and families explore issues such as social difficulties with siblings and classmates, attention and behavioural issues at home and school, emotional issues such as defiance, aggression, addiction and self-esteem and the vital role living a balanced simple life brings.

He is Co-Founding Director of Whole Child Sports, an institute that educates parents and coaches about the value of a healthy approach to child and youth sports and play.

He has also consulted for educational associations in South Africa, Hungary, Israel, Russia, Switzerland, Ireland, Canada, Australia, and the United Kingdom, Thailand and China. Kim has worked extensively with the North American and UK Waldorf educational movements. He has served as Director of the Collaborative Counselling programme at Antioch University New England. He is the Director of the Simplicity Project, a multi media social network that explores what really connects and disconnects us to ourselves and to the world. Together with his team they have trained over 1000 Simplicity Parenting Coaches around the world. Kim is the Founding Director of The Centre for Social Sustainability, an organisation that has trained thousands of teachers, parents and students in the Three Streams of Healthy School Culture that gives social, emotional and behavioural support to children who struggle in the school environment.

He is the author of best sellers *Simplicity Parenting, Soul of Discipline, Beyond Winning, Being at Your Best when Your Kids Are at Their Worst,* and co-author of the new *Emotionally Resilient Tweens and Teens.* His books have been translated into 27 languages.

He has appeared frequently on television including ABC, NBC, CBS, Fox; on radio with the BBC, Sirius/XM, CBC & NPR, and in print including being featured in *Time Magazine, Chicago Tribune, Parenting, Mothering, Times Union* and the *LA Times.*

Kim strives to deepen understanding and give practical tools for life that arise out of the burning social issues of our time. He lives on a farm in Ashfield, Massachusetts, USA with his wife and two children.

Cory Waletzko has taught movement and games at the Upper Valley Waldorf School and in the wider Northeast region since 2005. She is a graduate of Spacial Dynamics® and Bothmer Gymnastics and has worked for the Center for Social Sustainability, bringing Social Inclusion to students and staff in both public and private schools. Cory is a certified Waldorf teacher and has a Master's in Education from Sunbridge College and a Bachelor of Fine Arts from Carnegie Mellon

University. Before becoming a teacher, she was a professional dancer, actor, and musician. She is a co-producer of FEARless, a 'performers-potluck' initiative through which artists explore how fear affects our lives. She currently teaches Games and Movement, and Music at Northeast Woodland Chartered Public School in New Hampshire. She is interested in bridging social and cultural divides and how music, movement, and the creative process can help us do it. Play on!

Games in the Covid Time

Children are endlessly inventive. They will do almost anything to be able to play together. Take for example the family who, in facing a ban on children playing in close contact in the park found out that biking was allowed so long as the children did not 'mingle.' So they made a simple but amazing 'one way road' obstacle course for bikes that the dad and his two kids set up in the park. Within a day children from all over the neighbourhood had joined in. The course even came with a 'burning ground' rule that meant you could not touch the ground with your feet for more than three seconds otherwise your feet would catch fire and the tires on your bike would melt. The no-mingling rule was more than upheld, while crucially the kids got to play together. His children told him that this was, 'the best game ever', and that they had 'loads of new ideas for tricks and obstacles'. This book has a long genealogy. It began in the last century – now that sounds impressive – with *Games Children Play* (1996) written by Kim John Payne and then came *Games Children Sing and Play* (2012) by Valarie Baadh Garrett and Joan Carr Shimer. For much of this time Cory Waletzko was greeting children each day, eager to hear what games they might be playing today. And then came *Waldorf Games for the Early Years*. Now comes the book you are holding in your hand.

Countless thousands of children have played, run, tumbled, hugged, argued and laughed as they have played these games. This is also true of the many new games now described in this book as they have been invented, collected and tried and tested in the gamester tradition fuelled by children's deep need to play.

We were thrilled to be compiling this collection for you. As each month passed during the writing process our excitement grew as new games were added and old games renewed with new adaptions and new learnings described to help children who might struggle to play.

And then along came the Covid pandemic. How can children play when there is a need to socially distance? Should we delay the release of the book? With their long years of experience Hawthorn Press advised that we should press on saying 'This book is definitely needed.' We conferred and agreed. In spite of, or maybe because of, all the social and health upheavals of this time our determination and excitement to be sharing these games with you was undimmed. Sure, you will need to pass, for now, on a some of these games as they might depend solely on touch to work, but many others can be adapted to still be a whole lot of fun.

For example, an alternative to any tagging game would be that instead of physically touching with a tag, when the tagger gets within three feet of a person, they clap, then that person is tagged. A person can be rescued, if someone comes within three feet of the person who is tagged (or down on a knee) and the rescuer claps three times, thus freeing a person who has been tagged.

Of course, you will need to adapt whatever you come up with, to stay in line with your legal health requirements and community agreements.

Gamesters all around the world are a spectacularly inventive bunch. The healing power of play is needed now like it has seldom been needed before. And when this pandemic has ended children are going to need to 'play it out'. They are going to need to connect again, really connect. Can you think of anything that does this better than play and games? And we are so happy that this book will not only be of use during these challenging times but also long, long after it.

Your Servants in Games,
Kim John Payne, Cory Waletzko.

Tagging Games in the Time of Covid – Filling the Six-Foot Gap

This approach to tagging game modification was created by master movement educator Mashobane Moruthane (for more information, check out the Mashobane Ubuntu Initiative mashobaneubuntu. com or contact him directly at:

Email: mashobaneubuntuinitiative@gmail.com
Facebook: @mashobaneubuntuinitiative
Instagram: @thatafricanwaldorfteacher

This is an opportunity for us to create new ways to connect with one another. We don't have to feel pressured to 'do things like we used to' – we can create new rituals, new games that **enliven the space between us**.

In teaching the children about the six-foot gap, it's helpful to use imaginative pictures. When bringing the rule of the six-foot social distance space, you can describe a large dairy cow, steadfast and sturdy, calmly chewing cud on a warm, breezy day, she's not going anywhere! This is the 'cow' space (six feet), and when you have a cow space between you, you cannot be tagged.

Then comes the drama, when we get closer than six feet. The three-foot social distance space is no longer a large dairy cow between us, but a spritely little goat, happily bouncing all around, ready to switch directions at any moment. This is the 'goat' space (three feet), and when you get within the goat space of another person, you can 'tag' them – not with a touch, but with a clap! You can, thus, 'Get someone's goat!' For games that require rescuing someone who has been tagged, you can 'free' someone by getting within their 'goat' space and clapping three times, sending them up and on their way into the game once again.

When safety precautions keep us from physically touching one another, we can heighten our other senses – the sense of sight (watching the action of the chase), the sense of hearing (listening for the clap or claps), and the sense of space (relating to one another through our shared proximity).

Other Titles from Hawthorn Press

Waldorf Games Handbook For The Early Years

Games to Play and Sing with Children aged 3–7

Kim John Payne, Cory Waletzko & Valerie Baadh Garrett

Throughout the book the 142 games focus on children's growth and development, and how this is expressed in movement and play. Each game is clearly and simply described, with diagrams and drawings for how to play it. Parents, teachers, forest school educators and play leaders will find this a must-have resource.

136pp; 246 × 189mm; paperback; ISBN: 978-1-912480-26-5; Paperback

Simplicity Parenting

Using the power of less to raise happy, secure children

Kim John Payne

This new and revised UK edition of the popular US #1 provides tried, tested and doable answers to the rapid increase in anxiety in childhood and the ever-increasing need for balance in family life.

Here are four simple steps for decluttering, quieting, and soothing family dynamics so that children can thrive at school, get along with peers, and nurture well-being. Using the extraordinary power of less, Kim John Payne, one of the world's leading Steiner-Waldorf educators, offers novel ways to help children feel calmer, happier, and more secure.

352pp; 234 x 156mm; paperback; ISBN: 978-1-912480-03-6

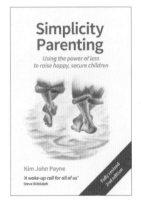

Ordering Books

If you have difficulties ordering Hawthorn Press books from a bookshop, you can order direct from our website www.hawthornpress.com, or from our UK distributor

BookSource: 50 Cambuslang Road, Glasgow, G32 8NB
Tel: (0845) 370 0063, E-mail: orders@booksource.net.

Details of our overseas distributors can be found on our website.

Hawthorn Press
www.hawthornpress.com